MY DESTINY

SURVIVOR
OF THE
HOLOCAUST

Georgia M. Gabor

Amen
PUBLISHING
COMPANY

Copyright © 1981 by Amen Publishing Company
All rights reserved.

Library of Congress Catalog Card No.: 81-68276
ISBN# 0-941204-00-6

Published by
Amen Publishing Company
1320 S. Baldwin Ave.
Arcadia, California 91006
(213) 574-8594

Printed in U.S.A.
by
Sinclair Printing Company
Los Angeles, CA

The following is an exact translation of an entry in my diary, written in March of 1944, at the age of fourteen and a half.

"I think, therefore I am. — We are only molecules, microscopic components of the ordered universe, but to our own selves we are the entire cosmos. Man is egocentric and ignorant. He stops at nothing — insincerity, mendacity, plunder, or even murder — to satisfy his selfish desires.

The road of life is full of obstacles, and we learn only through our own mistakes. We rarely regret our premeditated, logical actions, but often act impulsively, and thus plunge into disaster. Frequently we credit solely ourselves for our successful achievements, denying that much may be the will of God, part of OUR DESTINY."

— — —

I dedicate this book to the millions of innocent souls, be they Jew or gentile, who were tortured and annihilated by the Nazis during the World War II Holocaust. And to those still in captivity, in labor camps, victims of Communist Regimes.

I also dedicate this book to the living, to those who will never forget the martyrs, who will forever strive to prevent — and make sacrifices to conquer — any form of totalitarianism. Be that THEIR DESTINY.

TABLE OF CONTENTS
MY DESTINY
Survivor of the Holocaust

TABLE OF CONTENTS (Cont.)

INTRODUCTION

It was the summer of 1956. I was enjoying a break from my seminary studies by visiting my parents, who were stationed with the Air Force in Germany. I had heard of the World War II concentration camps and had a rather vague notion in my mind that they must have been terrible places. I was totally unprepared, however, for what I saw and heard from the Jewish guide who took me through the infamous Dachau Concentration Camp. He, indeed, had been one of its more "fortunate" residents.

I remember standing in the shower room, looking up at the water sprinklers that would gush forth cyclon-B gas on the unsuspecting victims below. I remember, too, the crematorium room next door, where the several huge ovens would receive the bodies from the shower room and reduce them to nondescript ash that would be scattered in various places in the camp.

I remember, also, thinking to myself: "What kind of people were these Jewish people? How were they able to survive with so little help from the outside world? Where are the survivors now? In what ways are their minds and bodies still damaged and crippled by this horrible experience?"

This book is the story of one of those World War II heroes! While it does not profess to be any more than one person's account of what went on during a most painful period in world history, one has the feeling that Georgia Gabor is writing for millions of people who could not bear to relive the agony, to write their own story; people who experienced more terror and pain than should ever be allowed among civilized men and women.

So, in a very real sense, this book is a kind of barometer of how unkind we can actually be as human beings! It is an extreme tragedy that this book had to be written at all. However, if full knowledge and disclosure of our basest nature and tendencies can prevent our past blunders from ever being repeated again, then this book — with all its joy and pain — will have served its purpose in elevating our definition of what it means to be human and, in turn, of being "our brother's keeper!"

Laurence C. Keene, Ph.D.
Assistant Vice-President
Pepperdine University
Los Angeles, California

BOOK
ONE

ANNIHILATION OF EUROPE'S JEWRY.

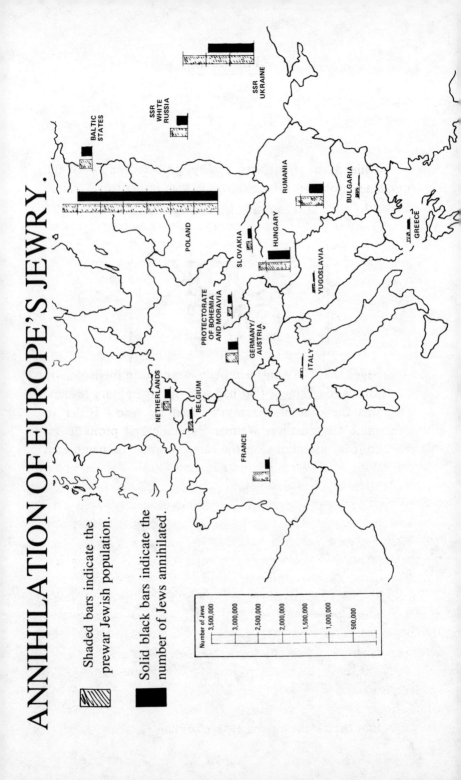

Shaded bars indicate the prewar Jewish population.

Solid black bars indicate the number of Jews annihilated.

BALTIC STATES

SSR WHITE RUSSIA

SSR UKRAINE

POLAND

RUMANIA

BULGARIA

GREECE

SLOVAKIA

HUNGARY

YUGOSLAVIA

PROTECTORATE OF BOHEMIA AND MORAVIA

GERMANY/AUSTRIA

ITALY

NETHERLANDS

BELGIUM

FRANCE

Number of Jews
3,500,000
3,000,000
2,500,000
2,000,000
1,500,000
1,000,000
500,000

PREFACE

While I, a child, was totally preoccupied with the mundane problems of growing up, an insignificant figure emerged "from the woodwork" and started to alter world events. Adolf Hitler, born on the same day as my father (April 20, 1889), having no more than a ninth grade education, at the age of 44 became the abominable Führer of Germany.

On November 11, 1918, the defeated Germany of Kaiser Wilhelm signed the armistice ending World War I. Unable to accept the fact that the German soldiers had been defeated on the battlefield, Hitler fanatically endorsed the false belief that Germany had been "stabbed in the back" by a traitorous government that had sold out its military leaders. This was the first of the myths used by Adolf Hitler to undermine the post-war Weimar Republic and promote his own political ambitions. In the early twenties he hammered this myth into the minds of his compatriots. It was not a difficult task. The German people were eager to find scapegoats for their defeat and subsequent humiliation. They convinced themselves that Hitler was right. The signers of the surrender were referred to as "the November criminals," and they were blamed as well for the establishment of a floundering democratic government that had replaced the old autocracy of the Kaiser.

In September 1919, seeking an organization that expressed his secret convictions against the Jews, who in his mind were profiteers and intriguers who had sold out Germany, Hitler attended a meeting of the German Workers Party. The party leaders expressed his bitterness, mouthed his hatreds. He joined them and within six months established himself as their most bombastic spokesman.

A Germany seething in the convulsions of defeat and severe economic depression was fertile soil for a demagogue who saw himself as a savior. He would avenge the wrongs done Germany. He would lead the master race to its rightful destiny.

Within that year he had asserted, "All the highest things men strive for, religion or socialism or democracy, are for the Jew only the means to an end, to satisfy his greed for money and power. The effect is to produce a race-tuberculosis of the Folk. . . . Rational anti-Semitism must be directed toward a methodical. . . elimination of the privileges they possess, . . . final aim must be the deliberate removal of the Jews."(Payne, p. 131.) His early success was due in no small measure to his emphasis upon anti-Semitism.

Hitler succeeded in mesmerizing the German people, because he himself represented their frustrations. He had been wounded and gassed*, his pride ravaged, as his nation tasted bitter defeat in World War I. An ignominious armistice, in which the treaty of Versailles heaped an economic and military burden on a dejected nation, sheared it of resources essential for recovery. By mid-1920, the National Socialist German Workers' Party, with the swastika as its symbol, had announced its "25 Points Platform," which was little more than the extension of Hitler's philosophy.

In 1920 there were other groups promising salvation for Germany, among them the communists and socialists. They saw Hitler and his policies as their mortal foe. They harassed his meetings and tried to break them up by demonstrations. When Hitler could not cow them with words, he turned to force. By 1921, the first units of storm troopers were organized. These strong-arm squads grew into the S.A.,

---

* Hitler inhaled a significant amount of chlorine gas filling his trench, which caused temporary blindness and mental damage.

a terrorist army of storm troopers that cleared Hitler's way to power.

The storm troopers, in Hitler's words, "had been trained and brought up to realize that only terror is capable of smashing terror." They were used to provoke incidents and to beat up political opponents as part of a widespread campaign of intimidation. Fear, Hitler demonstrated, was a potent weapon to control friends as well as destroy enemies.

By 1923 Hitler had transformed the insignificant German Workers Party into a new and dynamic organization—the National Socialist Party. Naziism was born.

Nazi tactics followed. Black-shirted storm troopers paraded through the towns of Bavaria, flaunting red and white flags and wearing arm bands, carrying the black hooked cross that dated to the dawn of civilization — the swastika.

In November of that year Hitler decided that the moment had come to seize power in the state of Bavaria. Besides storm trooper Rőhm, he had surrounded himself with a group of loyal Nazis who would eventually form the nucleus of the power elite of the Third Reich — Gőring, Hess, Streicher, Rosenberg, Frank, etc.

By mid-1925 *Mein Kampf,* dictated by Hitler and recorded scrupulously by Rudolf Hess, was published; a blueprint for the total destruction of the bourgeois society (à la Marx's and Engel's philosophy) and the conquest of the world. In his book Hitler expressed with manic force his hatred for the Jews, the insignificance of men, the necessity of a führer figure possessing supreme authority, the immeasurable superiority of the German race, its need for a much enlarged living space, etc. He also displayed a basic brilliance and a deep understanding of the effective use of propaganda.* If men like Daladier, Stalin and Roosevelt had read it with attention and heeded it, World War II and the death of multimillions might have been avoided.

But in the year 1927 most Germans did not listen to the appeals of the Nazis. Like most of the world, Germany was enjoying prosperity. With employment at its peak, industry booming and money stabilized and plentiful, the Germans were satisfied with their state of affairs. Hitler did not offer them more prosperity; he predicted disaster. They mocked him. He and his party became the butt of jokes.

During this period, when the Nazis failed to capture the attention of the German people, Hitler awaited a brighter day by devoting all his energies to building an intricate party structure. The Hitler Youth Movement came into being, with its own departments of school, press, and culture.

By 1929, though the Nazi Party had won only twelve seats in the Reichstag, Germany's parliament, the Hitler machine was functioning efficiently as a complete state within the Weimar Republic. It had its own government and its own army, a phenomenon inconceivable for a political party in a true democracy. Thus, while a prosperous world smugly ignored the Nazis, the Nazis laid the foundation for the coming of the Third Reich.

---

* "The receptivity of the great masses is extremely limited, their intelligence is small, their forgetfulness enormous. Therefore, all effective propaganda must be limited to a very few points and they should be used like slogans until the very last man in the audience is capable of understanding what is meant.

"The people in their overwhelming majority are so feminine in their nature that sober reasoning motivates their thoughts and behavior far less than feeling and emotion.

"Their feelings. . . do not have many varieties of shading, only love or hate, right or wrong, truth or lie, never half this and half that, or partially, etc. . . .

"The masses, however, are slow-moving, and they always require an interval of time before they are prepared to notice anything at all, and they will ultimately remember only the simplest ideas repeated a thousand times over."   *(Mein Kampf, 1939)*

On October 24, 1929, the stock market on Wall Street crashed, ushering in the Great Depression. Like almost everywhere in the world, in Germany millions of people became unemployed, hungry, and despairing.

Adolf Hitler's contentment came from the understanding that economic disaster breeds political unrest, and political unrest is fertile soil for an ambitious tyrant. With the old system of government crumbling under the weight of the depression, the Germans entertained great fears, indulged in bitter hatreds, and sought change, no matter how extreme. In these circumstances Hitler's propaganda machine launched a full-scale campaign against the Republic, the money barons, the Jews — blaming them for Germany's plight. The people were looking for a scapegoat for their misery; Hitler gave them many on which to vent their anger. At the same time, in glowing but ambiguous terms, he extolled the Nazis as the "new men" to make Germany strong and feared, and to restore dignity and security to every German. His oratory was hypnotic, his promises fantastic. The German people were eager to listen and respond.

The election of 1930, after a year of depression, gave the Nazis six million votes, making it the second largest party, and in the 1932 election, the majority party. On January 30, 1933, fifteen short years from the time he wept over Germany's defeat in World War I , Adolf Hitler was appointed Chancellor of the German Reich.

Once in power, the Chancellor moved fast. Within the year the following orders were issued: a law imposed the death penalty for "crimes against the republic security"; a nationwide boycott of Jewish businessmen, doctors, lawyers, and other professionals was proclaimed; all free trade unions were taken over by the Nazi labor chief; throughout the day and night all books by "non-Aryans" were burned in every German city and town; all parties but the Nazi Party were outlawed; finally, Germany withdrew from the League of Nations.

With the death of President Hindenburg, Adolf Hitler declared himself Führer and Reich Chancellor on August 2, 1934. By now the concentration camps created in 1933 were bulging with his opponents. Not only political prisoners and Jews, but also devout Catholics and Protestants, for as Borman often stated, "National Socialism and Christianity are irreconcilable."

Hitler himself envisioned a Nazi religion, organized under the "National Reich Church." The main articles of this church spoke for themselves:

- The National Church is determined to exterminate the foreign Christian faiths imported into Germany.

- The National Church demands immediate cessation of the publication and dissemination of the Bible.

- On the altars of the National Church there must be nothing but *Mein Kampf* and a sword.

- The Christian Cross must be removed from all churches and must be superseded by the only unconquerable symbol, the swastika.

Such were the tenets of Hitler's church. To establish it, he had to destroy Judaism and Christianity. He went at the task with maniacal vengeance.

During the spring of 1935, rearmament and universal military service were reintroduced, and Hitler reserved for himself the title of Supreme Commander of the Armed Forces. In September of that year he proclaimed the infamous anti-Semitic "Nuremberg Laws," which deprived all Jews of their citizenship, relegated them to a caste of untouchable slaves to be drafted for manual labor, and prohibited them from marrying Aryans. In March of 1936, his troops occupied the now French Rhineland, and in October he established the Rome-Berlin Axis. This was the first step taken by the Nazi-Fascist block on the road to war.

During those years my country, Hungary, had its own problems. After World War I, although we regained our independence from Austria, the Trianon Treaty had crippled my homeland, giving nearly a third of our territory to our neighbors: to Czechoslovakia on the north, Rumania on the east, and Yugoslavia on the south. Further, Béla Kun usurped power and established a very cruel and much hated communistic dictatorship. As a response to the plea of several statesmen of the former parliament, London-and-Paris-backed Admiral Miklósh Horthy led a successful counterrevolution in 1920, thus freeing Hungary from the short-lived "Red Regime." Horthy's regency lasted until the Germans forcefully removed him in October of 1944.

As for the life of the Hungarian Jewish population, it was quite similar to that of Jews residing in Western European countries prior to the rise of Hitler. Through the centuries none of these countries were fond of the Jews, but we were highly assimilated, and due to our relative wealth, a large percentage was powerfully influential. As Germany and Hungary kept absorbing a substantial number of penniless refugees, first those escaping from the 19th century pogroms in Eastern Europe, then from the territories given to Eastern countries by the Trianon Treaty, anti-Semitism started to raise its ugly head. Anti-Jewish feelings began to flare up not only because Jews had been staunch supporters of the Western nations who had dismembered Hungary, but mainly because there was a significant number of Jewish officials in Kun's infamous "Red Regime." *

The first Hungarian anti-Semitic laws were relatively mild. They limited Jewish participation in high government and civil service offices and commerce, and later their mem-

---

* Most of those were Trotskyite Communist agents, recruited and indoctrinated while in prisoner-of-war camps during World War I. The overwhelming majority, the middle-class Jews, strongly opposed the Reds.

bership in intellectual guilds, bars, and associations. The *Numerus Clausus* law of 1920 specified that only 6% of the universities' students could be Jews. (That ordinance, however, was eliminated in 1928.)

During the thirties German military movements and anti-Jewish activities increased with incredible speed. As a trumped-up response to the assassination of a minor official of the German embassy in France, a nationwide pogrom was precipitated by the Nazi propaganda ministry. In Germany every synagogue was burned to the ground, thousands of Jews were brutally murdered, and an extreme amount of property destroyed. A $400,000,000 fine was levied against the Jews, and every Jew worth over $2,000 was made to pay. Able-bodied Jews who could not manage to leave the country were drafted into slave labor, while the sick, old, and very young were systematically destroyed. Able to pursue genocide on a grand scale, with little interference and worldwide indifference, Hitler was encouraged to start out on the conquest of Europe. In the same year Germany marched into Austria, where another quarter of a million Jews fell under the swastika.

Hitler kept pressuring our regent to join the Axis and settle "the Jewish question," promising in turn to help Hungary realize her territorial aims. Since our geographic position made us an island between the eastbound German-Italian forces and the westbound Russians, neutral we could not remain. Horthy had three possible moves: oppose Hitler outright and expect our country to be occupied and treated as Austria had been; turn to communist Russia for help, as Roosevelt suggested in his reply to Hungary's plea; or join the Axis, i.e., "cleanse" his country of the Jews and engage his people in a full-scale aggressive war. All the options detrimental, at first Horthy tried to appease the Führer with mild concessions, such as allowing free movement of his troops across our land. Also, our government issued another anti-Jewish law, limiting participation in the political, economic, and intellectual area to no more than 20%, emphasizing their total exclusion from federal employment or holding a rank in the military.

Before the end of the decade, Hitler's demand for the Sudetenland threatened to explode into war with England and France. These two Allies were not prepared to risk the explosion. Daladier and Chamberlain met with Mussolini and Hitler in Munich, and signed the infamous pact that allowed Germany to occupy Czechoslovakia without bloodshed, in March of 1939. Her 350,000 Jews, who made up a respected and well-educated middle class, were speedily deprived of all their property and dignity, and not much later suffered the fate of the German Jews.

Within the same year, the official start of World War II was marked by Hitler's attack on Poland, followed in two days by the declaration of war by Britain and France upon Nazi Germany. Due to a German-Soviet pact in August of 1939, Germany from the west and Russia from the east invaded Poland in September, occupying and partitioning it between the two conquerers within that year. The fate of the Jews in that country, for so very long greatly anti-Semitic, need not be described. The many infamous concentration camps and crematoria on Polish territory testify mutely and in great detail to the agony and terror there.

Hitler, encouraged by his almost unresisted conquests, accelerated his expansionistic policies: by early 1939, German troops had invaded Denmark, Norway, Belgium, Luxemberg and Holland; by June, France had surrendered; and by October, Italy, who had already declared war on Britain and France, attacked Greece. In November Antonescu, with the aid of his Nazi-like Iron Guard, usurped power in Rumania, and soon joined the Axis.

Meanwhile, Hungary kept demanding the return of her lost territories. Finally, in 1939, we got back a portion on the northern border from Czechoslovakia, a part of Transylvania from Romania, and a small section on the south from Yugoslavia, but for a high price. In November, Hungary also joined the Axis.* Soon after, new anti-Semitic laws were enacted: the first defined a Jew as one who had at least two grandparents of that religion; the second reinstated the 6% *numerus clausus* at the universities and college preparatory high schools; further ordinances specified that only 6% Jews were to be allowed to hold membership in professional guilds, bars and associations, and only 12% to be employed in a purely intellectual capacity.

In early 1941, Bulgaria joined the Axis. Finland also became an ally of Germany, and she, too, began issuing anti-Jewish legislation. In April, Germany invaded Greece and Yugoslavia; in June, the Axis powers attacked Russia; in December, Japan attacked the United States at Pearl Harbor; and, finally, before the year was over, Hitler and Mussolini declared war on the United States and vice versa.

Within that year Hungarian Prime Minister Bárdossy, without consulting members of the cabinet or congress, gave permission to move German troops across our land, discontinued diplomatic relations with England, declared our entry into war against Yugoslavia and Russia, and on December 12, 1941, also against the U.S.A.

During the first half of 1942, the Axis powers were forging ahead in all four directions, victoriously. But by November, with the Allies' landing in North Africa and Russia's counterattack at Stalingrad, the war's direction had reversed.

---

* Hungary did stipulate, however, to give military assistance to the Axis powers *only* if one was attacked by such a country which was not involved in the war at the time of the signing of the pact.

During 1943, the Germans withdrew from Africa, the Allies landed in Sicily, and Italy surrendered and declared war on Germany. By January of the following year, the Allies had landed in Anzio, and the Russians had pushed the Germans back to the prewar Polish border. Thus, by the time Hitler's troops occupied Hungary, on March 19, 1944, it was not unrealistic for our Jews to lull themselves into the belief that the end of the war was too near for them to be harmed significantly by the Nazis.

However, as Part II of this book reveals, it was grossly naive to so underestimate the power and cruelty of the German National Socialists.

The famous thousand-year-old Saint Stephen's
crown, given by the Pope to István,
the first Hungarian king.

Grandmama Blum.

Mother, Father, and Author. Budapest, 1931.

Uncle Lacó.

Aunt Bözse.

Author.
Budapest, 1940.

Author.
Siófok, 1936.

Mother, Father, Author.
Siófok, 1938.

Our apartment on Ráday Street.

PART I: GROWING UP IN HUNGARY

CHAPTER 1: STRANGER THAN FICTION

"Look! I can see the lights of Tel Aviv!" My heart throbbed and my eyes filled with tears as I leaned across my husband's lap, to look out the tiny window of the airplane. Like a halo, the lights of a pulsating city illuminated the end of the horizon. This was my first glimpse of "Eretz Israel", the original homeland of all Jews.

Gracefully, like a giant bird the airplane descended and allowed us to disembark. Our small tour bus vibrated rhythmically while speeding along the serpentine road, bisecting alternating patches of emerald green fruit groves, twisting among newly erected village homes, Bedouins with their grazing goats and sheep, then the seemingly endless stretch of pale gold sandy rocks huddled to form the myriad tiny hills so typical of the Israeli desert. The setting sun turned the scenery from pale brass to glittering bronze, as we reached Jerusalem, the fulcrum of our tour.

During the next two weeks we all tried but failed to keep our emotions constantly cloaked while we observed the sites — from historically significant ancient ruins and excavations, which verify miraculous events described in the Bible — to the modern wonders of turning deserts to manmade oases and industrialized cities. Anyone would find it difficult to deny the influence of a Super Power while observing the testimonials commemorating a people's resistance to the innumerable attempts of powerful forces during the past six millenia, all aimed at annihilating the mere handful of people of Jewish faith; and the accomplishments of these barely three million heterogeneous and mostly penniless immigrants, establishing and defending a politically stable and econom-

1

ically flourishing country in a desert, surrounded by hostile nations, all within a mere three decades.

Many people view Israel as the land of miracles and the home of their ancestors. Soon after my husband and I set foot on the Promised Land, these phrases took on literal meaning for us.

My husband, an only and lonely child, never knew his father. His parents were divorced before he was born, and his mother did not possess a picture nor would she ever speak of his father. After her death my husband, then a young adult, questioned his only relative, his aunt, about his father. All she could reveal was that, to the best of her knowledge, he had come to the U.S. from Russia, was married for a short time, after the divorce emigrated to what was then called Palestine, where according to hearsay, he subsequently remarried and fathered four children. With such meager information my husband had never before attempted to locate his father, but now that we were in Israel, he was determined to try.

On our first free day in Jerusalem, we got into a taxi and asked the driver to take us to whatever office might keep a record of all immigrants. A few blocks later we were deposited in front of a tiny old duplex, displaying a sign: "Search Bureau for Missing Relatives." With the attitude of having nothing to lose, we entered a small overcrowded room. We introduced ourselves to the lady behind the first of two desks, and my husband promptly stated the purpose of our visit. The lady nodded approvingly, implying that we were in the right place, and then proceeded to ask and record every bit of information my husband could supply. Upon the speedy conclusion of that activity she thumbed through a few boxes of microfilm, pulled out and illuminated several, then looked at my husband and asserted: "I found only two even remotely likely candidates. The first one's name

2

matches what you gave, but he had no children nor even a wife, and passed away three years ago. The second one has also passed away, but he did marry here and fathered four children. Although born in Russia, he was raised in the U.S., came to Israel in 1934, not in 1932, and his first name was Solomon, not Samuel."

"No other? S. Weinstein is such a common name!"

"Strange but correct, sir. Yet even more unusual is the fact that three of his children emigrated, and the one who remained is the only Uziel Weinstein in the entire Israeli telephone book! Shall I phone him?"

Stranger than fiction, within a ten-minute interval my husband found four half brothers and sisters, in the land of miracles and home of our ancestors.

The next day we traveled to Beer Sheva, to meet our new relatives. Rapidly flowing tears merged as the brothers embraced each other. Similarity in appearance alone made their common origin undeniable.

They examined family photographs, which revealed unmistakable genetic resemblances. Curled up on the couch, the brothers exchanged accounts of their childhood and youth. Not until Uzi's three beautiful daughters were tucked in and on their way to dreamland, was it my turn to relate my life story.

CHAPTER 2: FIRST BRUSH WITH DEATH

I was born in 1930, into a well-to-do Jewish family. Father was a very handsome, forty-one-year-old, prominent attorney; Mother, an exceptionally attractive lady in her late twenties. I was an only child.

While I was a baby we resided in an elegant, seven-room apartment in Budapest. We had a live-in maid and a cook, and I had a German-speaking governess. That I might become more graceful, my parents enrolled me in ballet school at age four. Oh, I remember our recitals! How I enjoyed being a swan in the Swan Lake ballet, and an officer of the court in *Kukorica János,* an Hungarian operetta. I can see some incidents as clearly as reflections in a mirror.

I recall a happening shortly after my fourth birthday. Mother decided to dismiss the governess and to enroll me in an English nursery school. I hemmed and hawed, but Mom took me anyway. She sat and watched for the first hour or so, but then she was asked to leave. That did it! No way could she leave me behind! I threw such a tantrum that I was ordered to leave. Mother was too embarrassed to return with me the next day, and therefore decided that I was to have, instead, a part-time German governess and an English tutor two afternoons a week.

By 1935, with the rise of Hitler and National Socialism (Naziism) in Germany, an undercurrent of anti-Semitism became evident in Hungary also. My father, who had twice held the position of "Városatya" (a selected legal advisor to the Ministry, with duties similar to that of an alderman or congressman) and had been for years the chairman of the city's Social Democratic Party, lost his position and many of his most prominent clients. We had to discharge the cook and move to a smaller, five-room apartment, at 31 Ráday Street. This was a large, three-winged building, about a mile from the elegant shopping center of downtown Pest, and about the same distance from the Ferencz József bridge, that led across the Danube River to the half-millenium-old Citadelle and the King's Castle in Buda.

4

In 1936, I entered first grade. A tantrum didn't help this time. Although it wasn't easy, I had to adjust to the new environment. The second day of school stands out clearly in my mind. At snack break each of us received a small bottle of milk, to supplement the sandwiches which we had brought from home. While fidgeting with my lunch bag, I carelessly deposited the bottle on my slanting desk top. Needless to say, it landed crashing on the floor. Noticing my complete disinterest in the matter, my lack of attempt even to clean up the mess, our teacher, Miss Olga, slowly walked over to me and in a gentle voice asked, "And what do you think should happen now?"

Being a smart but spoiled little child, I looked at her strangely and replied, "Nothing! My Mom will come in and pay for it."

As time went on, I did adjust to school. I got along well with teachers and grown-ups, but made no friends among the children. Partially this was due to lack of time. We went to school six days a week, and to maintain a straight A average I had to study for hours daily at home. Besides, I took English and piano lessons twice a week each, and practice for those added several hours to my daily schedule. And partially, because I found my peers very immature. My almost exclusive out-of-school contact with children of my own age was to tutor anyone who asked me, which I enjoyed immensely and pursued when time permitted. My recreation consisted of visiting Grandmama Blum, Mother's older sister Aunt Bözse, and her younger brother Uncle Lacó every evening. They all resided in a nice apartment on Gyulai Pál Street, a mere fifteen-minute walk from our apartment. On Sunday afternoons Mother used to take me ice-skating, or to a matinee at the opera, theatre or movie.

I used to look forward to Sunday forenoons also, usually going for long walks with Father, listening intently to his explanations while visiting a museum, college campus or the site of some historical event, and to the stories about his childhood and youth. Father was born on April 20, 1889, in Tokaj — where the famous wine comes from — a small town of about 1,000 people then. He had had ten brothers and sisters, nine of whom had passed away before I was born. I knew only one of his sisters, who had had a bad marriage and had committed suicide in 1933, leaving behind my only cousin, Pista Halász, eight years older than I. Dad's parents were poor folks. My grandfather was a cantor in the temple, supporting thirteen on a meager salary. Really fourteen, because for lack of a local public school his children were educated by a poorly paid live-in tutor.

Father started to earn money at age four, when he got the job of opening up and cleaning the temple yard at five o'clock every morning. At sixteen he left home for the capital, to get a college education. He earned his keep and tuition by tutoring. At twenty-one he graduated "Sigma Cum Laude" (with highest honors) receiving his doctorate in law. Having an exceptionally beautiful tenor voice, he was offered employment with the Hungarian Opera Company, but turned it down in favor of becoming an attorney.

The stories about his youth and incidents connected with some of his famous clients used to fascinate me. Dad reminisced about times when he went hunting with Count Eszterházy; the pleasant weekends he had spent at Franz Joseph's Court, negotiating a delicate matter between the Austrian Emperor and a prominent Hungarian lady; his dates with Rozsi Bársony, a famous Hungarian actress; and stories about distinguished ministry personnel, government matters and court cases.

The summers used to be the highlight of the year. Typically, Mother rented a cottage on the shore of Lake Balaton, a few hours' ride from the capital, while I stayed at a nearby children's camp. I saw Mom every day at the beach, and Dad when he joined us at the resort on weekends.

One summer, however, I had very little pleasure. In 1938, shortly before the school year was over, Aunt Bözse, whom I loved very deeply, was taken to the hospital. I was told it was nothing serious and that she was to be home in a few weeks. So we went to the resort town of Siófok as usual. Mother kept telling me Aunt Bözse was getting better and would soon join us. Thus, it should not have surprised me when one Sunday afternoon my teacher-counselor informed me that my parents were not coming to visit, because they were going to Budapest to bring back my aunt.

I stared at her for a moment, then asserted with great conviction, "That is not true. My aunt is dead!"

She looked at me bewildered and tried to convince me that I was imagining things. — I now see myself as clearly as if it had happened yesterday: running into the cottage, into our walk-in closet and locking the door from the inside. Now I see myself in pajamas, dashing across downtown of the resort and charging into my parents' apartment. — My premonition was correct. There were Mother, Grandmother and Uncle Lacó sitting "Shivah". (An Orthodox Jewish religious custom, in which close relations of a deceased person confine themselves to the house, remove their shoes and simply sit and pray for the duration of a week after the burial.)

The camp director arrived shortly, white as a ghost and gasping for air, stuttering as he tried to give an account of the mysterious incident concerning me.

"The whole staff and most of the children searched for her for hours before one of the youngsters stumbled onto the locked closet door. We broke it down and found her sitting in a corner, staring as if hypnotized. We undressed her and put her to bed, but she did not awaken. She slept silently through the night. The next forenoon she occasionally mumbled, as if having a dream. We called a doctor. Though the child slept through the examination, the doctor found nothing wrong physically and could not make a diagnosis. He suggested to wait another day, then if no change, to take her to a hospital. We kept trying to reach you, but to no avail."

How very strange! My aunt was indeed getting better, and the doctors did suggest that she come to the resort to rest. My parents and counselor did tell the truth! However, at the exact time the counselor delivered my parents' message, a main artery in my aunt's brain ruptured, and she passed away instantly. Was my two-day-long coma to allow my soul to accompany hers, perhaps, while she adjusted to her new environment in the other world? We shall never know, for I had no recollection of anything beyond locking myself in the closet. But, contrary to my nature, I did not cry like the rest of the family. I was very solemn and withdrawn for the next two days while staying with Mother and the relatives; then I chose to return to camp and behave as if nothing had happened. For a very long time after, I dreamt about Aunt Bözse nightly, always waking up calm, content and with a smile on my face.

CHAPTER 3: A LITTLE GIRL GROWS UP

In 1940, at age 10, I had to change schools. In prewar Hungary, one had to decide his educational aim at the end of the fourth grade. Our choices were: continue "elemi" (elementary school) for four more years; go to "polgári" (equivalent to the commercial course in a U.S. high school) for four years, i.e., fifth through eighth grade; attend a "gymnázium" (college preparatory) from the fifth through the twelfth grade. Needless to say, I wanted the latter. But! By now we had *numerus nullus* in universities, and *numerus clausus* in the gymnazia. This meant no Jews were allowed to enter (and only 2% to conclude their studies) in universities, and only 6% of the gymnazia's student body could be Jewish.

I recall Father saying to me, "My child, if you truly wish to go to a gymnazium, I will leave no stone unturned to get you in. But remember, to stay on the top is up to you." And so it was. Mother and I checked out the schools, and we chose the Zrinyi Ilona Leány Gymnazium. Father contacted an old friend, a cabinet member, and within weeks we were notified of my acceptance.

My new school was located on Práter Street, a mere ten-minute walk from our residence. It was a highly rated girls' school. Students attended it six days a week, from 8:00 a.m. until 1:00 p.m. or later, depending if one signed up for extra-curricular courses, such as piano, ballet, drama and the like. We studied eleven specified subjects — some daily, others only one to three times a week. They included Hungarian, German, religion, mathematics, history, geography, biology, plus several minors from the fifth grade on, with the addition of Latin and physics in the seventh grade. I studied a great deal, not only because we had substantial homework assigned in every subject daily, but because we Jews had to know much more than the others to get the top grades.

Shortly before the end of the school year my studies were interrupted, when in the spring of 1941 I contracted my first serious sickness. During the 1930s, Hungarian doctors believed that tonsils should be saved. So, I put up with three or four tonsillitis attacks per year. But this time one of those innocent ailments turned into rheumatic fever. In the days before penicillin, that was a deadly disease. The constant high fever frequently attacked the heart, and patients had to be kept wrapped in ice-cold, wet sheets day and night for weeks. My poor mother and grandmother, our maid and a nurse, kept praying and attending to me for three weeks, until the crisis passed.

The doctor said my heart was badly damaged, and would never endure physical strain. To avoid another, possibly fatal attack, as soon as I gained strength, the tonsils had to be removed. So, before our usual resort vacation, I had a tonsillectomy. But I was not about to miss the fun! I refused general anesthesia, tolerating only a local freezing, insisting on sitting in a dentist's chair, holding our family physician's hand and watching the whole ordeal in a mirror. I put up such a tantrum that the surgeon decided to give it a try. He performed surgery as he had never done before. And I behaved with gallant bravery. Mother nearly fainted when I walked out of the operating room, carrying my tonsils in a glass jar.

The rheumatic fever had left a permanent mark. No physical education, no long walks, nor any sports for me! At least not for years. So, that summer we went to Szárszó, a resort at Lake Balaton, and I stayed with Mother in a small hotel. With such restriction on physical activity, frustrating boredom would have set in had it not been for the owner's daughter, who taught me how to make lovely jewelry from beads. I became so skilled that when we returned from our vacation, I asked Lili, my third cousin, to display my art pieces in her cleaning store's window and take orders. I earned the equivalent of several hundred dollars during that summer and fall.

The heart murmur subsided as time went on, and by the spring of 1943 I was allowed to resume, except for sports, a fairly normal physical existence. It was toward the end of that school year that Erika Viltschek, one of the sixteen

10

Jewish students in my entire school, told me that her brother wanted to be introduced to me. Until that time I had had no interest in boys, so I told her to tell him that he could meet me in front of the building any day as I came out of school. And so it was. The last day of school a young gentleman stopped me as I exited, clicked his heels and bowed, properly introduced himself as Bandi Viltschek, and asked if he could walk me home. He was so handsome, intelligent, polite and pleasant that I could not resist saying "yes" when he asked to be allowed to see me again.

This was the start of the first real "love affair" of my life. Except for our respective summer vacations, we saw each other daily and were nearly inseparable. Bandi was a year older than I, also an all "A" student, so with the advent of the new school year we began to do our daily homework in each other's company. Afterward we frequently practiced conversing in English or German, playing the piano, cards or chess, or going for walks.

I vividly recall my first kiss! It was a late August afternoon, and we were sitting on the couch, separated by an exquisitely carved chess set. I was deeply in thought about my next move, when suddenly Bandi leaned over and kissed me on my cheek. My reflex reaction was instantaneous and almost cruel. With all my might I slapped the poor boy's face. At first he looked at me with amazement; then, with his face turning from pink to crimson red from both embarrassment and anger, he rose, stared at me for a moment, and walked out without a word. He did not contact me for days. Although I was miserable, my pride did not allow me to telephone him. Finally Bandi did call, apologized and asked to be allowed to visit me the next day, my birthday. Of course I allowed him to come! I had regretted the incident a thousand times by then! The next afternoon he arrived with a beautifully wrapped box of candy, thirteen red roses, and photographs of me he had taken and processed himself. They were better than any portrait I had ever had, for Bandi was a very skilled amateur. But what thrilled me most was the comment he wrote in English on the back of one of the pictures: "To the first and only girl whom I love, loved, and shall always love. Your Bandi."

Shortly after the 1943-1944 school year began, my parents enrolled me in dancing school. We learned the fox trot, waltz, rhumba, tango and even the minuet. I was quite pretty and a good dancer, thus soon became popular.

One Saturday three cadets attended our open house. They sat and watched for a while; then one approached me and asked for a dance. As the next number began, the second cadet walked over, clicked his heels, bowed to me, then waved my partner to step aside. The third cadet did not even wait for the music to stop before he, in the same manner as that of his friend, cut in. We barely managed to take a few steps when the first young gentleman reappeared. Moments later, when the second tried to cut in, my partner refused to yield. Feeling humiliated and furious, Number Two slapped Number One with his white glove which, according to old custom, required the challenged one to respond by drawing his sword. Within an eye-blink, two swiftly moving swords were shimmering in the multicolored light of the rotating crystal chandelier. I felt both flattered and worried as the dancers stepped aside to watch the dueling pair.

It was quite an achievement of the instructors to separate the by-now-furious cadets. Meanwhile the room was emptying, as the predominantly Jewish group of parents, concerned about possible repercussion if their youngsters would get involved in a fight with the Aryans, began to leave with their children. My mother, too, went to the checkroom for my coat. She returned just as the young cadets were separated. At the same time, the instructor wisely declared

A Little Girl Grows Up

the dance to be over.

For me, however, the incident had not yet ended. As my mother was dragging me toward the exit, the first cadet reached out, got hold of my hand and asked politely to be allowed to escort me home. I observed my mother's frightened face, but thought it wiser not to anger the already irate young man, so I graciously accepted his offer. On the way home I made it a point to tell him I was Jewish. He heard, but did not react. Reaching my home, he asked to be allowed to call his family, to tell them he would return late, implying that he wished to visit with me for a while. Although I left the room, I could not help but overhear parts of his conversation: ". . . I'm fine. Just wish to visit with . . . on Ráday Street. . . Dr. Balla. . . Jewish. . . So what, I'm not marrying her!. . . It's my business, don't order me around! . . . And if I don't come home right now?. . . " But he did! With face crimson red, he said he would return, then instantly left.

My escapades did not last long, however, for in November Bandi found out about my popularity with the opposite sex and declared our friendship finished. The next day I felt miserable. Before going to bed I felt so bad that I started to cry. Mother tried to console me, then hugged me lovingly and kissed my forehead. As if she had touched a ghost, she stepped back and began observing me strangely. She ran for a thermometer, stuck it into my mouth and proceeded to undress me quickly. I don't know which one of us got more scared when we noticed that my torso was covered with little red spots and my skin had mysteriously turned a brownish-yellow color. In less than a minute my temperature registered 104°. Mother called Dr. Anna Szász, chief of the Children's Hospital, wrapped me in sheets dipped in ice-cold water to reduce the fever, then sat at my bedside and proceeded to pray.

As usual, Father was not at home. For the past several

13

years Dad had the habit of closing his office at 6:00 p.m., having a light supper with Mother and me, then going to a nearby cafe which many of his clients in the wholesale food business frequented. Both he and the clients were heavy card-players, winning or losing thousands per evening. Father would play and conduct business often until two in the morning. Except on very special occasions, my parents never went anywhere together. Even my Sunday forenoon walks with Dad had ceased years before, and Mother and I had become inseparable.

I recall seeing the concerned expression on the face of Dr. Szász, the tears rolling down Mother's face, but nothing beyond that. It was several days later before the crisis passed, my fever dropped, and I emerged from the unconscious state. It was nearly a month later when I finally recuperated from scarlet fever, combined with jaundice.

During the Christmas vacation all my new boyfriends came to visit, except my real love, Bandi. To celebrate my recovery, Mother had arranged a surprise New Year's party for me. It would have been a surprise had Bandi not called early that evening, saying that he would forgive me if I would kick out all the boys from the party and have him as the only male. We negotiated and settled with the compromise that I would use my recent sickness and weak heart as an excuse to end the party at 10:00 p.m., so after that we could be alone for a while.

And so began 1944, the year of pain and horror, beyond imagination.

CHAPTER 4: BEGINNING OF THE HORROR

By the beginning of 1944, even the Axis Powers knew they had lost the war. The only question was the length and cost in human lives before the total defeat. The news media spoke only of great victories, but the letters from the Front, which was by now on Polish territory, and increasingly heavy and frequent bombings, implied the contrary.

One day a family friend came to say good-bye. He had, through the Hungarian Zionist Federation, found the opportunity to go to Palestine, and he was leaving with his family. He proposed we do the same.

My father, although a highly knowledgeable and brilliant man, responded, "We don't need to take such chances. Hungarians would *never* tolerate the mass torture and murder of Jews, like the Germans and Poles have allowed in their ghettos and concentration camps! The stories we hear about German-occupied lands could never happen here. Our Jews are assimilated. Prominent in all segments of society. Such things couldn't happen to *us!*" And so, everything remained in status quo until March 19.

Before dawn, my family was awakened by the piercing ring of the telephone. Mother grew increasingly pale as she listened to her girlfriend's warning. Joli's boyfriend, a colonel in the army, had just informed her that German occupation troops had crossed the Austro-Hungarian border at 1:00 a.m. and, meeting no resistance, were proceeding on their roughly hundred-mile-long journey toward Budapest. He had called to warn her to stay in the house in case there would be trouble.

Father consoled us women by asserting that it was

probably only heavy troop movement through our country to the Russian front, to reinforce the retreating German militia. This pacified us and we went back to sleep. But in the morning, we found our radio's program schedule changed. All we could tune in was German gobbledygook!

Rebi, our maid, had Sunday afternoons off, so at noon she left. A short while later she returned. With her face white and body trembling, she cried, "Oh, something terrible has happened! Budapest has become a ghost town! All the stores are closed, even the movies and restaurants. There are no busses, cars, or even pedestrians on the streets. Life has stopped. I'm awfully scared!"

Being curious and naively brave, I began to nag my mother to go for a walk, to find out what had happened. Although reluctant and afraid, Mom finally succumbed. Walking through desolate streets, we soon spotted the parliament and other official buildings on the horizon. They looked like match boxes on top of swarming ant hills. As we got closer, the black dots took the form of Gestapo men (Geheim Staatpolizei, i.e., Secret Police) and SS (Schutz Storm Trooper), plus a multitude of soldiers surrounding motorcycles, trucks, heavy artillery, and many tanks. It took only a glimpse for us to realize that Rebi had reason to be scared, and Joli's warnings were not to be taken lightly. Within mere hours and with hardly any bloodshed, the Germans had occupied the nerve center of Hungary.

Regent Horthy's diary and official documents released after the war reveal what preceded that black day.

On the eve of March 15, three weeks before Russian troops reached Hungary's northeastern border, Regent Horthy received a message from the German ambassador that Hitler requested his appearance at Schloss-Klessheim on the seventeenth. Escorted by his war and foreign ministers and the chief of general staff, Horthy complied with the request.

On the forenoon of the eighteenth, once alone in Hitler's chamber, the Führer stated that he was aware of the regent's secret negotiations and that he planned to unite forces with the enemy. In spite of Horthy's denial, Hitler said he could not take chances and therefore he had already issued orders to his troops for the probable occupation of Hungary. Horthy pleaded and tried to reason, but to no avail. He walked out.

Meanwhile the Germans had staged an air raid, put the castle under a smoke screen, and informed the guests that bombs had severed the telephone lines.

At 6:00 p.m. the regent requested permission to return home, but he was told that first he must sign certain documents which demanded: nomination of a new quisling government; unconditional inclusion of Hungary in Germany's war economy; general control of water and railways; extradition of Axis deserters and refugees; Hungarian workers for German factories; and strict application of the Nuremberg laws against 1,000,000 Jews. Further, Hitler demanded that Horthy sign a declaration that the German troops entered Hungary with his government's approval.

Although the regent refused to sign the documents, at 8:00 p.m. he and his party were allowed to leave. His home-ward-bound train was halted at the Austrian border, delaying his arrival, with various excuses, until 11:00 the next forenoon. The delay gave time for eleven German divisions, planes, and heavy artillery to occupy Budapest, to close off (with the aid of Rumanian troops) the eastern half of the country, and for the Gestapo to surround the regent's castle, to round up and arrest anti-Nazi conservative elements, nationalist government officials and public figures, union leaders, journalists, and of course, many influential Jews.

The Allies quickly responded to the occupation with a

series of massive bombings.* Although we had had civil defense training and drills, people did not know how to react when hearing the seemingly unending series of explosions, starting within seconds after the sirens had sounded late Sunday afternoon on March 19, 1944.

Conforming to our previous drills, while my parents proceeded to shut off electric and gas lines, I gathered the emergency items to take with us to the shelter. I barely reached the storage room when I heard an ear-piercing blast, as if a bomb had hit next door. Carelessly, I ran to the window, just in time to see a nearby building go up in flames and collapse. Hundreds of people were running into the streets, shoving and screaming, trying to get into any and all moving vehicles. Within seconds cars were crashing into each other. Going to the nearest shelter (the cellar of each apartment building), the tenants were hysterically screaming, crying, cursing and shoving one another down the staircase. At the end of the raid there were far more injuries resulting from accidents due to panic than from falling bombs.

For Jews, however, the subsequent heavy air attacks became a minor fear or concern. For many, being killed by a bomb would have been a merciful end, far preferable to the tortures that awaited them.

On the afternoon of the occupation, Gestapo officers appeared at the Israelite Community of Pest's headquarters on Shíp Street, and ordered all Jewish leaders to gather the next morning for a conference. At 9:30 a.m., on March 20, two Gestapo officers and a translator appeared and promptly began issuing Eichmann's orders: a Jewish Council to be named by noon of the next day; the Germans, who were

---

* Premier Kállay had made a secret pact in 1942 with the Allied powers that we would not fire at their bypassing airplanes; in turn, they would not bomb our cities.

from then on in charge of all Hungarian Jews, would deal with all Jewish matters only via the Council, to whom all their co-religionists must be obedient; by 5:00 p.m. of March 21 the Council was to prepare and submit a list of all Jewish organizations and agencies, and the names of their leaders; all Jewish publications were ordered to have prior approval of the IV.B.4. section of the Gestapo, located in the Astoria Hotel; and finally, that no Jew was allowed to leave the city.

On the 22nd of March, after the lives of members of his family had been threatened, the regent appointed Sztójay as Prime Minister. Seven days later, the new cabinet held a meeting and established ordinances to "solve the Jewish question." From then on, new anti-Semitic edicts were issued almost daily.

The first decree, issued on March 29, required that Jews file a detailed report if they owned or operated any type of motor vehicle, or had a telephone. The next series of orders, issued two days later, dealt with employment and professional practices. Jobs of all Jewish government employees were to be terminated; Jewish employment of non-Jewish household help had to stop by April 15; subsequent practice and membership in the Press and Actors' Guild by April 30, and in the Lawyers' Bar (60% Jewish) by May 31; safe deposit boxes were immediately sealed, and Jews could draw no more than 1,000 Pengő (approximately $36) per business day from their personal accounts.

The next ordinance, issued on March 31, to be effective as of April 5, specified the identification of Jews. Anyone who had even one Jewish grandparent was considered a Jew and had to wear a canary yellow, six-pointed star (10 x 10 centimeters in size), made of cloth and sewed onto the left side of the chest area of the outer garment, worn whenever appearing on the street. The edicts were publicized via all the news media, publications of the Israelite Congregation and the Central Jewish Council, and placards posted on advertising pillars, bulletin boards and sides of buildings.

The bombings were now frequent and heavy. Due to this, schools terminated their year abruptly on April 5, the day when (coincidentally?) Jews had to begin wearing their Star of David emblems.

My day started with tears. I had hardly stepped out of our house when a filthy street-kid stepped in front of me; with obvious enjoyment, he called me "a dirty Jew" and spat a mouthful of saliva into my face. A nearby policeman observed the scene, but did not move a muscle. Feeling defeated and utterly helpless, wiping away the saliva and my tears, I proceeded to school.

We picked up our report cards, registered for the next year, and by 11:00 a.m. were ready to go home. As usual, many students gathered in small groups at the entrance to the school to chat for a while. Marika, the only other Jewish student in the fourth gymnazium (eighth grade) and I remained near a corridor window, watching the youngsters gradually disband and go home. But this time several little groups kept lingering much longer than usual. About an hour later we heard loud noises and saw two upper-grade Jewish girls exiting the building. Twenty or so students on the street surrounded them instantly and proceeded to beat them mercilessly. We were scared — mighty scared!

Five of our classmates were still standing across the street. We looked for help inside, but by now the building was deserted. Since there was no other open exit, with our hearts beating like drums, we finally took the plunge. Stealthily we stole out of the building and tiptoed along the walls, in opposite directions. I managed to get to the first intersection, about fifty yards, without being noticed. By then all five of my classmates, whom I had seen from the window, had taken after me. Having had a very weak heart and consequently very little physical exercise for the previous two years, a souvenir from the rheumatic and scarlet fever and jaundice, it took my classmates no time to catch up with me. I was never before so petrified. All I could do was pray. As if God had heard my plea, one of the girls yelled out, "Györgyi, wait for us!" I heard her, but without turning around kept panting, sobbing and running.

All of a sudden I felt a tight hug and a kiss on my wet cheek. Another, with tears in her eyes said, "What in the world took you so long in school? We waited and waited and though we will be in trouble for getting home so late, when we saw what happened to those upper classmen, we just had to stay to escort you home safely!" — There was a long moment of silence. I had to say "thank you" to someone above.

By now the Jewish Council was fully organized, its members and structure approved by Adolf Eichmann, head of the SS Special Operation Unit to liquidate Jews. The chief organ of the later-named Federation of the Hungarian Jews, the Central Council, consisted of eight prominent and wealthy members. They were to be aided and advised by the twenty-seven member Budapest Great Council and the twenty-two member National Great Council, composed of congregation leaders and rabbis. Administration of all their activities was divided among nine departments: Presidential, Finance, Social, Economic, Cultural and Statistical, Converts', Loan, plus the Dwelling and Travel Departments, in which my father had agreed to assist.

The multitude of anti-Semitic ordinances that followed fill three volumes of "Vádirat A Nácizmus Ellen".*The

---

* *Indictment Against Naziism,* by Dr. Ilona Beneschofsky and Elek Karsai, Magyar Izraeliták Országos Képviselete Kiadása, Budapest, 1958, 1960, 1967; also, *Zsidósors Magyarországon,* (Fate of the Hungarian Jews), by Dr. Jenő Lévai, Magyar Téka,1948.

following were only a few of the decrees issued during the month of April: all motor vehicles and radios of Jews had to be reported and later turned over to the authorities; their telephones were to be at once disconnected; all types of firearms, ammunitions and explosives, and licenses to possess such, had to be turned over to the police within eight days; Jews could not own or manage pharmacies after June 30; all Jewish organizations and institutions had to be liquidated without delay, their assets turned over temporarily to the Hungarian Jewish Coalition; entrance to the Chamber of Physicians was at once denied, with members losing their power to vote or to hold office, and after June being allowed to treat only Jewish patients; stores owned by Jews had to be inventoried, closed and turned over to the authorities by April 28; intellectual employment of Jews (such as office workers and salesmen) had to be terminated before June 30; also, termination of services by all Jewish public and civil servants had to be concluded by the last day of June.

The following two ordinances affected not only specific segments, but the Jewish population at large. By April 23 our rations had been severely reduced. From May 1 our *monthly* sugar and cooking oil allotment became 10 oz.; our *weekly* ration of only beef or horse meat went down to 3 oz.; and milk, now only for infants and pregnant women, was not to exceed a *daily* 8 oz. Although other edibles were not as yet rationed, their availability was far below the demand.

The edict of April 16 required Jews to report — and later to relinquish — all their assets, except furniture, household goods, and clothing items, if their total worth was below 10,000 Pengő ($360).* To be listed in any case were oriental rugs, all luxury items (such as name-brand watches or photo

---

cameras), and all objects of art. Further, to be deposited with the designated authorities were all objects with pearl, precious stone, gold, or platinum content; stocks, bonds, securities, etc., and all cash above 3,000 P ($108.)

May did not bring relief. As long as some segments of the population still had an income, orders kept coming in rapid succession. Licenses of those involved with printing or any kind of duplicating, and later those of all other profit-making trades, were revoked; new writings of Jewish authors could no longer be published, and all existing works of certain authors were destroyed by submitting them for paper recycling. Other ordinances specified that Jews could not appear in public beaches, swimming pools and bathhouses, nor in certain hotels, restaurants, bars, nightclubs, theatres, movies, etc. Further, they could travel only in the last trams of streetcars.

How did the Jews react to all of these edicts? Like a mouse in the jaws of a cat. Why? For many reasons. Hungarian Jews (about 5% of the total population), especially those of Budapest (about 16%), were so assimilated and integrated into the social and economic structure that, naively, they could not believe that the gentiles would tolerate their eventual elimination. The Central Council kept reiterating that the orders should be followed for self-protection, that resistance would induce severe retaliation against the individual and the entire community; that the government, under German advice, was so well organized and informed that any disobedience could easily and speedily be detected. Also, fear of the Gestapo's cruelty and deportation to concentration camps deterred most from disobeying the edicts. Finally: by then we knew the Germans were retreating and that the Front was already on Hungarian soil. Therefore, we expected to be liberated within the very near future, before the Nazis could begin our liquidation.

In spite of these reasons, two of the above decrees were disobeyed by many, frequently with detrimental results. One was the reporting of assets. Like my family, most Jews hid some of their valuables in devious ways, such as sewing jewelry and money into shoulder pads and mattresses, or giving them to gentile friends for safekeeping. The punishment, if discovered, ranged from enormous fines to torture and deportation of both parties involved.

My parents hid a large diamond ring in a bar of soap. This, together with several gold, platinum and smaller diamond objects, and cash which my father had kept in his office vault, we gave to Mr. Duka, and a suitcase full of artworks, furs, and cameras to the Szilárds.

Wearing the yellow star was the second edict often disobeyed. Tens of thousands — including myself during the last months of the war — chanced to appear on streets without it occasionally, and many more thousands never put it on. Those of the latter group either went into hiding and never surfaced, or acquired false identification papers and moved to an unfamiliar area.

In order to enforce the ordinance, thousands of "razzia" teams had been established. Usually a Gestapo or SS man, accompanied by a Hungarian, comprised a team that patrolled streets and requested pedestrians to identify themselves. If the individual could not produce proper identifications to prove his Aryan origin through his grandparents, he was assumed to be a Jew breaking the law. Those caught were typically tortured and/or deported to a concentration camp. Thus, false or forged Christian identification documents, acquirable for enormously large sums of money, enabled the owner to move to some distant place where he would not be recognized, and thus to evade the fate of a Jew.

For the price of several thousands of dollars many children, like my boyfriend's sister Erika, were taken in by distant gentile farmers, as relatives escaping from the heavy bombings of a city. Bandi and I also had the opportunity to go, but we did not want to be separated from our parents, nor from each other. My father had found in his files a set of documents — birth certificates of three generations — which had belonged to an orphan client of his, who was about my age and had resided in another city. These he made me hide, in the eventuality that they might save my life.

How did all these anti-Semitic laws affect our lives? Very severely. By June most of the Jews of Budapest were unemployed and without an income. Except for those who could barter their skilled labor, or dared to do black-market trading, most retrieved piece by piece their hidden valuables and, chancing deportation if caught, converted them into cash or exchanged them for food. The poorer ones at first relied on their relatives for help, but when those resources were exhausted, they turned to their Christian friends.

A large segment of the gentile population had aided Jews in some manner. At most a fifth were anti-Semitic by conviction. Perhaps another fifth aided the Gestapo and our quisling government for personal gains, such as promotions, favors, and rewards. About a third did not get involved; they disassociated themselves from the persecuted elements, and continued making the best of their status quo. The remaining fourth, however, helped our people to a lesser or greater degree. Their aid ranged from loaning money, keeping valuables or occasionally giving food to one of their unfortunate friends, to actually hiding Jews for months in their own homes. These Christians took an enormous chance, for they were constantly warned that anyone aiding an "enemy of the public" was to be severely punished. "Hiders", when caught, suffered the same fate as those they hid.

Even those city folk who benefited from the new era, by acquiring positions they could not have hoped for prior to the persecution of their countrymen, suffered the effects of the war. Nearly everyone had relatives who had died or had been injured in battle. Many by then had lost loved ones, or at least property, due to the frequent and heavy bombings. But the worst effect was the scarcity of necessary commodities and food. The Germans removed a significant portion of our livestock and food products; due to the general mobilization, agricultural production had greatly diminished; in view of the situation, farmers began to hoard their yield; bombed railways and roads and lack of non-military trains and trucks made shipping difficult. Thus, the capital's food supply was far below the need.

Until now my family had been relatively well off. Father had hidden enough cash to satisfy our needs, and mother had always kept a large supply of household commodities. We did not yet lack even food. I recall many a time when in the morning we opened the front door and found a sack of flour or sugar, a portion of a pig or a lamb between blocks of ice, a huge can of fat or a crate of fruits and vegetables sitting on our doorstep. Who else but father's clients in the wholesale food business could be the donors? We never did find out.

Meanwhile I, a 13½-year-old child, was still relatively content. With Bandi, who visited me daily, I often went food-hunting in nearby stores, stood in lines to cash in our ration tickets, visited elderly family members, or passed the time playing chess, reviewing what we had learned in school, or discussing abstract philosophical topics or politics. In the evenings I used to read or knit, and make coded entries in my little black diary. But the last few edicts of this three-month period affected severely even my life.

My first boyfriend, Bandi. Bp., 1944

Zrínyi Ilona Leány Gymnázium

26

The ordinance of June 5 stated that Jews could shop for food only between 11:00 a.m. and 1:00 p.m., and for non-edibles between 1:00 p.m. and 3:00 p.m. Those who served Jews at any other time would be jailed for two to six months.

On June 14 the Pest's newspaper, and the next day the Hungarian Jewish paper, carried lengthy and detailed articles about the latest city ordinance, requiring Jews to move into designated houses. The official ruling, issued on the 16th (and disseminated via 52,700 copies) specified that: by 8:00 p.m. on the 21st all Jews had to move into "star-houses", buildings which displayed a 30 x 30 centimeters, yellow, six-pointed star on a black background. Each family was entitled to occupy only one room (except doctors, lawyers and engineers, who could have an extra room for preserving their records); and those who were moving were allowed to gather and lock into one room of their vacated residence any of their personal belongings.

The chaos that followed is indescribable! People were running around frantically, bidding, as at an auction, for choice dwellings. Everyone tried to move into a "good location", far from target factories, close to relatives and shopping facilities, into buildings with large rooms, etc. Understandably, those who already lived in star-houses wanted their families and friends to share their homes, or else to profit in money or merchandise-barter. Thus, people dug out whatever valuables they still possessed and began searching and bargaining. Most Jews spent that night tearfully packing.

As if that were not bad enough, the next day the ordinance was revised, adding a few but removing a lot more buildings from the "star-list". This began an epidemic of insanity. About a third of those who spent perhaps their last penny to rent a hole in the wall were now both penniless and homeless. But, survive one must, so the frantic search continued.

The next problem that faced the Jews was finding a vehicle to move with. Since "star-wearing elements" had been for a long time forbidden to use any motorized vehicle or even to own a bicycle, only horse-drawn carriages and push-carts could be used. But how likely was it that one could secure such a vehicle when out of 36,000 houses, only 2,681 (scattered mainly in Pest) were identified by the star? And 28,000 dwellings had to be vacated by nearly 200,000 people, within at most five days! Some paid as much as their monthly wage for the use of a horse and carriage, while most brought along only what they were able to carry.

Due probably to the fact that the moving was much slower than anticipated, on the morning of June 21 a new ordinance extended the time until midnight of the 24th. But! On June 22 another update appeared, adding two while removing 700 from the star-houses list. Those poor souls had only two days to move.

The Dwelling Department of the Federation worked day and night setting up branch offices and temporary shelters to help people relocate. Even so, thousands ended up home-less, their certain fate to be deportation to a concentration camp.

My family was still among the most fortunate ones. Grandma Blau, my father's mother, did not have to move. Grandmother Blum found a good place nearby with a close friend, and my father's position at the Federation enabled him to select a choice place for the three of us.

Erzsébet Boulevard 57 was a beautiful four-story build-ing, relatively modern, located in an elegant section of the city. The house was structured so that the front apartments faced the main boulevard, while ours faced a quiet, small side street. It had three rooms, a small entrance hall, a kitchen and bathroom. Only an aged lady with her ailing forty-year-old daughter lived in it. The two largest and nicest rooms were to become ours. But Bandi and his mother (his father was already in a labor camp) were not as fortunate. Twice they had been able to find a suitable place, but the last change would leave them without a home. They kept searching until the last minute, when even my father's office was unable to help. I began to cry and plead. My parents, anticipating the horror to follow and warm-hearted as they were, decided to give up the smaller room and invited the Viltscheks to move in with us.

Before we moved, my father chose to seal his office, leaving everything everywhere in its place, except a commode, wardrobe, desk, bed and a sofa bed, besides our clothes and a very few personal treasures. These we brought to our new home on a wheelcart Father had borrowed from an ex-client. We even left paintings, lead crystal, porcelain and antique ornaments, normally valuable but then unsalable, in their original locations, anticipating that either the Germans or the new residents would break the seal anyway.

The next city ordinance restrained the movement of Jews, allowing us to leave our houses only between 2:00 and 5:00 p.m., and only for "appropriate reasons", such as to go to a doctor or to shop.

In spite of all the miseries, I was still relatively happy. Although the residents of star-houses were both Jews and Aryans, the four youngsters in our building were all Jewish. The oldest was Laci, almost sixteen; then Bandi, fifteen; then I, nearly fourteen; and the youngest, Laci's brother Miki, thirteen years of age. We made a good team. We spent practically day and night in each other's company.

Since the frequent air raids forced us to spend more hours of the twenty-four in the cellar than upstairs, we made the basement quite liveable. The manager had removed some of the partitions separating the storage areas of the tenants, moved the typically stored wood and coal, cleared the ground and sectioned the area into two large parts, one for the Aryans and one for Jews. Our parents put wooden planks along the stony earth walls and a huge rug on the damp, raw floor. They furnished our area with mattresses, cots, dining tables and armchairs, a bureau, desk, and a metal stove. They kept extra clothes, pots and pans, books, and even our games down there.

During the day, between air attacks, we stayed mostly in my apartment, the roomiest and best equipped. Between 2:00 and 5:00 p.m. the four of us would take turns standing in lines to cash our ration tickets, allowing each other time to occasionally break the law and visit nearby relatives or friends. My poor Grandmother Blum was so lonely; by then she could not even get in and out of her wheelchair. Two or three times a week my mother or I ran over to see her, even if only for minutes, to return before curfew. Fortunately, she had had a Jewish nurse who remained with her, taking only food and lodging as payment. Thank God for our mysterious friends who kept leaving food packages on our doorsteps even in our new location! Though we shared all with my grandmothers and the Viltscheks, there was enough, so none of us were ever really hungry.

We four youngsters were in every respect — age, I.Q., personality — very congenial. Bandi would teach me Latin, history, and algebra from his ninth-grade textbooks; I taught Miki eighth grade topics; and Bandi and Laci often reviewed or studied ahead. The rest of the time we discussed political theories, philosophized, quizzed each other from the dictionary or encyclopedia, practiced speaking English and German, and played cards, Monopoly or chess.

We also pursued a most unusual form of entertainment: experiments in mental telepathy. Although the brothers demonstrated no unusual talent, the frequency of successful communication between Bandi and me far superseded all statistical probabilities. I would think of something, such as, "Bring me a glass of water," or "Ask Laci to come up," and Bandi would know and carry out my mental command on the average of two out of five times.

In the evenings, while our parents usually visited with the other Jewish neighbors, Bandi and I would stand in the window of his room, his arm around my shoulders, gaze at the stars and listen to the music from a nearby cafe. Oh, how we loved to hear the gypsy band play "Argentina" and "Bolero"! And we talked about getting married after the war, after he became an engineer and I either the same or a lawyer, and where we would settle down, what kind of furniture we would buy, and how we would raise our children.

On one beautiful, starry night, Bandi could no longer resist and kissed me on the mouth. It startled me. Suddenly, a strange, hot flash ran through my veins and I responded instinctively and passionately. Wisely, Bandi pulled back and gently led me into the kitchen, claiming a sudden surge of hunger and thirst. Moments later our parents returned from the neighbors, which meant bedtime for all of us. I tossed and turned, pondered and worried. Finally, I awakened Mother and asked, "Mommy, if I kissed a boy, would it cause me to get a baby?" My mother let out a sigh of relief and replied, "It is late now, go to sleep, my child. Thank God you are still naive enough to ask such questions."

Mother's answer did not put me at ease, but I had to wait until after breakfast to be alone with Bandi to ask him. In tears I blurted out my fear: "What happens if I got pregnant last night?"

He looked at me with amazement, smiled at my innocence, then led me to the bookshelf and took out several volumes of the encyclopedia. Still smiling, he said: "Today I'll teach you human biology." I learned the facts of life, but he did not kiss me on the mouth again.

Several weeks passed uneventfully. Then, toward the end of July, the scenery in front of our house changed. The beautiful Royál Hotel across the street was taken over by the Germans. SS and Gestapo officers filled the building and the nearby streets. Although they did not bother us, their presence intensified our constant fear. But, to avoid upsetting each other, we rarely aired our deepest thoughts and emotions.

One day our neighbor Ema, whose apartment faced the hotel, took us youngsters up to the attic, to show us her workshop. Before the war she used to earn her living by selling garments she had knitted on machines. The attic had a large room full of equipment and a small storage room with a heavy metal door. There was a window which gave a view of the "lichthof", a mere six by eight-foot opening running the height of the building, designed to give ventilation to the bathroom and toilette of typical city apartments. Below, there was a straight four-story drop to a block of cement, and above, roughly an eight-foot rise to the gutter of the adjacent building.

This scene made such a strange impression on me that for days I could not block it out of my mind. Finally, a thought crystallized. If the Germans came into our house to take us away, I would attempt an escape through the workshop. I told my plan to my parents and buddies, but they all laughed at me and ignored my comments. Yet, I filed the thought carefully in the back of my mind.

As the air attacks increased, more and more rubble had to be cleared away fast to save trapped and injured people and to allow traffic to flow. The shortage of manpower became so great that Jews were allowed to voluntarily join the "rubble-force". The job was very hard, but although we were supposed to work only after every raid, we worked when our hearts and needs dictated it. The authorities found it too cumbersome to verify each Jewish volunteer's presence.

The activity had two great advantages. First, members wore a black X across their stars and were allowed to be on the streets during curfew after each air raid, which gave a chance to those who dared to run emergency errands. Second, among the rubble we often found food and valuables. For these reasons, although against my parents' will, I joined the rubble-force.

Sometime in August, the building across the street, next to the Gestapo-occupied Royál Hotel, got a face-lifting. We soon found out that the new offices were to belong to the big shots of the Arrow Cross Party, the Hungarian Nazi Party. As our fears increased, all we could do was pray and hope for a speedy Russian victory.*

The Jews of Budapest had no factual knowledge of what had been happening during the past half year outside the capital. We were not allowed to leave the city, had no radio, no telephone, little contact with gentiles, and only censored mail. We heard rumors of deportations, which, to preserve our sanity, we chose to ignore. How much the Central Committee or Great Council members knew, I would not venture to guess. Many of their activities were highly secretive. If my father had any knowledge, I could not know, for contrary to the past, when he often discussed his court cases at the dinner table, he never spoke about his contacts or activities at the Federation office. Having no relatives or close friends outside of Pest, I gave only infrequent, fleeting thoughts as to what might be happening to Jews elsewhere in Hungary.

One day in early September, during a long air raid, one

---

* The Front was already on Hungarian soil, along the southeast border of our country.

of the bombs hit very close to home. Our tiny cellar window crashed, beams vibrated, even our potbelly stove's pipes came crashing down. Everyone prayed. We feared we would be buried alive. After ear-piercing screams and cries from the direction of the street, there was a long silence. Upon the "all clear" sound, we all ran up the stairs like a stampeding herd. Our prayers were answered. Except for cosmetic damage, our building stood unharmed. However, the Arrow Cross Headquarters was in partial ruin.

It gave me great joy to run across the street, quickly clear some rubble, and before others got there, collect some precious booty. After my speedy return, while my parents and friends viewed my acquisitions with perplexity and apprehension, I plotted a grandiose escape. I visualized myself wearing a sample of each type of my newly-amassed treasures: a khaki-green skirt and shirt, with an Arrow Cross necktie, armband, and pin-on insignia! Later, when I voiced my brilliant plan, Mother nearly passed out and Father firmly forbade me to wear any of it.

The next day Mom packed my newly-acquired treasures in a dirty old paper bag, among some other clothes, and brought them over to Grandmother Blum. Later she admitted that she feared I might have been seen, and thought that since all the tenants in Grandmama's building were old folks, they were beyond suspicion or search. I was happy to hear that my treasures were not discarded, because my sixth sense told me — and it was infallible — that someday they could come in handy.

Our worst sufferings began on that black-letter day, October 15. Just after 1:30 p.m., the manager stepped out into the courtyard and with joyous shouts exclaimed: "Ladies and Gentlemen. Regent Horthy has just announced on the radio that THE WAR IS OVER! He has ordered all Hungarian soldiers to put down their guns and surrender." Everyone, Christians and Jews alike, ran out into the courtyard and hugged and kissed each other, amid happy tears.

I, alone, did not rejoice. My sixth sense told me to take a bath, dress warmly, remove the stars from my clothes, put the set of false identification which my father had long ago secured for me into my inside pocket, and stuff the outside ones with raisins and nuts. (Still available high-level of nutrition with small mass.) Thus, while everyone was childishly happy, I was preparing physically and emotionally for the worst.

The real horror of "The Final Solution" began for us at approximately 3:00 p.m., when Ema came running out of her apartment, screaming hysterically that she was under rapid fire, that her room was full of bullets. Within seconds, we all heard gunshots and loud voices coming through the entrance of our building. I did not hesitate. I ran into Ema's apartment, up the stairs to her workroom and to its window. Hearing footsteps behind me, I turned and saw Laci. He knew my crazy plan. Since there was no time to discuss details, I let him take the lead. Being an outstanding athlete, he managed to jump upwards from the window sill, catch the gutter of the neighboring roof, fling himself over and extend his arms toward me. The more-than-three-foot jump would have scared me enough to abandon my plan, had I not heard heavy footsteps and German voices coming from Ema's apartment. Thus, I climbed onto the sill, stretched my arms out, and, lifting my eyes to heaven, jumped upward. Laci managed to catch my wrist and fling my body onto the roof of the adjoining building.

We lay motionless on the glass roof of an artist's studio for a few minutes, until we heard a devastating bursting sound and felt the building vibrate. After the calm we began to creep across the cracked but unbroken glass, reaching for the gutter along the inner edge of the pyramidal roof. Due to the use of coal stoves, apartment buildings needed several chimneys for ventilation. These chimneys had to be cleaned periodically; therefore, we soon reached a six-inch-wide wooden plank, used by chimney sweepers, which ran along the roof's crest. Naively, we began to walk along it.

A dozen or so steps later I tripped, lost my balance and fell, fortunately on my stomach, with my head toward the peak. The roof being sharply slanted, my body began to slide rapidly downward. There was nothing to grab onto. A few seconds later I would land on the asphalt pavement, four flights below. As I kept getting closer to the edge, I felt my muscles tightening and my body becoming rigid from fright. I was literally petrified. Either that or the Lord above had saved my life. My feet got caught in the gutter, stopping my slide abruptly.

The next problem, of getting back up, seemed unsolvable. As I looked around helplessly, my eyes fell upon Laci's army-type boots. "What about it?" I heard myself think out loud. "Shoelaces," was the reply of a mysterious voice I seemed to hear. I called to Laci to remove his laces, join them and extend them down to me. He sat crosswise on the plank for strongest support, and pulled as I grabbed the end with one hand and clawed my way upward with the other. My heartbeats could have awakened the dead, but I finally reached the plank. Our second daring maneuver had met with success.

After this accident, we dared not go further. We lay on the plank and whispered, shivering from fear and the bitterly cold evening wind. We had a good view of a sizeable portion of the city, but for what seemed an eternity there was nothing to see. For hours Budapest was again a ghost town.

The temple clock had barely struck eleven when we saw under the starless sky a faint light moving toward us. Soon the undulating illumination was enhanced, and a hum became audible. As the light's intensity and the hum increased, so did our heartbeats. Time seemed to creep. Finally we could make out the details of that strange vision. Thousands of people were marching down the boulevard, torches in one hand and guns in the other, singing a revolutionary song. They all wore Arrow Cross uniforms.

As the parade proceeded, periodically four or five marchers split off the group and went into nearby houses. The pattern of that activity implied that these men went into star-houses. We lay motionless while they passed below us. By the time the end of the procession had passed, we saw the front approaching the parliament. We heard shots in the distance, then all was dark and silent again.

After some contemplation and discussion, we concluded that getting down safely via a chimney or sliding down on gutter pipes, even if we did manage to reach either, was imaginative but impossible. Further, we reasoned, whatever the Nazis had intended to do, they had already accomplished. Thus, we decided to return to the attic.

Sliding like worms along the plank and then the roof's crest, we retraced our path. At about 1:00 a.m. our acrobatic maneuvers culminated in success, and we landed loudly on a heap of rubble. We crept to the storage room and found the metal door intact, but locked. As we discussed in a whisper the possibilities of opening it, a young voice called out, "Is that you, Laci?" The door flung open upon his response, and there stood Miki with a flashlight in his hand. He pointed at the makeshift bed made out of wool and knitted yard goods, upon which we joyfully collapsed.

Miki filled us in on what had happened. "I knew of your hair-raising plan, and when Laci ran after you, I followed him. But by then the Nazis were so close behind me that all I had time for was to run into the storage room. I heard the Germans tramping up, going straight to the open window, exchanging comments, going down again; then I heard the whistle of a flying grenade, followed by the deafening noise of the burst." (That was what had cracked the glass roof we had been lying on and had split the machines in the work-room into slivers.)

"As you originally anticipated, the metal door protected me. I sat here, utterly petrified, as I heard two shots and many screams and cries coming from the flights below. After several minutes all was quiet again. Around midnight I crept downstairs. In your hall I saw the dead bodies of the ladies who shared your apartment — one shot in the heart, the other in the head. The rest of the apartments were empty. Judging from the humming noise coming from below, the people had been taken down into the cellar."

We told Miki about our escapade and what we had seen, and concluded that Szálasi and his Arrow Cross Party must have captured Horthy and his cabinet and had taken over the government of Hungary. With this dismal thought we fell asleep.

It was still pitch dark when heavy steps and loud voices awakened us. They led directly to our door and, as it could not be opened, a voice commanded, "Machen Sie Auf! (open up!)" No one budged.

Then another voice said, in Hungarian, "Open or we'll shoot you!" None of us moved. Only seconds had passed when the first voice ordered the second person, in German, to shoot the lock and throw in a grenade.

That did it! I yelled out, "Please, don't shoot! We are only frightened children. I'll open it!"

Two armed Nazis stepped in and shined a flashlight at us. They frisked Laci and Miki thoroughly and threw handcuffs on them. Miraculously, I was not searched. (The false papers were in my pocket.) Nor was I handcuffed. The German shoved and kicked the boys, making them tumble down the stairs. The Hungarian put a machine gun against my spine and ordered me to move. They forced us toward the cellar.

Along the last flight, while the boys were still being kicked and shoved, my captor proclaimed: "You filthy swine, you'd gladly deny your God to save your miserable life, wouldn't ya?"

Heaven knows what gave me the guts, but I halted sharply, turned around, looked him straight in the eyes and asserted, "Neither my God, nor my religious beliefs would I deny. Not even to save my life! When you'll kill us, we'll go to heaven. When you people will die, you'll go to hell."

Strangely, instead of shooting me or roughing me up, he merely said, "We'll probably die prematurely, but prior to it we shall cleanse the earth of all Jew-pigs!" Feeling proud of myself and strangely secure, carrying my head high, I proceeded to the cellar.

As the German Nazi kicked the door in, our parents and Bandi came running toward us. They were ever so happy to have us with them again. After the hugs and tears, Mom explained that Bandi, suspecting where we were and worried about what might have happened to me, could not bear the strain and had become hysterical. When the SS guard came closer, to shoot him, his mother kneeled down and begged the Nazi to go to the attic, where I was supposedly hiding, and to please find me and bring me down.

I was filled with mixed emotions. Although I was happy

to know my loved ones were still unharmed, I felt we had had a fair chance to escape the other Jews' imminent fate, and that I could have helped those dear to me far more as a gentile, using my false papers, than as part of the imprisoned group. My parents did not share my optimism and confidence. They were convinced that I was too immature and dependent to survive on my own, and feared that *when* (not if!) I got caught, I would not only be killed but tortured to death for claiming to be an Aryan, the utmost crime a Jew could commit.

The next forenoon three of the six guards were replaced. The new set consisted of two German and three Hungarian Nazis, plus one Hungarian soldier. As time went on, we all began to feel sick. For a day and a half we had had no access to food or water, nor to warm clothes, while sitting in the bitterly cold, damp cellar.

First, Mr. Schwarz went into convulsions. Some of the elderly required medicines, which they had had no chance to bring along when the Nazis rounded them up. I took a chance and went toward the Hungarian soldier. He raised his machine gun but allowed me to get close to him. I pleaded to be allowed to go upstairs to bring medicine, food, and clothing to these poor, sick, old people, but he said it was out of the question. No Jew was allowed to leave.

Around midnight, without a sound or move, Mr. Schwarz passed away. The Nazis had no compassion. Even the dead had to remain in the cellar! But the Hungarian soldier was not yet used to such cruelties. He motioned me to come to him, then whispered that soon, when the three old guards were to be replaced, he would take me upstairs.

Meanwhile Mrs. Green was getting worse. Her husband could not bear it any longer and yelled out toward the guards, "What sort of men are you? Letting a harmless old woman suffer so!" Upon this one of the Arrow Cross men walked over, lifted his pistol, and shot both Mr. and Mrs. Green. I helped move the two bodies to the furthest corner of the cellar and began to sob.

Around 2:00 a.m. the new guards arrived. During the temporary commotion my soldier motioned, and we quickly sneaked out of the cellar. Entering our apartment, I could not hide my horror as I stumbled and fell over the stiff and deteriorating bodies of my landladies. Every room had been ransacked, and except for the furniture and some badly worn clothes, everything of even minor value was gone! The only food left was a sack of barley and some rice. I grabbed the edibles, sweaters and coats, and whatever medicines I could find, then asked my soldier if we could stop in the other residences to gather more needed items. He agreed. I tied the corners of an old blanket and stuffed into it whatever I thought to be of use.

My soldier seemed kind and compassionate. In the last apartment, as I was ready to return to the cellar, he asked me to sit down and said, "Child, I feel real sorry for you. I hate to see you slaughtered like all the rest of your co-religionists will be. Soon after I bring you back, you ask another guard to let you go to the W.C. (toilette). Next to it there are some planks covering the cavity under the stairs. Go toward the W.C., then quickly beyond, squeeze between the planks and stay in that big hole, motionless. I'll be relieved at dawn, then I'll take you out." I expressed my gratitude and promised to follow his instructions.

After we returned and I distributed the contents of the bundle, I whispered to Mother the soldier's proposition. Although she was frightened for me and tried to talk me out of it, I proceeded as planned.

Time crept very slowly. The hole was pitch dark and small, and I had room only to sit crouched over. Hours later a hand reached in and dropped a soft object. It was a ham sandwich. I gobbled it up and dozed off. A strange ticklish feeling awakened me. Rodents were running across my body, en route to the corpses nearby. A sliver of light coming from upstairs, shining through the cracks of the wooden stairs, allowed me to read my watch. It was almost noon. The only sound to be heard was made by the rats, as they squeaked and chomped on the flesh of the dead.

I couldn't stand it any longer. I crawled to my entrance space between the planks, and as quietly as possible squeezed through. To my luck the nearest guard was many yards away, turned in the opposite direction. I stepped into the toilette, then back to the big room. Everything was status quo, except that Laci's father had died from a heart attack. Everyone was glad about my return, and strangely, so was I.

I looked for my benefactor, but he was not in sight. Bandi later told me that shortly before my return he had gotten into an argument with the three Arrow Cross men, one of which finally pulled a gun and shot him. The other two carried the soldier's body upstairs, then returned to their duty.

As if having returned from years of absence, I scrutinizingly looked around. Our little group was a pathetic sight to behold. Huddling together and sobbing, quietly bearing pain, hunger, cold and fright, without a ray of hope, resigned to go to the slaughterhouse like cattle!

The "star-house" we lived in, and the roof through which I tried to escape on Oct. 15, when the Arrow Cross Party usurped power.

Soon after dark, new Nazi wardens arrived. They at once ordered the Jews to go up the stairs and gather in front of the house. I thought of escape, but with twelve armed men guarding fewer than sixty of us, there was no chance. They lined us up twelve abreast and commanded us to march along Erzsébet Boulevard. As we passed other star-houses, groups of Jews were attached to the ends of the columns.

Mr. Salamon, a few rows behind me, tripped on a cobblestone and fell. His poor old wife bent down to help him up. The people behind them halted. The SS on our left whirled his whip in the air and with obvious sadistic delight landed it like a lasso, around the necks of members of the captive herd. The Nazi on our right aimed his submachine gun and shot the helpless couple, then commanded the flock to continue marching, in straight lines, and to "step on the Jew pigs if they're in the way."

After a couple of miles or so we were ordered to turn into a side street. It was so narrow that twelve of us abreast completely filled the road, the guards using the two narrow sidewalks. It was a bitterly cold, damp, cloudy, starless night. All of a sudden, out of the complete darkness, two enormous lights shone upon us. I could not see the ends of our columns; by now there must have been many hundreds of us. As we marched into the beams, only the frequent cracks of the whips broke the still of the night. Finally a thundering roar was accompanied by flickering lights, as the enormous tiger-tank began to roll toward us. Dad behind, Mom and I were in the center of the second row. As the tank approached, a brainstorm hit me: since its belly was about a foot above the ground, if we were to throw ourselves flat on the road, we might escape being crushed to death. I grabbed Mom's hand and whispered my idea to her. She looked at me, made no sound, just kept marching like a zombie. The closer the tank got, the harder we all prayed. Only an outright miracle could prevent our slaughter. And, as so many times later, the Lord manifested a miracle! We heard some loud voices behind the tank, then barely a foot before our first row, the mechanical monster came to a screeching halt.

The miracle ended soon after the tank was ordered to back up and we to proceed. The frequent sounds of whip-lashes and pistol shots suggested the limit of human endur-ance. The dead were quickly replaced by new groups taken from the star-houses as we passed them along the way toward the old "Jew-town". We reached our destination, the Rum-bach Street Temple, at about midnight. The temple gates were flung open and we were whipped into our cage. People behind us kept shoving, but we could hardly move. The tem-ple, designed for a few hundred worshippers, had several times that many in it already. How could it accommodate the additional 500 or more of us?

My parents and friends fought our way up to the bal-cony. People—everywhere! Sitting in each other's laps, lying on the footboards and prayerbook benches, squeezing one another in the aisles. And the cries — of people dying from hunger, pain and diseases! And the smell — the horrible smell of people vomiting, defecating and urinating, mingled with the fetid odor of deteriorating corpses!

A few hours later my father and some other elders managed to congregate at the altar, to plan some organization to reduce the suffering. First, all dead bodies were to be isolated. But where? Only the men's and ladies' rooms had doors. So, since most people could not fight through the crowd to reach the toilettes anyway, corpses were passed along above our heads and piled up ceiling high in the two tiny bathrooms.

Next, we needed air. Someone smashed a window, but at once we were under machine gun attack. We dared not attempt it again.

Starvation was bad enough, but dehydration was more of a problem. The waterpipes had been damaged; thus, even the two sinks in the toilettes failed to yield the life-preserving liquid.

And then came the rats! Rats which used to live in sewers and feed on garbage were as hungry as the Jews. Food had been scarce for so long that edibles were never discarded. The rats' new food source became the ever-increasing supply of corpses. And our heap kept growing by the minute. We carried our dead loved ones to the "altars" like rat-worshipers' offerings.

With the advent of time the heap grew faster than the beasts could consume the flesh. In the absence of sufficient oxygen, the rest of us gradually lost the energy to move, talk, or even to cry. The foul smell of vomit, feces, and rotting corpses — which by now overflowed the capacity of the toilettes — took away even starving people's hunger; thus, we just vegetated hopelessly, awaiting death.

Nearly three days after our arrival — but four or almost five days for the earlier groups — an unexpected gush of air reached the balcony. Pandemonium erupted downstairs. It took a while for us to learn that a huge drum, filled with some restaurant dishwater, was shoved into the temple. Starving animals would have used better manners descending on a prey. Men shoved, kicked, scratched, some even jumped from the balcony, to reach the life-saving liquid.

The Lord must have heard our prayer, for during the night a new gush of air brought us out of our semi-coma. This time the air kept coming, the noise level increased, and soon the crowd began to move. It took an hour or so before we, on the balcony, were able to descend. Once outside, a dozen or so policemen were grouping us by our residences. This time not Jews', but Arrow Cross men's dead bodies decorated the road as, with loaded pistols pointing in the opposite direction, protecting *us* now, the policemen escorted us back to our homes.

Upon arrival we found the corpses of our landladies gone, but so was almost everything else. Except for the furniture, a bedspread and some ragged old clothes, only my diary, books and dishes had been left for us. Bandi found a hidden sack of barley, which his mother boiled and shared with us. After our "feast" we stretched out on our beds and went contentedly to sleep.

Rumbach Temple, where over 2,000 Jews were held captive for days.

Group of Jews, like us, blinded by the headlights while herded toward the oncoming tiger tank, which was to mow the people down.

CHAPTER 8: SAFE-PAPER

Next morning, on October 20, about 10:00 a.m., we were awakened by shouts. "All Jewish males age 14 to 60, and females age 16 to 40 are to gather at once in the yard!" I was too young and Mother too old, but Father, Bandi, and his mother had to go.

Bandi was so scared that he froze. I acted quickly. I ordered him to bed, rubbed his face with a rag to flaming red, and with a sliver of wood dipped in the blood that dripped after I pricked my finger, I drew spots on his face and hands. I barely finished "decorating" him when we heard the Nazis kicking in the door and yelling, "Heraus! (Out!)"

I walked out toward them and, wearing a dumb little girl's expression, in a squeaky voice said, "Don't go in there, you'll catch scarlet fever! The kid in there is very sick. He has a big fever and lots of spots on him. He scratches like crazy. If you go in, you'll catch it too!" The Arrow Cross man

smiled, but pushed me out of his way. The German kicked the door in, took one look at Bandi, turned around, and without a word left the apartment. Needless to say, his Hungarian counterpart followed without further ado. This saved Bandi, at least for a while.

When the manager assured the Nazis that all the Jews of the specified ages were gathered in the yard, with submachine guns pointing at them, they were taken away. My father, Bandi's mother, Laci and his mother, . . . very few Jews were left behind!

Our secret guardian angels must have visited us during the wee hours of the morning, for when we arose the next day, Mom and I found all sorts of edibles, just as before, on our doorstep. During the day, the manager was kind enough to call Grandmother Blum's Aryan neighbor, so we found out to our great relief that nothing had happened to the Jews in her building and immediate vicinity.

The next few days passed uneventfully. Mother spent some time visiting Mr. and Mrs. Bolgár, our neighbors in their seventies, but most of the time she just lay on the bed speechless, with a blank expression, or quietly sobbed.

On the morning of November 6, there was a polite knock on our door. Opening it I almost fainted, recognizing Jákob, Bandi's childhood buddy, bedecked with an SS uniform. Noticing my paleness, he quickly explained that since the October 15 purge, when he had lost his entire family, he had been hiding among the rubble. In one such area he had found a dead SS, whose clothes he was currently wearing.

After the three of us regained our composure, Jákob informed us that the Swiss, Swedish and Portuguese Consulates were issuing a limited number of "protective passports", documents asserting that after the war the owners could legally enter, settle and become citizens of the issuing countries. Hoping that the Germans, to avoid possible conflict with those neutral countries, would treat the recipients as foreign citizens and not as local Jews, he came to find Bandi and help him secure such a paper. I offered to go with Jákob to get papers for both me and the Viltschek family, and begged Bandi to stay home, not to take the chance of appearing on the streets without the star, without false papers, and on top of it masquerading as an SS. I knew that Bandi was not a shrewd and conniving character, and my intuition told me that he would get into grave trouble, but Bandi felt a deep concern for me and preferred to take the chance himself. After an argument the two of them left, and as I had anticipated, neither returned. Only after the war did I find out about the tortures they had suffered when caught, and later while interned in the Dachau Concentration Camp.

The next morning before mother awoke, I sneaked out and went to the Swiss Consulate, armed with my false papers and coat without the star. Thousands of people were already crowding the building, all pushing to get in. I elbowed my way through the crowd. Nearing the entrance, I saw a young officer exit, whom I recognized at once. He was one of the three cadets who drew swords over me in dancing school, only a year ago. I called to him and, to my delight, he recognized me also. We walked a little distance away from the mob; then I told him about my fate and mission at the consulate. Although he seemed a bit afraid of being seen with a Jewess in case I was recognized, he was sufficiently compassionate and daring to go along with my wild scheme.

First, he went back into the building and within an hour managed to secure a "safe-paper", as these protective passports were later commonly called, made out in my name. Next, we walked for several miles, in and out of used furniture and office supply stores, acting as though we were looking to buy a typewriter. We tested a great many before we found one that matched the type on my safe-paper. While the owner was not looking, I typed above my name, "Dr. Balla Ernő & wife, former Blum Rózsi," the names of my parents, after which we quickly left the store. The first open portrait photographer was able to make copies of my parents' pictures from the ones I always carried in my wallet, and also to make several photo duplicates of the now complete document. And so, at the end of a very busy day, I returned to my frantic mother with my precious acquisition, a safe-paper for her, Dad, and myself.

A few days later a postcard arrived. Father wrote that he had been taken to a labor camp, but his unit was to be relocated and en route would be shipped through Budapest. He wrote that they anticipated spending the night of November 12 in or around the Dohány Temple, the big one on the edge of the Jewish section of the city. He asked us to try to send to him, with an Aryan, some food, medicines, and warm clothes.

Needless to say, I was off again! The very next air raid provided the opportunity. I went to clear rubble during the night, stuffing men's clothing and edibles into a big potato sack I had found and had managed to hide and drag with me, unnoticed by the Nazis. My poor mother was bordering on insanity worrying about me, but her sheltered little child had grown into a daring and conniving young woman; I was mentally maturing by years with the passage of each day.

I kept up my rubble-looting escapades until the last minute. On the 13th of November I was up at dawn, got dressed in the most childish clothes I had found among my acquisitions, and before Mom awakened, carrying the clothes and stuff in the potato sack on my back, I was off to see Father.

Thousands of people crowded the streets around the Dohány Temple. No one wore the star, but some were obviously Jewish. Policemen guarded the temple yard and nearby buildings, holding in their hands the list of names of the men stationed in each house. I elbowed my way through the crowd. Reaching the front row, I recognized one of the policemen. He was one of those who had attacked our Nazi captors and liberated us from the Rumbach Street Temple a few weeks before. Logic told me to hide, for if he saw me without the star, it was his duty to turn me over to the Nazis; but my sixth sense told me to trust the guard. I took a daring chance. Dragging the sack behind me, I crept under the rope barrier, then bravely walked up to him. Before he could speak, I whispered to him that I anticipated that he might recognize me, but that I was willing to suffer any consequences for being able to see my father again. I left it up to him either to take me to the proper building, or to turn me over to the Arrow Cross men. The policeman pondered for a moment, then smiled and looked at his list. He found my father to be stationed in that very house. Shielding me from sight with his body, he pushed me through the entrance. I leaned against the wall, shaking like a leaf. Soon I heard him yelling upstairs, calling Father by name, ordering him to come down to the door. Dad seeing me without the star, and I seeing how he had aged, eyes sunken and only skin and bones — upon sighting each other, we both almost fainted.

We barely had time to exchange hugs and kisses when my policeman stuck his head in and motioned that the two of us should simply walk out. I whispered to Dad to put on the overcoat I had brought and walk out with me, arm in arm, smiling. My father looked at me tenderly, and with tears in his eyes said, "No, my dearest. You, as a cute little girl, might get away with some camouflage. But I, who have lived by the law all my life, do not know how to pretend. Besides, being an able-bodied male, I would be caught within the block. And then you, too, would suffer. I know what the Nazis do to masquerading and escaping Jews. I could not bear to see you being tortured. I am almost fifty-six years old. Anyhow, my life is nearly over. You just watch your step and take care of yourself! Do not take any more risks on my behalf!"

Our conversation had to end, because my policeman motioned me to leave immediately. We kissed each other once more, I gave Dad the stuffed potato sack and safe-paper, then stole out of the building. I had barely turned the corner when a truckful of armed SS men arrived. Had we walked out as the policeman suggested, Dad and I would surely have been caught. I cried all the way home, as if I knew that this was to be the last time I saw Father.

Upon my return, Mother was raving mad. She had planned for both of us to go together, wearing our stars, during the permitted hours. Not being aware of my intentions, she did not know where I had disappeared. Horrible thoughts had been crossing her mind. Seeing no sense in depressing her with the truth, I said I had had a nice, long talk with Father, that he looked well and was in a cheerful mood, and when I gave him the safe-paper he was sure he would soon be released. Hearing these words and having me home safely, put her mind at ease. At 1:00 p.m. we both went running to Dad, but by then the streets were empty. The temple's caretaker told us that Father's labor force had been evacuated hours before.

One of the 1,983 "star-houses", where the nearly 200,000 residents of Budapest dwelled between June and December of 1944.

51

November 15th was the last day for Jews who had safe-papers to find a living space in a designated few blocks of the city. The Nazis figured that 72 houses would suffice, since only the Swedish (4500), Swiss (7800), Spanish (100), and Portuguese (698) consulates and the Vatican (2500) issued such affidavits. Thus, assigning 15,600 Jews where previously 3969 people had resided seemed relatively simple and speedy. (The roughly 20,000 undistinguishable Swiss forgeries, however, complicated the situation, so the authorities granted two additional days to complete the relocation.)

Mom decided that at 2:00 p.m. she would go to begin standing in line at the housing bureau on Szent István Boulevard at Pozsonyi Street, and I, after cashing our bread ticket, was to join her there. I felt ill at ease letting Mother go alone, so, instead of walking, I removed my coat displaying the star and chanced getting on the streetcar. Blocks before my stop, however, clearly visible was the huge line around the tall office building. I also spotted a "razzia" team hard at work in front of the Nazi-house, located between the bureau and my streetcar stop. Just as a precaution, I rode a stop beyond and walked along the several city-blocks-long line, looking for Mom. A long distance from the entrance I spotted an acquaintance. She told me that my mother had left earlier, to get home before curfew.

Realizing it was almost 5:00 p.m., I hurriedly crossed the street and hopped the first streetcar. As we rode by the Nazi-house I saw the patrol stopping people. They must have found some Jews, for I observed them hitting two men with the butts of their submachine guns and shoving them through the entrance.

I made it home safely, but upon arrival found out that when Mother had returned and did not find me at home, she became so worried that she had decided to take the chance of going back to look for me. Anticipating what might happen,

I took off after Mom. Not wearing the star and getting off a stop beyond, I again reached the crowd safely. There were still thousands of people, all gentile friends of Jews who had returned to their homes by then. (It was months later when I found out that there were people in the consulates who forged affidavits, issuing them by the thousands.)

I walked back and forth along the line for awhile, but Mom was nowhere in sight. It was close to 6:00 p.m. when a truckful of Nazis arrived at the scene. The armed men jumped off the still-moving vehicle, and with the speed of lightning began herding all those in line toward and into the 1 Szent István Boulevard Nazi-house.

I acted like a disinterested pedestrian, walked forward nonchalantly, stepping into the nearest open store and browsing around just long enough to see those poor people being whipped, beaten, and herded away. When the last Nazi passed by, I casually walked out of the store, crossed the street, hopped the first streetcar, and returned home. As I had feared, Mom was not there; nor did she return later.

Early the next morning, very scared but motivated by my deep love of my mother, I dressed in my most childish-looking clothes and, without the yellow star, rode across town to see Mr. Ferenc Nagy, an ex-client of Father, the Arrow Cross Party's chief of the eighth sector of Budapest.

Simulating the behavior of a nine-to-ten-year-old, I walked up to the armed guard and requested to see my uncle Nagy. He looked at me puzzled, for it was unusual for a child to wish to confer with such an important person. Not wanting to allow him too much time to think, I put on a very convincing act of bursting into tears and blurting out that our house was hit during the night's air raid, my parents were killed, and I had no other relative but Uncle Ferenc. The guard looked at me with pity, motioned for me to enter, and commanded the inside security man to take me upstairs. I was positively petrified, but hid my emotions remarkably well.

When we reached a huge padded door, he instructed me to wait outside. As he opened it, I saw Mr. Nagy behind an enormous, exquisitely carved, antique desk. This was it! I had to act instantly.

Being very small, I managed to bypass the guard standing in the doorway, made a beeline dash to and around the desk, jumped into Mr. Nagy's lap, and whispered to him to get rid of the man. Pale as a ghost and hands trembling, he did as I asked. I gave him a chance to recuperate from the shock of my appearance, then in a very mature tone described what had happened to my parents, and since I did not know where my father was, nor even whether he was still alive, I asked Nagy to at least get Mother released. His response was that he did not think he could do it. I looked him straight in the eyes and replied, "Mr. Nagy, if it were not for my father getting you out of many black-market shady deals, you would not even have the opportunity to help. You'd be in jail today! As it is, you are a powerful man. You order torture or death of many Jews daily. We both know that with a phone call you could kill or free anyone recently caught. You owe at least that much to my father. Besides, some day you'll have to account to the Almighty for all the sufferings you've caused. It will be nice to have at least one good deed to recall!"

After a seemingly eternally long silence, Nagy softly said, "I'll see what I can do." He called his guard and told him to give me some money and to put me on a bus. — The Lord had performed another miracle!

I spent the rest of that day and the next alternately thinking, praying, and crying. *Would* Mr. Nagy do anything? *Could* he accomplish such a feat? Mom was trapped in another Nazi-house; did Nagy have enough influence? What if they had already shipped all those people to a concentration camp? If not, they would not keep them all in that building overnight. Where had they been taken? Could Nagy find it out? Had they been tortured? Was she still alive?

Logically, the chance of my mother being released was almost nil. I couldn't bear the thought! I wanted to go to Grandmama — I felt so terribly lost and alone — but I had to be home in case Nagy liberated Mom.

On the third morning, about 10:00, there was a knock on the door. Outside stood a dirty, old, dumb-looking soldier. He asked my name, then handed me a folded piece of paper. Tears poured down my cheeks as I read: "My Dearest Child. As you perhaps figured, I was caught by a razzia after curfew. They took me, and many others, into the Arrow Cross house. Later all of us were taken to the Óbuda Brick Factory. And there a miracle happened. Before nightfall the loud-speaker called me by name. Ten thousands of people — they called only me! I reported to the chief Arrow Cross man and he turned me over to this nice soldier. He brought me back to the safe-house, where space had been already assigned for both of us. This kind soldier told me he had been instructed by a very important person to bring you here today. I have no idea how or why this all happened, but God's hand is mysterious and we are often not to know His reason. Pack up whatever you can carry and let the soldier bring you to me."

My first reaction was pure ecstasy! I packed a bundle, dressed up warmly, put my diary in my pocket, and then I had to ask the crucial question: "Should I or should I not wear the star?" The soldier looked at me stupidly, then replied, with a heavy uneducated farmhand's dialect:

"You're a Jew, ain't ya? You gotta wear one of them stars!"

We got on the streetcar and off at the correct stop, a few hundred yards before that infamous Nazi-house, 1 Szent István Boulevard. My heart beat like a drum. As expected, a razzia team stood in front. They returned my soldier's salute with a "Heil Hitler" and "Kitartás, éljen Szálasi!" (Fortitude, long live Szálasi!) We passed them by about a dozen steps before they realized that I wore a star. Since soldiers as yet in Budapest had never been assigned to guard Jews, they knew something was illegitimate. The Nazis turned, reached out, and grabbed us. Without a question or chance to explain, the Hungarian informed my soldier that he would be court-martialed and jailed for walking patronizingly on the street with a Jew during curfew, while the German grabbed my arm and dragged me down to the cellar. As they shoved me in, I landed practically in the arms of a high-ranking Gestapo officer. He caught me and smiled, then pinched my cheeks while calling me a cute little Jewish wh . . ., stuck a luger in my ribs, and set me down beside himself on a nearby bench along the wall.

Every minute detail of the sight I saw shall remain vividly in my memory, as long as I live! Picture a huge cellar room. About a hundred people facing a wall, arms above their heads. Women on the left, humming a German marching tune; men on the right, whistling the same. About a dozen SS and Gestapo men, plus another dozen Arrow Cross Party members, walking between the rows and whipping those pathetic skeletons with a cattail whip to the rhythm of the tune.

I said skeletons, for by now each stood in a pool of blood, bodies shredded by the seven straps of the whip, an empty eye socket or an ear ripped off of some, blobs of flesh dangling here and there, and some raw bone exposed on all.

A once beautiful young girl in line just in front of us turned her one-eyed face toward us and begged, "Please, make them stop!" My officer got up, pulled out his whip, shredded her body in a few more places, and when she collapsed, kicked her twice, then shot her in the heart.

In the far corner of the cellar an old rabbi was crouching down, mumbling from his prayer book. A Party man standing nearby picked up a hand-carved antique armchair and held it above the old man's head. A young uniformed girl rushed over and passionately exclaimed, "Daddy, don't hit the Jew with that chair, you might damage it!"

A cavelike portion of the cellar contained the ghastliest sight. Naked men and women were nailed to the wall by their ankles, hanging upside down, their bodies slashed and carved. One had had her breasts cut off; another had lost his genitals, a third was without arms; a young girl's stomach was split open. . . . Dozens there were brutally mutilated.

What crime could they have committed? Most likely no more than just trying to stay alive. I closed my eyes and prayed.

Suddenly the air raid sirens sounded. Evidently the cellar was needed as a shelter, which meant they had to get rid of us. The whips snapped as they herded the half-dead bodies toward and through a large black hole in the wall. I knew not what was on the other side, but felt it couldn't possibly be worse. I also knew that my body was destined to serve the Gestapo men. With lightning speed, I plotted a course to change my destiny.

During the momentary confusion the officer had to issue commands, so he turned and moved the luger away from my ribs. This was my God-given chance. I wore a reversible coat, light grey outside and navy within. My hair was long and pulled severely back, held away from my face with pins. In the instant the gun barrel left my rib cage, I reversed my coat, ripped out the pins allowing my hair to cover my face, and descending on all fours, crept rapidly toward the black hole. I heard the officer searching for me and cussing, but by then I was through the dark opening.

Well, I had been wrong. I had underestimated the Nazis' cruelty. The other side was the true hell! It was a narrow tunnel, dug under the foundation, seemingly endless. It was not high enough for us to stand erect and barely the width of our shoulders. After the last remnant of a still-breathing human was squeezed in, the Nazis closed the hole.

A normal mind is not capable of imagining the suffering that followed. All, except me, were bleeding somewhere and had raw flesh exposed. As we were squeezed like sardines, any movement caused the unprotected tissues to rub against another's shred of clothes, or the rocky earth which paved the tunnel. For lack of ventilation, breathing became difficult. Soon excruciating cramps set into our leg and back muscles from having to partially squat. The fear and pain caused people to vomit and eliminate, of course, upon each other. To top it all, these "ideal" conditions soon brought the local rats.

At first, the tunnel was filled with horrified screams, which soon turned into cries, then sobs; finally, only the squeaks of our cohabitants could be heard. Those who did not die passed out from pain and lack of oxygen.

Finally, a ray of light and a gush of cold night air brought me to consciousness. A piercing voice kept yelling, "Heraus, Heraus!" (Come out!) I tried to move, but bodies blocked my way. On my stomach, like a worm, I worked my way outward. The ever-increasing cries and shrieks indicated the presence of living beings under and ahead of me.

At the exit of the tunnel, as soon as we stood up erect, two Nazi soldiers proceeded to frisk us. Rings, broaches, and watches were grabbed off; earrings ripped out; gold-crowned teeth knocked out with butts of guns. We were counted — none knew why — then lined up eight abreast and ordered to march.

People around me kept dropping like flies. Our new Nazi guards did not use their whips, but with sadistic delight shot those who tripped or collapsed. As my sensations and memory began to return, I kept running my hands over various parts of my body, searching for bullet holes, whip marks or rat bites. Slowly I recalled that I got away from that officer unharmed, and figured out logically that since I did not smell of fresh blood, the rats had had their feast without me. Soon the bitterly cold and damp night air dulled my senses, so even the backache and leg cramps seemed to have disappeared.

We must have walked a few miles already when I noticed a Gestapo officer walking briskly between our lines, shining a lantern into some of the women's faces. — We were a large bunch by now, since, when passing other Nazi-houses, more victims were attached to our group. — The officer was only one row behind me when I heard him murmur angrily in German, "That young Jew b... must have dropped dead or been left stuck in the tunnel." With feverish speed I messed up my hair, pulling it more over my face, and since my previous pale grey coat was now almost black, he passed me by, still cussing. During the march I had sufficient time to properly thank the Lord.

Before we crossed the Danube River, our group was ordered to halt. We had to watch one of the Nazis' favorite entertainments.

There were about fifty men and women lined up along the river bank, arms extended sideways and wrists tied with heavy ropes to the wrists of adjacent persons. The prisoners had to stand facing the river, toes touching the edge of the pavement. Parallel to and behind them, fifteen or so feet away stood SS men, one for each four victims, pointing their loaded submachine guns. As proper at military funerals, someone at the far end played a German march on the bugle. As the last note of the composition sounded, the SS men in perfect unison pulled their triggers, moved their guns first left to right, then right to left, firing until each victim's body had tumbled into the river. We listened to the cracking of the floating ice blocks, and watched the gunmen as they remained momentarily silent and motionless. Then we continued being herded along the bank, being forced to watch the gradually emerging bodies of the dead.

Soon we had to cross a bridge connecting Pest to Buda. The capital was structured so that the suburbs contained the industrial plants and factories, Pest the large apartment and office buildings and stores, while Buda was scenic and hilly, mainly residential with decreased street traffic. The icy roads were covered with snow, knee-deep, making our journey much more painful and difficult. Those of us whose strength held out and who did not stumble or collapse, reached the Óbuda Brick Factory slightly before dawn. We were herded into the brickdryers. Then our guards disappeared. The brickdryers were open structures, about eight feet wide and a hundred or so long, with widely spaced poles supporting the thin roofs. We could not notice the two-foot high sides, for the freshly fallen snow had reached far above our knees. My hands and legs by now were frostbitten, and my body was numb from exhaustion and cold. As I was about to lie down to go to sleep, an old man's voice behind me said, "No, child; keep moving, or you'll literally freeze to death." I sat right up and struck up a conversation.

Mr. Szamos did most of the talking. "There are tens of thousands of people in the complex. Some, still alive, brought last week or daily since. My group arrived two days ago. We got no food as yet. The area is surrounded by a wire fence, some think electrified. The guards don't bother much with us, just patrol around the trains, the factory, and watch us from the top of its roof. They seem more bored than cruel. Except the SS in the 'patio'! They entertain themselves when some shy idiot asks to be allowed to go to the latrine. With their usual demoniac delight, the guards escort them to a huge pit dug in the center of the yard, fifty feet wide and the same in depth. They command the poor souls to go to the edge and squat down. When they do, the SS men laughingly kick them into the hole, from where there is no return."

I asked if he knew what our fate was, to which he replied that the day before, thousands of able-bodied men and women had been selected and marched out of the complex. No one knew where to.

By then it was dawn. I walked around a bit, primarily to warm my body, but also to survey the area. I saw the hole Mr. Szamos had described, brickdryers filled with a multitude of the dead and living, more inside the huge building, dozens of SS with and without dogs scattered around, and in the very far distance, the barbed wire fence surrounding the place. When the sun rose higher and it got a little warmer I returned, collapsed, and fell asleep.

I was awakened by movement and noise. The loudspeaker bellowed: "All those who have valid Swiss protective passports line up near the front gate!" I searched each opening of my clothes before I recalled that when the Nazis frisked us at the tunnel exit, they took all our papers and valuables. I felt awful — but at least I was alive and unharmed!

Time passed very slowly. It seemed tenish when the speaker sounded again, this time calling for all children under sixteen years of age. Mr. Szamos wished me good luck as I joyfully ran toward the exit.

Red Cross personnel looked us over, handed each of us a piece of bread and cellophane-wrapped margarine, then began to line us up. Meanwhile, grown-ups were running up to us in tears, dragging and carrying their children and infants, begging us older ones to take care of and save their innocent babes. The Red Cross people did not object, and the few SS guards nearby seemingly couldn't care less. It took over an hour to assemble our group. Each one who was a pre-teen or older was to carry an infant or a very young child. We didn't mind. We were being saved from the horrors the helpless adults had yet to face!

Although our little bundles were heavy, the return trip seemed shorter and easier. We were all relatively able-bodied, happy to walk toward what seemed like safety. Besides, the dozen or so SS guards treated us humanely.

The sun was high above when we heard the air raid sirens. The Red Cross people seemed concerned, but instructed us to move on. Soon, however, approaching tanks and trucks forced us off the road. That portion of our path led through Rózsadomb, an open hillside, scattered with trees and bushes. Hiding behind them, we watched the retreating Germany convoy.

The convoy was small and poorly equipped. Within minutes and without resistance, the low-flying attacking planes destroyed nearly half of the soldiers and their equipment. We soon resumed our journey. Feeling protected by the Red Cross and seeing the Germans retreat made us feel very happy. But our joy was soon to turn into a nightmare.

On Török Road we approached a huge old fort, which we could see housed thousands of Germans. Mere minutes later, we sighted a Gestapo car speeding toward us. We had to halt while the leaders of our guards rushed to greet the officer. They conferred briefly; then the car turned around and we were ordered to follow it.

They led us into the circular courtyard and lined us up into a U-shape, five rows thick, all facing the center. Ten feet

apart and facing each column of five stood the SS executioners, pointing their cocked submachine guns at us. And then
the bugle choir began to play the familiar "Death March".
The tune was somber and reverent. The passing seconds
seemed like hours. Since any means of escape was totally impossible, death obviously inevitable, we mentally re-lived our
lives and prayed the Lord our souls to take.

God, why? What crime have these nearly five hundred
children committed? Some of them had spent only a few
months on this earth. The Red Cross — where were those nice
people? I could not see them anywhere. My mind wandered.
— Will I be with Aunt Bözse in the other world? Is it
peaceful and without suffering over there? Who else is waiting for me on the other side? Maybe Uncle Lacó, Grandmama, or even Daddy had already gone to their repose!
Mommy is probably still all right in the safe-house, but for
how long? And Bandi . . . when he was caught, he was probably tortured like those people in the Nazi cellar. He was
strong and healthy, but how much pain can a human endure?
. . . Well, it's just as well, I'll be less alone in the other world!

As the tune was approaching the finale, I quickly
prayed, "Dear Lord, forgive me if I have been bad sometimes;
I know I've aggravated my parents and I've been bratty on
occasions; lately I've even disobeyed Mother several times;
but Lord, I've always *tried* to be good! I've always tried so
hard to follow Your Commandments! I have never hated
anybody. I've always given my pennies to poor beggars and
have never refused to help anyone if I possibly could! I used
to go to temple every Friday, and I even fasted on Yom
Kippur. Honest, I've always tried hard to please You! I know
it's too late now to ask You for a miracle, so all I ask is to be
allowed to come to You, to have peace and rest, and be with
my loved ones in the other world."

I felt serene and peaceful as I closed my eyes and waited for THE moment. But instead, I felt a big, strong hand touching my left shoulder firmly. I looked, but saw no one nearby. Was it an angel or Mr. Death? I will never know, for next I heard loud voices, shouts, commotion, then saw a very high-ranking army officer storming into the yard. He motioned the bugle choir to stop, then turning to our executioners, began to shout in German. "Idiots! We are rapidly retreating! The Russians are slaughtering our forces! We need every able-bodied soldier and you are wasting time with these brats? Get them out of here! Fast! Then regroup and move on to the Front!"*

Heavenly music to my ears! Could it be true? Have I fallen asleep and dreamed it, or was I already in heaven? No, it turned out to be merely another divine intervention.

The SS men lowered their guns and, pointing toward the outside gate, ordered us to line up and march. Without a sound, the little ones again in our arms, we followed their command. Outside the fort — from whence they came nobody knew — the Red Cross ladies were again alongside us.

The sky was red as the sun approached the horizon, and behind the clouds, far, far away, like a mirage, appeared the most beautiful rainbow I'd ever seen. "Oh, Lord, how omniscient and omnipotent You are!" — I knew then that He had destined me to survive the Holocaust.

---

* The Front by then was only about 30 miles east of Budapest.

The Óbuda Brick Factory and its drying structures, used as a marshaling yard for tens of thousands of Jews awaiting to be marched to labor camps or to be deported to concentration camps.

The original dozen or so guards were still with us, leading us along the Danube River, passing the famous Fishermen's Bastion and the Royal Castle in Buda, across the Chain Bridge, downtown Pest, by the Dohány Temple, and finally into a large apartment building. Once all of us were inside, our Nazi guards turned around and left. The Red Cross ladies locked the gate-door from within and distributed us into large, empty apartments. The rooms were big and clean, furnished only with beds, cots and sofas, besides the little stoves used for heat.

Soon uniformed nurses came with soup, bread, margarine, and herb tea, as much as we could consume. They issued each of us a blanket, towel, soap, toothbrush and paste, hairbrush and comb, and metal dishes and silverware. They lit a fire in our stove, medicated our wounds, infections and frostbites, and tucked is in for the night.

We spent the next day getting to know the setup and each other. Our apartment had sixteen girls, my room only seven. We were between 12 and 15 years of age. The neighboring apartment was the nicest. Its rooms faced not the courtyard but the street. The largest room was reserved for recreation, since it was furnished with a piano, tables and chairs, and many games. The other rooms were occupied by teen-age boys, about thirty of them. Allowed to walk around freely but only within the three-story building, we found some of the apartments locked and seemingly empty. On the floor below us all the flats had been converted into nurseries, offices, a sick bay and a central kitchen. Our supervisors were mostly elderly ladies, clothed in Red Cross and nurses' uniforms.

We were not the first group to be brought to the orphanage. It had been established a month before, after Szálasi's Arrow Cross Party usurped power, when all the young and middle-aged Jews were taken away, and so many old people and children were left helpless. We were the second group brought back from the Óbuda Brick Factory. The first was a week before, teen-age boys, about thirty of them, our neighbors.

In view of the general circumstances, conditions in the orphanage were relatively pleasant, except for some of the strict rules. We had to go to sleep — oil lamps out — by 9:00 p.m.; we could visit in other apartments only during the afternoons; lastly, we were forbidden to leave the building.

A good night's rest and food were enough for me to recuperate. I was ready to take any chance to get to Mother. So, I went charging into the office, insisting to be allowed to leave. But the Red Cross ladies would not hear of it. They tried to reason that there was a good chance that my mother had been relocated and I could not trace her; they claimed it was far too dangerous to be on the street; they said they heard there was a ghetto being built somewhere, and all Jews were being rounded up and taken there. I alternately pleaded and argued, but to no avail. At most they were willing to post a letter for me. It would have pacified me had I known Mother's address. But the soldier who was supposed to have taken me to her did not tell me the exact location, and the note she had sent did not state it.

Suddenly, a thought flashed through my mind. If Mom was alive, by now she would have contacted Blum Grandmother! Besides, I wanted her, too, to know that I was safe and well. I got pencils and a pile of Red Cross stationery, and ran upstairs to share them and the news that we could send out mail, with my new acquaintances. We wrote, but got stuck before completing the envelopes. None of us seemed to know our address. We were brought here at night, no one had ever left the building, so we only guessed that we were on Király Street. So, with a pile of letters in my hand, I ran to the office for information.

The response seemed very strange. We were not allowed to receive mail, nor to know our exact location, not even the last names of the grown-ups. Even the reason for this secrecy was withheld from us.

Feeling depressed, helpless and defeated, I brought the letters back. We questioned the kids in all the occupied apartments, but they knew no more than we. They said that nobody ever came or went out of the building, except the few times when the adults went for and brought back children. Even sending letters had until now been out of the question. Thus, to make the best of the situation, we all left the tops of the envelopes blank and wrote a "p.s." inside, describing the building and the view of the street from the windows as best we could. One of the ladies took the letters and promised to get them mailed.

A few days later, just before "lights out", a nurse brought me a package. With shaking hands and throbbing heart, I ripped the paper off. The bundle contained a skirt and blouse, a pair of Mom's wool pants and a pair of her shoes, a set of my old underwear, a prayerbook, a handbag of mine, and a letter. Joyful tears poured down my face as I read it. Grandmama wrote that she was feeling well, her nurse had been managing to round up some food, she had not heard from Uncle Lacó nor from my dad, and although my mother was not yet able to leave the safe-house, everything was fine with her. Via an Aryan friend Grandmama had managed to find out my location and promised to get that information to Mom. Except for that note, the package was the very one Mom had brought to Grandmama to hide when in September I had returned with my prized acquisitions from having cleansed the rubble of the across-the-street Nazi headquarters.

The next morning I read and re-read the letter, chanted a long prayer from the book, then examined the contents of the package more carefully. Sure enough, the skirt and shirt were the khaki ones, their pockets stuffed with the Arrow Cross neckties and insignias. To my pleasant surprise, my bag contained not only some money, but also my rubble-force workbook, a good I.D. that came in handy later.

As I was carefully rewrapping the Nazi paraphernalia, the shirt's pocket felt strangely stiff. Reaching in, I pulled out a neatly folded paper. To my amazement, it was a very important and frightening document. I copied it in shortened code into my tiny black diary and swiftly burned the original.*

APRIL 7, 1944

Confidential Decree of the Department of Interior With Respect to Deporting Jews to Concentration Camps. Order of Laszló Baky, Hungarian Regal Secretary of Interior, 6163/1944

The Hungarian Regal Government shall cleanse the country of Jews within a short time. I am ordering the cleansing to take place by regions, resulting in the delivery of all Jews in concentration camps, regardless of their sex or age. In larger towns and cities a portion of the Jews will later be placed into houses or ghettos, designated specifically by the organizing authorities.

Exempted temporarily are those specially skilled Jews who are employed in mining, factories engaged in war production, or strategically important farms or plants, and where immediate replacement would hinder production. Jews in all strategically non-essential positions are to be at once replaced by the best qualified available Aryan employees. . . .

The collection of the Jews shall be done by the local police and gendarmerie. The German Security Police (Gestapo) will be present on the locations and serve in an

---

* The following is a complete verbatim translation of the original edict, as it appears in "Vádirat a Nácizmus Ellen".

advisory capacity. Emphasis is made that they are to be supported and cooperated with harmoniously, without any opposition or disturbance.

The regional municipal authorities are ordered to establish appropriate collection camps at once. . . .

Only such buildings or areas should be designated which are currently occupied predominantly by Jews. Their non-Jewish residents are to be relocated into equivalent quarters, vacated by Jews, within thirty days of the conclusion of the cleansing operation. Arising expenses, regulated and determined by the authorities, shall be temporarily covered by _____ .

Simultaneously with the concentration and deportation of the Jews, the local authorities shall designate commissions, who, together with the police and gendarmerie shall lock and seal at once the vacated residences and businesses. These keys, together with the names and exact addresses of the Jews, shall be turned over to the commanders of the concentration camps in individually sealed envelopes.

Perishable items and live animals not used for further propagation or cultivation shall be turned over to the city or town governments, or appropriate local authorities. They shall be dispensed to satisfy the needs of the military, public security authorities, and lastly, that of the local public.

Money and valuables (gold and silver objects, stocks, etc.) shall be taken over by the above specified authorities, and, after brief documentation, shall be turned over to the city or regional government authorities, who in turn shall deposit them within three days in the local branch of the National Bank. These branches are to be selected by those authorities in charge of the cleansing operation.

The captives shall be transported by trains. These Jews should be allowed to carry with them only the clothes they wear, at most two sets of underwear, food for at least fourteen days, plus the maximum of 111 lbs. of luggage, including their mattress, bedclothes and blankets. To take along money, jewelry, precious metal or any other valuables is to be forbidden.

The concentration of Jews shall take place in the following sequence: Kassa, Marosvásárhely, Kolozsvár, Miskolc, Debrecen, Szeged, Pécs, Szombathely, Székesfehérvár, and lastly in Budapest, the capital.

The gendarmerie and police commandants have at their disposition all the available armed divisions and their trainees.

Commanding Headquarters shall assure the safeguarded sealing of their region's borders until the concentration of Jews has been completed in the adjacent regions. The gendarmerie and police divisions shall stay in close touch and function in harmony, to accomplish the cleansing activity cooperatively and simultaneously.

Jews not to be found in their residences shall be tracked down in the usual manner, referring to this ordinance during the tracing activities. Meanwhile, their businesses and residences shall be treated the same way as those of the captured Jews.

I have ordered the Central Jewish Council, residing in Budapest, to immediately establish, equip and staff temporary aid-stations and hospitals in Nyiregyháza, Ungvár, Munkács and Máramarossziget. These doctors shall also attend to hygienic and sanitation matters in the concentration camps.

I am calling it to the attention of the authorities that all alien Jewish refugees, without exception, should be treated as Communists, that is, they are to be placed in the concentration camps.

Dubious individuals should also be transported to concentration camps, at which place shall their religious status be verified.

This ordinance of mine is to be held in the strictest confidence, and the commandants of the authorities to be involved in the cleansing activities are held responsible that no one should have any prior knowledge about the cleansing operation.

A copy of this decree is to be sent to . . .

Women, children, and the old folks of towns and villages — not yet taken to labor camps — were herded first into ghettos, then to concentration camps. The yellow stars depict their difference and hence their destiny.

By June of 1944 — within a mere three months — all but the capital of Hungary was "cleansed" of her nearly half million Jews.

70

CHAPTER 12: BENEVOLENT DECEPTION

One day in late November Jancsi, from the front apartment, called us over to look out the window and watch a strange activity. Storm troopers were supervising old men hauling huge planks of wood, then nailing them together to barricade a nearby intersection. One of the boys thought it was to be a lookout tower, while another guessed it was to be a blockade when the Russians would reach the city. The next day the structure was completed. As best we could see from a distance, it looked like a wall, fifteen or so feet high, reaching from the building on one side of the intersecting side street to the house on the other. We all agreed that Jancsi was right; it must be some sort of barricade.

A few days later one of my roommates rushed in, gossiping that she had overheard the boys talking about me. Rizsa said he wanted me to be his girlfriend. Péter said he did too, but he didn't think I'd let a boy even kiss me. Rizsa said he was in love with me and was not going to give up. So, several boys made a bet that Péter, who was far better looking and more the Don Juan type, had a better chance than Rizsa. Hearing the story I thought it was cute, but since I loved Bandi deeply, I ignored Cica's comment without a response.

The next afternoon several of the boys came over and brought their phonograph and records. We talked and danced. Later, exhausted from the exercise, I stretched out on the couch. Rizsa, and several other kids, sat down beside me. I don't remember what we conversed about, but suddenly Rizsa leaned across me, pinning my shoulders down, and began to kiss me passionately. Since I wasn't strong enough to merely push him up and away, I grabbed his hair and tugged at his head. As he tried to yank his head out of my clutches, my fingers slipped, my nails scratching him deeply on the skull and behind the ears. Red from embarrassment, he left instantly. We girls laughed and forgot about the inci-

71

dent. But the next morning we saw Rizsa coming from sick bay, his head bandaged like that of a mummy! Conditions being unsanitary and his body resistance low, my nails must have carried enough germs to cause Rizsa to acquire a bad infection. Although I felt he had asked for it, I could not forgive myself for causing him such pain.

My physical needs were being satisfied and I considered our orphanage the safest place in the city, but being shut off from the outside world was driving me crazy. While scheming one afternoon about how I could sneak out and go to Grandmother, Péter came running and yelling, "Györgyi! Come quickly! Your mother is downstairs at the gate and nurse Olga won't let her in. She's ordering her away!"

I didn't walk but flew down three flights. The gate-door had a tiny window, with metal bars outside. I could see my mother's face, but nurse Olga stopped my approach. I shoved her aside, but the door was locked. I screamed and shook it like a fierce gorilla, but 200-pound Olga put her big hands over my mouth and asserted, "Your mother *must* go away! We cannot take the chance of letting *them* in. And we cannot protect you if you leave this house."

I stopped screaming and she let me talk through the window. A policeman stood beside my mother. She said he was O.K.; he was paid to escort her and me back to the safe-house. However, as much as she loved and missed me, she said, I was probably safer here. She barely had time to give her address and kiss me through the bars when the policeman motioned her to get going. I went to plead with the other nurses and Red Cross ladies, begging, crying, ranting and raving, but to no avail. The cage remained locked.

I began to plot my escape, but before I had a chance to execute my plan, the Nazis intervened. The next morning, Friday, December 1, we were awakened by banging doors and shouts from downstairs. Listening to my sixth sense, I washed and dressed, and packed all my belongings. Then I opened my prayer book at random. By coincidence, it was the morning service. Tuning the whole world out, I began to read the Hebrew passages. I do not know what happened after that; I was in another world. The next thing I noticed was a German SS standing beside me, sticking his submachine gun to my ribs. He said, "Heraus!" I looked at him in a daze and, mustering my best German, I told him that I would not go out until I had finished that particular prayer. I don't know why but he stepped back, put his gun on his shoulder and reverently waited for me to finish. When I closed the Bible he opened the door for me and, like a gentleman, escorted me downstairs.

By then everyone was lined up in the yard; the Red Cross ladies, nurses, even the kids from sick bay. As soon as I stepped into the nearest line, my SS gave the order for all of us to march.

Like a well-regimented herd of cattle, we moved silently down the street, turning left or right as commanded. We passed the wall we saw from the window, that one and several others. They had blocked each side street that ran into or crossed Király Street. We soon arrived at the big temple. There was no wall there, just a group of armed Arrow Cross men. They relieved our SS guards and brought us to a house on Wesselényi Street. There was no wall there, either; it was the nucleus of the prewar Jewish section. When we all had filed into the building, the gate-door was locked and we were free to move about within.

The Red Cross ladies were still among us, but no longer in charge. One of them later told me that they were all Jewish, faking the whole setup, trying to use the title and symbol to get us food and things, and to protect us as long as they could. They knew the Nazis would find out eventually, but the Russians were already a mere ten or so miles from the southeast border of the city and were rapidly advancing, and each day increased our chances to survive until liberation. This explained why they did not want me to leave and why they were afraid to let in my mother and her police escort.

We were now inside the ghetto, a 3 X 7 block area*, enclosed by the barricading walls at the limiting intersections. Free to move within the empty building, I chose to bunk in one of the large apartments. Thirteen of us, boys and girls who knew each other from the old place, occupied the large living room. It had a piano, a huge couch, and an old, badly worn Persian rug. I staked my place on the rug and went to explore.

To my surprise, the house still had a manager who was not Jewish. Acting ladylike and very charming, I invited myself into his living room. He was willing to answer my questions. He told me that this area was part of the ghetto, but there were still many Aryans living within. They had already been issued apartments outside and had to move out by midnight of December 7. Thousands of Jews were being brought in daily. The ghetto was enclosed completely; walls were barricading all the exterior intersections, and those windows of buildings which faced out of the ghetto had been filled with stone debris or boarded up completely. He said there were, however, still four streets without walls — one each to east, west, north, and south — to allow for the exchange of people. But Jews once in could not get out, because the exit streets were heavily guarded.

I said I was only a half-Jew from the orphanage and begged him to let me go out into the ghetto, to see if my Aryan grandmother in the next block was still all right. He

---

* The area surrounded by Király Street, Madách Park, Dohány Street, and Kertész Street was defined as the ghetto. It contained 291 buildings, and as of December 1, 3556 Jewish and 11,935 non-Jewish residents. It was planned to house more than 63,000 Jews.

hemmed and hawed for a bit, but finally let me go. With my heart in my mouth, I ran the few blocks to Síp Street, to Grandmama Blum.

The gate-door was unlocked and the house seemed to be deserted. Her apartment was open and empty. I guessed, but still hoped. With tears pouring down my face, I knocked on every apartment door. All were dark and silent. The manager's residence had a light on. I knocked. Recognizing me, she flung the door open, hugged me tightly and began to cry. She was Aryan, too, but everyone liked Grandmother. All choked up, she told me that several days ago Nazis came in, took away all the able-bodied Jews, then walked around and shot those still inside their homes. They shot Grandmama and left her in the wheelchair. Later, she and her husband were ordered to gather the bodies in the yard and to set fire to the pile of corpses.

We both cried for a while, then with a very heavy heart, I left. It wasn't far to Dob Street, where Grandmother Blau had lived. I was prepared not to find her alive either, but was not ready for the scene that faced me.

She had lived in an old people's home, where the management and residents were all Jewish. I first walked around outside of the building, looking for a light somewhere. No light. As I approached the entrance, I was hit by a fetid odor. My heart pulsated as I flung the gate-door open and walked through the hallway toward the rancid odor in the yard. There I saw a huge pile of corpses, faces unrecognizable, the little flesh left on the bones decomposing, and an army of carnivorous rodents carousing.

I was too sick to cry! I walked out, closing the door behind me, crossed the street, sat on the sidewalk, and waited for my stomach to stop churning. Then I sullenly walked back to our house.

It was a bitterly cold night. Our apartment, like most

others by now, had no windowpanes. Since there was no wood or coal to make a fire, we kept all our clothes on and lay next to each other, trying to keep warm. I tried to fall asleep, but failed. Finally I called out, "Who else is still awake?" Most of the kids answered. I then asked each to tell what he or she knew about our situation. When all had finished, it seemed that I knew the most. At first I hesitated, but thinking that knowledge was better than being in the dark, I proceeded to enlighten them. Someone began to swear, some to sob, some to pray. The rest just lay there like mindless zombies.

Soon I made another inquiry: "Who has the guts to try to escape?" Among the several counter-questions of "But how?", one voice said: "I do!" I responded to the many that I had no plan as yet, but trying to leave as gentiles before December 7 seemed most feasible.

The previous voice said, "I'm Ernő, count me in!"

Pista piped up, "You fool! *She* may, but *you* will never make it. I tried and that's how I got here." We asked him to explain.

Pista proceeded. "Have you heard of 'pants-check'? If not, I'll tell you. You females don't have that, but we Jew-boys are all circumcised. And as you well know, Aryans are not. The Nazis aren't so dumb. If they catch a guy whose papers aren't 100%, they make him remove his pants. Circumcised? Jew! The others they let go. I don't have to tell you what tortures await Ernő. He'll never make it!"

Ernő began to laugh. "I didn't know that! That's superb! Györgyi, start planning the forgery!" By now everyone was awake and somebody produced a candle. He wanted to see Ernő's face, for he thought the poor boy had gone crazy.

Our religion mandates circumcision for *all* male babies on the eighth day of their lives. Evidently it was common knowledge that in Germany and Hungary the alteration at the tip of the male's genital undeniably distinguished gentiles from Jews. Ernő, still finding the situation hilarious, proceeded to tell us that since birth he had been a hemophiliac; that is, from the smallest cut he could bleed to death. He said he had considered it a curse, for he could never lead a normal life. The slightest scrape or cut necessitated doctors or hospitals. Obviously, he was exempted from that religious ritual. And now that curse could save his life! Although no one else had the courage to attempt escape, they all volunteered to help us prepare papers. The details to be worked out the next day, we were ready to go to sleep.

CHAPTER 13: RECIPROCITY

The next day, December 3, was a busy day. Among our precious belongings Ernő found his old Boy Scout membership card, a patent document equipped with essential information. I, of course, had my rubble-force workbook, another valuable I.D. All we had to do was change the religion and the names, to prove that we were Aryan siblings. There was no hope of securing papers to prove our parents' gentile descent, but I thought we would bluff that somehow. The next step was to secure chemicals to wash out the old ink and to mix a batch that matched it.

All thirteen of us went hunting. Twelve of us searched the empty apartments in the building, while I, between 9:00 and 11:00 a.m., when Jews were allowed outside their homes, scavenged in the rubble on the streets. By noon the loot was gathered, and we were ready for the main production. A rotten potato, a bit of lemon peel, and some lighter fluid served well to make the ink disappear. I had found several bottles of ink, a pen, and bits of artists' paint. While Pista practiced imitating handwritings, I concocted a matching batch of ink. Before dusk the papers were finished. Ernő's last name was Balog, so it was not hard to change his name and my Balla to Ballag; "izr. (izraelita)" meant Jew and "ref. (református)" stood for Protestant, so we changed "izr." to "ref." No, it wasn't perfect. But since by sheer coincidence we happened to look very much alike — both small, slim and thin-boned, high cheekbones, olive complexion, brown eyes and hair, etc., — with a little acting, considerable luck and a great deal of prayer, I thought we had a chance.

I had also brought some boards back from my scavenging. The other kids had found a jar of jam, canned potatoes and sardines in the empty apartments, plus wood and coal in the cellar. So, we boarded up the windows, lit a fire, put food into our tummies and went to sleep. For Ernő and me, tomorrow was "D day".

The next forenoon we walked the length and width of the ghetto and observed the traffic on the streets and at the gates. Non-Jewish children, adults, and old folks were all rushing about, carrying bundles or pushing their belongings on big and small wheelbarrows. Since streetcars and buses no longer ran in the Jewish section, horse-drawn carriages were the vehicles most commonly used by the moving gentiles. By 1:00 p.m. there was a long line at each of the four exits. The one at the Dohány Temple was the most crowded, and the people were getting noticeably restless and impatient about the delay. There were only two Nazis and four policemen checking individual identifications. Instinct told me to choose that exit.

I formed my plan and instructed Ernő. He was to act as

my shy and helpless brother, and I was to do all the talking. We waited until dusk. By then our forgery was not obvious, the line at the gate was nearly endless, and the restless people were shoving, yelling, and cursing at the Nazis. When two relief policemen arrived, we made our move.

Dragging Ernő by the hand, bypassing everybody, we made a dash toward one of the policemen, waved our I.D.'s in front of him, and continued running outward. Naturally he yelled after us, to stop and to return. We at once re-treated. Then, like a hysterical dumb child, I started raving that we must run and catch up to that horse-drawn carriage ahead, before our parents found out that we had jumped off, to run back for the bundle I'd forgotten behind, and . . . The policeman looked confused, but he asked only for our papers. Nervously I held them up to his eyes, while holding on to them tightly. Then I began to rant and rave again. Seeing our pictures and fingerprints satisfied him, but he asked for additional proof of our Aryan status.

I looked at him strangely and exclaimed, "You haven't heard a word! I told you our parents, who have just shown all the papers to the comrade across the street, are on that horse-drawn carriage yonder. Now you must let us run and try to catch up before the horses get too far away and . . ."

Two men behind us raised their fists and yelled, "Damn it, let those brats go! We can't stand around here until mid-night! . . . Ya, let 'em go!" The policeman motioned us to pass. We let out a big sigh of relief. We had made it!

Our first objective was to cross the city safely and locate my mother. Encouraged by our success, having some nifty false papers, I thought the best way to get to and around in the Swiss-protected section was by wearing Arrow Cross out-fits and insignia. I changed my clothes in a public toilet, fixed Ernő up with a Party necktie, arm band and pin, and assuming the arrogant Nazi personality, we proceeded as planned.

After walking halfway across the city, we located Mother's dwelling. In character, we banged forcefully on the gate-door. A woman came to the small lookout window and asked us what we wanted. After the proper salute of "Heil Hitler, Kitartás Éljen Szálasi!" we demanded that Dr. Balla Ernőné be brought down to us. The woman paused, took a big swallow, then replied that Mrs. Balla was not there. I insisted that she must be and demanded that the Jewess be produced at once. The woman mumbled something, opened the door and asked us in. She locked the door again, looked me thoroughly up and down, wrinkled her forehead, and in a soft voice said, "My child, are you not Györgyi, Mrs. Balla's daughter?" Having been recognized, I wondered if it would still be useful to act. My hesitation to reply confirmed her suspicion. She hugged me, broke into tears and said, "Your mother constantly talked about you. She even showed me a picture of you. All she wished was to have you here, with her. I made my cousin, the policeman, go with her to bring you here. She lived only for you. Why did they have to take her! And just yesterday! . . . "

I interrupted the lady, trying to find out the details. She finally stopped crying and explained that just the day before Arrow Cross men had come, lined up the residents, chose the four youngest, my mother and three other women, and took them away. The lady, who was the house's manager, didn't know where the women were taken, but said these incidents had been happening daily for more than a week. Also, that she saw one of the groups thusly rounded up being taken straight to the Western train station and herded into cattle wagons marked "Dachau" and "Mauthausen" (concentration camps).

I could not bear thinking of Mom's fate, nor looking at the lady or the house a moment longer. I had to keep my composure and choke my tears long enough to get out of that section. We walked fast, properly saluting every German and Party member, and when we reached a nearby park, we sat down on a bench and I let loose my emotions. I cried until I had no tears left. My two grandmothers dead, my father and now my mother also gone, I felt hopelessly alone!

The sun had set and night was approaching. We had to find shelter quickly. I remembered a neighbor family on Ráday Street, before we had moved to the star-house. Their teen-age daughter was mentally retarded. They used to be so grateful whenever I went over to play with or to tutor her. Maybe they would hide us, at least for the night?

It was nearly 10:00 p.m., when entrance doors were customarily locked for the night, by the time we got to the house. Since I was known in that vicinity, Ernő walked a few steps ahead, to warn me if someone was approaching. Fortunately we reached the apartment without being seen. We knocked. Mrs. Kelemen almost fainted when she recognized me standing in front of her door. Although she was afraid to let us in, it was less dangerous than standing in the open doorway. Once inside, I told her of our recent escape from the ghetto, of the fate of my parents, etc., and asked her for some food and shelter. She served us bread and cold cuts, and left to confer with her husband. We had gulped down every morsel long before her return. She informed us that we could sleep in the maid's room, for just *one* night, but that we must not let her daughter see us, for the child might scream or run to tell someone who might report us. Well, one night was better than none.

Early the next morning, before the household awoke, we managed to leave the building unseen. I recalled a Christian client of my father, who lived near by. He and his wife owned a grocery store, and whenever I had stopped by, they always gave me candy. They even hid some of my parents' valuables. Wearing our Arrow Cross outfits, we approached their home. To our dismay, the building was a heap of rubble. Even the neighboring houses were almost completely demolished. It was now my partner's turn to suggest a hideout.

Ernő had only one Aryan friend, whom he had not seen for many months. The boy's father was a mechanic in Ernő's family's factory, and when the Germans came, he was promoted to foreman. He also got a job managing a large apartment building. Ernő did not know how the parents felt, but he had gone to school and chummed around with their son Gólya, and felt he could trust his old buddy. I was greatly worried, but we had no other choice. We were asking to be caught each moment we were on the streets.

Luckily we managed to get across town and to Thököly Road. Ernő hid behind the elevator while I rang the bell. Fortunately, Gólya opened the door. He was blond, tall, and very handsome, built like a typical Aryan, in his midteens. I asked him to come out to the entrance hall to meet an old friend of his. He almost fainted seeing Ernő with a Party insignia.

Not knowing who or what I was, Gólya hid his feelings and kept the conversation strictly about old times. Ernő, on the other hand, tried to vary the topics to sound him out. After close to two hours of chatting, Gólya finally opened up and said that although he was a Party member, he disliked seeing what was being done to the Jews. But his parents were totally dedicated. They believed that Jews had been secretly controlling the world economy, had cheated and exploited the gentiles, and that all Jews had to be exterminated to keep Christian blood pure and to save the world from future oppressive "Jew tyranny".

Meanwhile I had stayed out of the conversation, but since evening was approaching, a move had to be made. I felt that Ernő was afraid to ask, worrying that Gólya might report my impersonating a Party member. On the other hand, Gólya was afraid to offer. He feared that if I did not know that Ernő was Jewish, I would report him for aiding a Jew. It was a delicate and dangerous situation.

I silently prayed, then said, "Gólya, I know the dangers involved, but we must find shelter, at least for one night. Could you let us stay in the attic or in a damaged empty apartment?"

Looking amazed yet relieved, he said, "I'd never guess you were a Jewess! Stay here, behind the elevator, and I'll try to snitch a key."

The minutes seemed like hours, but finally he returned with a key and a bag in his hand. On tiptoe we followed him into an empty, ground-floor flat. He gave us firm and explicit instructions: voices to be kept to a whisper; not to use the water, not even to flush the toilette; not to answer knocks, except his special signal; if someone opened the door with a key, to hide under a bed; finally, we were not to leave under any circumstances. He opened the bag and gave us each a ham and cheese sandwich, and promised to bring us food on the following day.

Our new abode had a bedroom, living room, hallway, toilette, bathroom, and kitchen. In order not to be seen and heard, we had to cover and seal the windows, except for the one in the bedroom, where the missing glass had already been replaced by plywood. We chose that room to live in. It was furnished only with a dilapidated bed, but for the moment that was all we needed. Clothes and all, we dropped and instantly fell asleep.

In fear of being seen or heard, we slept the next day until afternoon, then just lay there and whispered until evening, when Gólya came. He brought us plywood, hammer and nails, black construction paper and tape to seal the windows, candles, matches and two old blankets, besides some sandwiches and a bottle of warm milk. He promised to return the next evening, and then he left.

During the next day's air raid we fixed up the place. We boarded up all the windows, and dragged a table and two chairs into our room. Gólya brought us food again that evening, but could not do anything about the cold. We soon got used to wearing our entire wardrobe at all times, except for a short while during the air raids, when the tenants went to the cellar and we could use the water to wash.

The next evening Gólya came looking very depressed and worried. His parents had noticed the alarming rate of disappearance of the food, and he no longer could explain it with a "growing boy's ravaging appetite." Although they seemed a bit suspicious, the issue was closed by putting Gólya on a diet. For us, however, the situation was indeed crucial. We still had some money, but no ration tickets. What could we buy without them? And how, and where? We had to leave our hiding place to search for sustenance.

Using the normal means of exit and entrance was out of the question, but leaving by the window that faced the side street was feasible. We waited until dark, when the street was deserted, then jumped out. The window was relatively low, the freshly fallen snow cushioned the noise of the fall, and the bushes protected us from being seen by the road traffic. So far so good, but where to now?

Wearing our Arrow Cross "decorations", we walked along the residential Thököly Road to the Eastern train station. The area looked like an anthill. A multitude of German soldiers were rushing to and from the trains. Most of the nearby buildings and stores were in partial ruin, but the big newsstand and coffee shop was crowded as ever. That was the solution to our predicament.

Almost all traffic had for a long time been restricted to

Eastern-Front transport trains, so hardly any civilians had reason to be in that area. Except for German and Hungarian soldiers, only a few Arrow Cross members could be seen. No Jew would have a reason nor dare to be around there, so it seemed least likely for us to be suspected and asked for I.D.'s. Furthermore, with all those Germans not having Hungarian ration tickets, we hoped to be able to find some available edibles.

Putting on a tough appearance, we entered the self-service coffee shop. We looked like little midgets among those robust German soldiers. We stood in the long line and read the menu above the counter carefully. "Stew: 17 P (equal to about 60 cents) plus 2 meat and 1 fat ticket. Pork-pie: same as above. Chicken soup: 4.50 P plus one meat ticket. Rice pudding: 3 P plus 1 sugar ticket." The menu looked depressing. But on the bottom, in small print: "boiled potato: 1.50 P; boiled cabbage, carrot, spinach or onion: 2 P; cooked peas or lentils: .90 P." Wow! No ration tickets! And with the 500 P ($18) I had, we could eat for weeks! And fresh vegetables – we hadn't had that for months! We gorged ourselves with four orders and bought a dozen more to go.

Retracing our steps, we got back to our house safely. Stepping on my shoulders, Ernő climbed in first; then, extending the old blanket, he pulled me in.

The next few days were peaceful and quiet. Gólya brought us two more dilapidated quilts, a flashlight, a chess game, and some books. He came to see us every evening, bringing a thermos full of hot ersatz coffee, a pitcher of juice or powdered milk, or whatever he could snitch unnoticed. By now all the windows had been boarded up with plywood and sealed tightly, so we could move about freely as long as we were quiet enough not to be heard. We didn't even mind the air raids, for when everyone else was down in the shelter, we could wash and flush the toilette.

A few nights later we got sufficiently hungry to chance a repeat journey to the coffee shop. Everything went smoothly until our return trip.

We were barely five or six blocks from the train station when the sirens sounded. Everyone had to get off the streets. We couldn't chance a strange cellar or a public shelter in fear that, during a long raid, Party members present there might start talking to us and discover our fraud. On the street, patrolling air raid wardens would surely pick us up. Our only choice was to lie down in the snow and, simulating stray animals, crawl on our bellies alongside the buildings.

We progressed nearly half a block when we heard voices from the nearby cross street. We kept crawling faster in the direction of the sounds. Barely before we got to the corner, we could make out the conversation. One voice, in perfect German, kept repeating that he could not go because his girlfriend was expecting him. The other, in very poor German, kept saying that it would tie him up too long and his parents would be worried. I crawled a few yards farther to observe the pathetic scene.

With guns in one hand and cat-tail whips in the other, a young SS and a teen-age Arrow Cross boy were herding along about twenty old men and women. The two were arguing about how they could get those "Jew-swine" or sympathizers to the nearest Nazi-house. The bombing per se did not seem to concern them, but the necessity of getting off the streets, sitting the air raid out, then marching the "filthy scum" for still quite a distance, plus the time involved in making their report, obviously caused both some problems. I felt the Lord provided me with the opportunity to repay Him for the many miracles that had kept me alive.

I whispered to Ernő to let me do the talking, but to support me with his actions. Making the sounds of two

86

youths being a bit tipsy, we walked noisily into the intersection. After the proper "Heil Hitler, Kitartás Éljen Szálasi!" I approached the two Nazis, and in my best German said, "Comrades, I couldn't help overhearing the discussion about your predicaments. If you both have to leave, what will happen to these filthy Jew-pigs? All your efforts in rounding them up will be wasted. And they can go on infecting our race and society! As dedicated Party members, my buddy and I cannot let that happen. Although we are off duty, we will gladly give up our evening fun to see to it that these scums are properly punished!"

My words seemed music to their ears. It was too dark to see our young faces and our incomplete uniforms, but my comments seemed explanation enough. Besides, they were both so anxious to be on their way that my suggestion appealed to them as the perfect solution.

They pointed out the old couple they had caught hiding the six Jews in their attic, the two boys of age without a draft card, the three women ordering meals in a restaurant and having no ration tickets, and the rest appearing on the street without proper identification. – Oh, what criminals! The world isn't safe with such "gangsters" running loose!

After I assured my "comrades" that they could go about their business with a clear conscience, that we would without fail see to it that all those swine were properly punished, the two Nazis thanked us, saluted, and went away content. To be on the safe side, Ernő and I yelled out some additional swear words while reprimanding the group. Then, when we were sure the Nazis were out of hearing distance, I turned to those poor souls and told them to disappear, fast. A woman tried to hug me, an old man kneeled down and kissed my knees and hands, and the rest encircled us uttering prayers, blessings, and various means of thanks.

I had to repeat myself firmly, commanding them to

crawl, as we had done, to avoid being spotted and picked up again. When the last one had faded from sight, we continued on all fours to our hideout.

CHAPTER 14: THIS FAIRYLAND

Following a few uneventful days, Gólya came with terrible news. He had overheard (fortunately) that our apartment had been assigned, and his mother was coming in the next morning to clean it. Our breath stuck in our throats before he had a chance to continue.

He put his arms around us and said, "But I have a plan. There is an enclosed area of the attic, above the third floor, that no one ever uses. It is next to the washroom, so you will have water and toilette facilities. There is some junky furniture, including some old mattresses. The only problem is securing food."

I gave him all my money and told him about the coffee shop where we had been eating. After he promised to keep bringing us food, we tiptoed upstairs.

The facilities turned out to be quite tolerable. The roomlike enclosure had no window, but it had a door and a functioning ceiling light. Also, it was warmer than our downstairs abode. Plus, the squeaking staircase would give us sufficient warning to hide when somebody was approaching. Our new hideout was a definite improvement. During the next few days we cleaned and furnished it, and began to get used to our hermit-like existence.

A few evenings later we heard Gólya's familiar signal, followed by two sets of footsteps. Who could it be? Friend or foe? Upon opening the door, we saw another young boy standing beside our friend. After the introduction, Gólya explained that Tibi was dodging the draft, so he would be in hiding with us. Also, that he had brought along a bundle of delicious foods and a substantial amount of money.

Tibi turned out to be a jewel. He was about seventeen, short, stocky, by no means handsome, but very intelligent and lots of fun to be with. Soon we opened up, telling him about our escapades. He, in turn, confessed that he was partly Jewish. Gólya came every evening, bringing us food, games, and Tibi's old phonograph with records. Considering the circumstances, we had a terrific setup.

Unfortunately, it didn't last long. One night the bombing was very heavy. Our house was only about a mile from the big train station, a small distance for high-flying airplanes, easy for bombs to miss. With an ear-piercing crash, a bomb landed dead center on the building across the narrow side street. The blast was sufficient to make our house shake like a leaf in the wind. A stone structure as high as ours could not withstand such vibration without being damaged. First the walls cracked; then part of the roof came crashing down. As if all that were not enough, a series of bursts from across the street forced chunks of bricks and parts of metal beams to fly in all directions, battering the front of our house.

Fear dulled our senses. I was lying on my stomach near the inside wall, covering my head with my arms, too petrified to move or even to look, when all of a sudden a flying hunk of debris came crashing through the front wall. The beam supporting the side partition of our room withstood the impact momentarily, but seconds later it, too, began to crack and squeak. Finally, with a thunderous roar, the inside wall and another portion of the roof collapsed.

Minutes went by before the stone and plaster dust had settled, and we could breathe again. From the distance we heard a series of large and small explosions, sparks bursting to flames here and there, then human screams turning into cries, then to sobs. Finally, it was dark and quiet again.

I ran my fingers over the exposed parts of my body, for I lacked all sensation. I seemed to be all there and felt no broken bones or blood. Then I heard Tibi's voice: "Are you two still alive? Are you injured? In pain? Can you move?"

I attempted to stand up while answering, "I seem to be all right. At least I feel no pain as yet!"

Ernő then responded, "If you guys are O.K., then come and get me out of here! I'm under the rubble."

The moonlit sky and distant burning fires gave us enough visibility to excavate Ernő. He had severe pains in his chest and lower right arm, most likely cracked or broken bones, but he had no open wounds and was able to crawl.

Tibi was in worse shape than he was willing to admit. His face was badly cut up, a front tooth was missing, his left shinbone pierced through the flesh and skin, and he was bleeding from several places.

The all-clear siren barely sounded when we heard Gólya's footsteps. He ran to relocate us before his parents came by to evaluate the damage. He brought the key to the last still-vacant apartment, on the top floor but luckily on the undamaged side of the building. He carried Tibi on his broad shoulders while I supported the tiny leaning body of Ernő.

The residents were slow to ascend from the cellar, which gave us enough time to reach the dwelling at the end of the third floor corridor. We heard some strange noises from inside as we entered the first room. Gólya laid Tibi down and motioned us to hush, while with his flashlight he worked his way inward from room to room. We soon heard loud whispers, then Gólya's chuckle as he came back for us and said, "This tops it all! Wait till you see the setup inside!"

Crossing two rooms, Gólya flung open the door of the farther one. It was large and elegantly furnished; a Steinway piano, wall-to-wall Persian rug, a huge china cabinet with porcelain and gold objects, lead-crystal hurricane oil lamps, etc. Two elderly ladies in elegant garb were sitting on a hand-carved sofa bed, graciously smiling.

Although very curious about this fairyland, my first objective was to attend to the boys. With lamps in hand, the ladies scattered about and produced, seemingly from no-where, nearly enough equipment to furnish a doctor's office. One put some coal in the built-in tile stove, which warmed the room to nearly 80° even before the other lady finished adjusting the extension-leaves of a small table and covering it with freshly ironed sheets. With Tibi on the "operating table", with Gólya's help they yanked his leg and snapped the shinbone back into place. They made him drink a full glass of pure brandy – which promptly knocked him out – while they cleaned the wound and tied wooden splints with bandages to his leg.

I was sent to the bathroom to get undressed and to wash myself from head to toe while they finished cleaning the rest of Tibi's wounds, putting him to bed in the adjacent room we had crossed before. They had even finished washing and examining Ernő, applying a stretch-bandage to his chest and arm and dressing him in women's pyjamas, by the time I emerged from the bathroom, all clean and wearing a robe of one of the ladies.

Ernő was given only half a glass of brandy, enough merely to kill his pain. Having only minor injuries, I was the last to be attended to.

They stopped a small, bleeding wound on my skull, cleaned the scratches and bruises I had gotten while excavating Ernő, and applied some salve to my frostbitten legs and hands. Then they went to the kitchen to bring us tea and food.

Concerned that he might be missed, Gólya assured us that we should be safe there, told us to follow the ladies' instructions, and then left.

The ladies returned with crackers and jam, scrambled (powdered) eggs and bacon, and a liquid made of milk powder. While we ate heartily, the older lady introduced herself as Özvegy Gróf Hochstein Istvánné (wife of the late Count Stephan Hochstein), but asked us to call her by her first name, Margit. The younger one, her sister, was Sári Berg.

Margit related that, although she was converted and married to a Catholic, this did not exempt her from the anti-Jewish laws. As early as June she and her sister had gone into hiding at the estate of a friend in Buda. However, the castle was hit by a bomb ten days before, so they had to find a new hiding place. The late count's friend had made the arrangement with Gólya's parents, for an enormously large sum of money.

Sári looked at her watch and interrupted the conversation by saying that since it was after midnight, we should all retire and talk all we wanted the next day. Ernő was put to bed with Tibi, I was to sleep on the living room's sofa bed, while Margit and Sári went to their own bedroom.

The next day, after having set the table for breakfast, the ladies awakened me. It seemed like a century since I had eaten over a lace tablecloth, from porcelain dishes, with sterling silverware — not since the good old days when we lived on Ráday Street. Could it have been just six months ago? I must have aged decades since!

Ernő came into the room in his baggy pyjamas. His cracked rib cage was tightly strapped, his arm in a sling made out of a kerchief. His face showed pain, but his words denied it. Tibi was moaning in the other room, then appeared in the doorway, hopping on one leg. We chuckled when he complained of headache and nausea, and assured him it was only a hangover from the brandy. Even so, he traded breakfast for some pain killers. We ate a hearty brunch of milk, eggs, potatoes — all dehydrated and powdered — plus a mouthwatering variety of smoked cold cuts, with lots of crackers and jam. I helped clear the table, wash the dishes and clean up a bit. Sári sent me to the storage room to put away the remaining food. To my amazement, it was jampacked to the ceiling with all sorts of non-perishable edibles. I thought to myself, "We sure lucked out!"

When finally we had all sat down in the living room and relaxed, the ladies were most cordial in answering our questions. We learned that Margit was a trained nurse; that's how she had met her late husband, when he was injured during World War I. She loved children, but they couldn't have any. Sári was a pediatrician, dedicated to her work, which was why she had never married. Although Sári was by no means poor, Margit had inherited and managed to hide a small fortune. Her husband's relatives had all lived in Austria, and her parents had died before the war. Having had no brothers or other sisters, the two ladies had only each other.

Tibi was too doped up to feel like asking questions, but Ernő wanted to know how much freedom of movement the ladies had. Sári replied that, although the managers were paid off to protect them, it was better if the other tenants did not see them coming in and out or in the cellar shelter, to avoid conversation and possible recognition. Movements or voices heard from the apartment were not a problem, since the neighbors would assume they were being made by new Aryan tenants.

Before I had a chance to ask another question, we heard Gólya's special signal at the door. He was absolutely thrilled about the way things had turned out. He said he no longer worried about hiding us, for if his parents found out, he could blackmail them with his new knowledge about the hidden ladies. He did agree, though, that none of us should leave the apartment, especially since we were so well supplied with all the necessities.

Ernő's bones turned out to be only cracked, and he was soon well on the way to recovery. Poor Tibi, however, was not doing so well. While the brandy lasted, he remained in a state of slight tipsiness, but later we had to rely on Gólya to replenish our pain-killer supply. Tibi was very brave though; he never complained and always managed to wear a smile and crack an occasional joke.

The days passed quickly and pleasantly. Gólya spent every evening in our apartment; he felt closer to all of us than to his own family and friends. The ladies were delightful: smart, highly intelligent, and very young in spirit. They loved and treated us as if we were their own children, and we grew to love them, too. We ate, we slept, we read; we played games, we danced to music from the records or the radio, and we talked openly without reservation.

Gólya assured us that only about a fifth of the Arrow Cross members were really dedicated and believed all the garbage shoved down their throats. Most had joined purely for the personal advantages. Through the Party they got better promotions, extra and unavailable food, better dwellings if needed, clothes and furniture if necessary, and even money. Prominent Party leaders — although some got their positions only by putting on a good act — had access to all sorts of luxury items, most of which had been taken from the Jews.

The only thing we wanted badly that Gólya couldn't get was a short-wave radio. Possession of one, according to him, was illegal even for Party members. The Nazis were fearful that people would find out the truth, no longer believe their propaganda, and possibly rise up. So, our only knowledge of the war's true progress was what Gólya heard from others, who got uncensored portions of letters from loved ones at the Front.

We knew the Russians were very close to Budapest by now, but it was still hard to judge the rate of their progress, the exact length of time before we were to be liberated. All we could do was pray, pray very hard, for speedy communist victory.

CHAPTER 15: SIX SHOTS ON CHRISTMAS MORNING

On the afternoon of Christmas Eve Gólya came upstairs, panting and pale, with a horrified expression on his face. He gathered us all, then pulled out a typed letter and began to read: "I know you are hiding some Jews. If they are not thrown out by midnight, I shall report you to the Party and you know what will be the fate of your entire family."

The note had no envelope nor signature. It had been shoved under their door, and Gólya had found it before his parents came home. None of us knew where to go, but one thing was clear: within a couple of hours, before it got dark, we all had to leave!

Tibi was first. Gólya was able to contact someone who was willing to help Tibi. With wet eyes he wished us luck, kissed us good-bye, then left with Gólya.

The ladies were too confused and helpless. For a long while they walked around aimlessly and cried. Sári finally decided that they should leave everything in the apartment as it was, get on the bus and go to Mr. X, their friend who had made the arrangements before, and let him take care of everything. We did not ask and, perhaps due to lack of clear thinking from the shock of the unexpected turn of events, they did not offer to take us along. Again we were on our own.

Ernő and I put all our possessions on our bodies; first, because the weather in December was always very cold, and second, because we looked less conspicuous without bundles. When Gólya returned we expressed our deepest gratitude to him and to the ladies, wished all of them God's blessings, decorated ourselves again with the Nazi insignias and, with tears flowing, we parted.

But where were we to go? Since I could not think of anyone who might risk giving us shelter, it was up to Ernő. The only suggestion he could come up with was the Red Cross orphanage he had been in before he was relocated to the one on Király Street. He did not know if it was a real one or an illegitimate one, whether it was completely evacuated at that time or whether only some of the children had been transferred, but for lack of any other idea, we decided to go there to see.

We walked mile after mile along the rim of the war-torn city, and the closer we got, the stronger my feeling became that some terrible danger lay ahead. I tried to convince Ernő that we should heed my intuition, which until now had been infallible, but he laughed at me, then became annoyed and said that if I wished to part he had no objection. Not wishing to separate, I suppressed my feeling and went along.

It was dark and icy cold by the time we reached the house on Andrássy Road. Candlelight shone through the cracks of the boarded-up windows, and childish voices were audible. An elderly lady responded to our knock. Ernő was delighted, for even in the dark he recognized her. It was the same Red Cross lady who had attended to him before. Of course we were invited in and welcomed to stay! The lady locked the gate-door and led us upstairs.

Many children, in clusters, were playing games in the big recreation room. Two little girls, who at once spotted and recognized Ernő, came flying into his arms. These boys and girls seemed very young, the oldest perhaps around ten. We sat down near the fire in the little potbelly stove and struck up a conversation with the older children. They said the orphanage was great. The back of the house was in ruins, but this room, the adjoining sick bay, the kitchen, plus the next apartment where they slept had been patched up, boarded in, and kept relatively warm. They received sufficient food and medication, and the lady and the old couple were very good to them. In spite of it all, my sixth sense kept saying, "Put on your coat and leave! Now! Right away!"

Soon the elderly couple came to meet us, bringing hot tea and some food. My mouth dropped in amazement when I recognized my old Jewish neighbors from the star-house, Mr. and Mrs. Bolgár. They were thrilled to see me alive and well, and the feeling was mutual.

When we finished eating the couple showed us around, then led us into the other apartment, where the children slept. They pointed out two empty bunks in the three-level beds. The beds had sacks filled with straw for mattresses and pillows, and each was equipped with two old, army-type blankets. We were to bunk with the older children; the lady with the little ones occupied the adjoining room, empty, except for a single layer of wall-to-wall straw sacks.

The kids crawled into their beds and started to undress, but I was not ready to join them. I asked Ernő to step outside and, once again, began pleading that we should leave. Ernő thought I had gone crazy. My fear was totally unfounded! Just intuition! Utterly illogical! He was, of course, perfectly right, but I insisted that everything about this war and our circumstances had been irrational. All our actions that kept us alive until now had been directed by intuition and chance.

I proposed a compromise: to leave right away, sleep among some nearby rubble, the next day find a livable room among the multitude of bombed-out buildings, eat in the cafeteria near the train station, and live thusly *only* until my intuitive feeling of foreboding subsided. Then we were to return.

Ernő had a more logical proposition. We were to stay here for the night, and the next day, if I still felt apprehensive, we were to follow *my* plan. Too insecure and afraid to leave alone, although ill at ease, I agreed. Still completely dressed, I went to bed and soon to slumber.

Loud footsteps and harsh voices awakened me at dawn. Suddenly our door was flung open and three uniformed Nazis, pointing submachine guns, entered. The familiar shouts of "Out, you pigs! Get moving! Fast!" followed. The children burst into hysterical cries as they crept out of their beds. The Nazis gave them no time to dress, not even to put their shoes or coats on. They herded everyone outside, into the snow-covered yard. By the time we got down the littlest ones were already there, huddling close to each other, crying and shaking from cold and fear.

After the Red Cross lady arrived with the last terrorist's gun in her rib cage, the men had lined us up into perfectly straight rows, separating the children with the butts of their guns. The six Nazis stood at attention while a high-ranking officer issued them orders. Soon the officer left and the sergeant assumed command. Four of the men remained facing us, standing at ease, while the sergeant and another went inside the house.

We all stood motionless, freezing to death. The littlest ones kept crying for a while, but soon became exhausted and soundlessly collapsed in the snow. The five-to-six-year-olds held out a little longer, but after about an hour, they too went down like the babes. The oldest ones, nine-to-ten years of age, took it like adults. They stood there in their pajamas and robes, barefooted, their lips and faces turning blue from the cold, their hair white from the freshly falling snow, without a move or a sound.

Ernő, fully dressed as I, looked at me apologetically, as if trying to say, "I'm sorry! Should have listened to you!" The Nazi motioned him to face forward; we had to stay at attention.

I was alone with my thoughts. "This waiting is pure torture! Why are they keeping us just standing here? What are they waiting for? Why don't they shoot us already? If that is not their intention, where will they take us? Most likely to the ghetto, since they must have just found out that this is another illegitimate Red Cross orphanage, run without an official permit."

I took a chance and glanced around. The Bolgárs were not there. Had the Gestapo found out they were Jews? Had they been killed already? I had not yet heard a shot. Ah! That was what we must have been waiting for! The couple must have hidden, and the sergeant and his aide must have been searching for them. Oh, God! I prayed they would not be found!

They weren't (I was to meet them later), but others were. In the still of Christmas morning, we heard six shots being fired. The sound came from the direction of the sick bay. I quickly turned and counted the children. There were thirty-seven in the yard, not counting the two of us. Mrs. Bolgár had told me the night before that the orphanage had forty-three at that time. Thus, it became obvious that the Nazis solved the problem of what to do with the sick. They simply shot them.

I remember calling to God as my legs gave out and I,

too, collapsed. Coma must have followed, for I came to only when commotion and the shouting started again. "Get up, you swine! Hurry! March, you rotting carrions!" Then the crack of the whips, spears and butts of rifles, and we were marching again.

The city was reverently quiet. Those who had gone to Christmas services had already returned. The warm noon sun was melting the freshly fallen snow under our feet. We moved very slowly, allowing the little ones to keep up with us. I counted. There were only twenty-eight of us. What had happened to the eleven missing babes? Were they shot too, or did they just freeze to death? We would never know.

We walked, and walked, and walked. On main roads and on side streets. Only three guards and the Red Cross lady walked alongside our pathetic group. By now we had walked a good three or four miles, but the little zombies didn't complain! Only the church bells and the sound of crackling snow could be heard.

Finally we reached Wesselényi Street. Just beyond the improvised hospital, near Akácfa Street, SS and Nazi guards opened a big gate and let us into the ghetto. Once inside, we were left again to fare for ourselves.

CHAPTER 16: DEATH IN THE GHETTO

The Red Cross lady assumed command and led us into a large former office building, near Kazincy Street. She proceeded with the fifteen littlest children to the cellar, leaving Ernő and me in charge of the older ones. We went upstairs one flight and chose the nearest set of empty rooms, once offices, to settle in. We all felt so very sick and exhausted that almost upon entering the first big room with a shabby rug, each of us just dropped down on the floor and fell asleep.

A thunderous noise and what looked like lightning awakened us. The next moment another deafening shrill, roar, burst, . . . then the ear-piercing shrieks and screams of children. I rubbed my eyes, yet was able to see only a cloud of thick grey dust.

What in the world had happened? I called to Ernő, but his reply was drowned by the children's screams. The seconds passed, but the cries did not subside. Nor did the grey dust settle.

Not being able to see, I instinctively began running my hands along each part of my body. Confirmed. I was all there, in one piece. I felt no pain, but found it most difficult to breathe. Was I dead? Just dying? It didn't really matter. Death in the near future seemed inevitable; the only question was how.

I began to creep around, feeling my way inch by inch. Recalling that Ernő and I lay down just inside the door, I crept in that direction. I flung open the door to the utter darkness and was hit by cold, fresh air. Convinced that I was very much alive and still well, I crept back inside and began to feel around. I grabbed the nearest shivering child and dragged her out into the corridor. Then I went back for the second, closest to the door. It was a little boy. By the time I returned for the third, Ernő was involved with the same rescue activity. The four children we had brought out were sobbing, but as far as we could tell in the dark, they were not badly hurt. The rest, however, were less fortunate.

By the time I re-entered the room for the fourth time, the dust had somewhat settled. Far and near bombs were exploding in rapid succession, and buildings in flames painted

101

the sky glowing red.

Some of the children were still screaming, but others were already beyond the stage of pain. The bomb that fell in the middle of the street blasted away our entire front wall. The beams supporting the floor and ceiling stuck out like pointing fingers, hanging in mid-air, ending in space. The two youngsters nearest the front wall were no longer to be found.

The children in the center row were horribly mutilated. One had been decapitated. He and the previous two were lucky; no more torture for them. They had died instantly, without time to feel pain. The next two were barely alive. One had an arm, the other both legs torn off. There was no hope for them. I prayed the Lord to take their souls quickly. A speedy death would have been for them the most humane.

The remaining two were only a little better off. Both were covered with blood and couldn't move. Ernő and I grabbed one each and, telling the ones in the corridor to follow us, we carried them down to the cellar.

The place was inhabited by forty or so elderly people, plus the Red Cross lady with her fifteen babes. As we got in sight, everyone ran to help. They cleared a large table for us, brought oil lamps, clean rags, water, and whatever first aid goods they had. Leaving the boys in the adults' hands, we went back for the other two. As we anticipated, by then they were both dead.

Somberly we returned to the cellar, trying to help. The grown-ups had already washed the blood off the boys, revealing some of their injuries. The eight-year-old's face was totally mutilated. His nose was smashed, teeth knocked out, and he had lost both of his eyes.

The nine-year-old had a large piece of metal lodged in his rib cage, near his lung and heart. He was still breathing, but bleeding heavily. We asked about the chance of getting him to a hospital. The response was that a Red Cross ambulance had been taking a few people to the Wesselényi Street improvised hospital once each day. Who they were, or how they were chosen, nobody knew. Most likely at random, so the Nazi propaganda machinery could tell the world how humane they were to the Hungarian Jews.

But, there was supposed to be a first aid station in the Central Council's building on Síp Street, operating around the clock. It had to be quickly decided whether the debris should be removed under such unsterile conditions by laymen, chance the metal's dislodging while transporting the boy, or leave him to bleed, possibly to death, while someone ran for help. The decision was grave.

While the grown-ups were debating, Ernő and I ran for help. The air raid was still on, but planes were no longer roaring above our heads. Reaching the building, we found a very poorly equipped first aid station, manned by two doctors, and at that moment without patients. The younger physician (in his late sixties) packed his case at once and followed us back.

The boy was still breathing, but unconscious. That was good, since pain killers were not available. The doctor removed the debris, bandaged him up, then attended to the smaller boy's face. He sprinkled on some disinfectant, bandaged his head, then sat down and prayed that the boy would die. He said the child's pain was so excruciating that no one could bear it without morphine. Such pain for what? The Nazis would wipe out all of us before they retreated, anyway!

After the doctor attended to the minor wounds of the other children, he murmured a Hebrew prayer and then he left. Ernő and I pulled up some orange crates, covered the boys with our tears, and then, from exhaustion, we too collapsed.

The scurrying about of the elders awakened us. Shouts

that "breakfast is here" sounded good. We joined all the others already standing in line. What arrived was a huge metal barrel, filled with a black liquid called coffee; then a man came with a sack containing "mud-bread". After an old gentleman lent me a metal cup, I too received my breakfast of one ladle of coffee and a palm-size, three-ounce piece of bread. The ersatz coffee tasted horrible. I was about to spill it out, but the elders advised me to consume it, since the body required liquid and the water from the pipes was not safe to drink.

The men who had brought the food from the central kitchen also brought a message. The doctor said that we should clean up and section off a large part of our cellar, set up an open-to-the-public first aid station, and, since we were on the opposite end of the ghetto, he might be able to get it officiated and thus secure some supplies for us.

We went to work like busy beavers. We took no break until the dinner arrived. It was delivered and served the same way as breakfast, except the liquid this time was "dishwater-soup". The elders said the name was likely to be based on fact, for the Germans were very economical. Instead of wasting leftovers from restaurants, they probably brought them in for the Jews. The taste of the greasy liquid and the variety of the little chunks implied the feasibility of the elders' comment. After our "delightful" meal, we continued to work.

Candles and oil for lamps being a necessity yet scarcely attainable, everyone retired right after dark. For lack of better furniture, the littlest ones slept on the few available vegetable crates, while Ernő and I, with a few bigger children shared a long, wide tabletop. We cuddled up closely, to warm each other with the heat of our bodies.

The next day started with sadness, yet, in a sense, relief. During the night our eight-year-old had passed away. He never came out of his coma. We asked the elders what to do. They whispered a bit among themselves; then one came forth and informed us of our choices. If we wished and had the strength, we could dig up the cobblestones and bury him in the street; or bury him under any easily accessible rubble; or burn him; or carry his body to Klauzál Tér, a tiny park a few blocks away. The latter appealed to us most. Our Red Cross lady handled the matter alone. She carried the small body and left it in the park.

Ernő and I went scavenging. We secured a table, some chairs and several mattresses, which we had dug out from under the rubble. Then we went to the Central Council's office, to exchange progress reports with the good doctor. He had managed to secure all sorts of things for us. We made one trip carrying first aid supplies, some metal cups and dishes, a bunch of old clothes, a few candles, and a can of petroleum for the lamps. We joyously returned for the shabby blankets and the big piece of glass, to let the light in through at least one of our cellar windows.

Trouble came, however, before we reached our house. Seconds after the air raid sirens sounded, we saw planes approaching. The Eastern front must have been so close that the German anti-aircraft equipment must have been moved far back, west of Budapest.* The planes flew so low that we could see the pilots. All the planes were American made, but manned by Russians.

I do not know why, but one plane began to sweep our street with machine gun fire. − Silly, but I recall trying to protect the precious glass with my body, leaning against the wall of the nearest building. − As soon as the dozen or so low-flying fighter planes passed, the heavy bombers came.

---

* We did not know it then, but the Russians had already encircled the capital completely, trapping the German divisions for nearly two months within an area of an approximate ten-mile radius.

We had just begun to run toward our nearby house for shelter when we heard the familiar ear-piercing whistle of a dropping bomb. We barely had time to throw ourselves on the ground and cover our heads with our arms when the whistle turned into a roar, followed by the terrifying crash. Moments later came the small burst of explosions, then the horrifying screams of people. I turned my head sideways and looked through my fingers. A full hit directly across the street!

As I stood there petrified, I thought to myself. Why? Why bomb the ghetto? Haven't we been suffering enough from the Nazis? Bombed by the Russians, our saviors? Maybe it was a mistake. No! The planes were flying low enough to be accurate! Was it just one man's hatred of the Jews? No! Our tiny area had been hit daily. In several locations. This implied various planes and numerous pilots! . . .

My thoughts were interrupted by some ghastly screams coming from nearby. Then I saw two flaming blobs falling from a second-story window. As they hit the ground, less than ten feet away, the blobs took on human shapes. Two women, their hair and clothes in flames. Fortunately, my intuitive reactions were instantaneous and wise. Grabbing a blanket from the supplies we were carrying and holding it in front of me, I ran to them and threw myself on top of one of the bodies. Seconds later the fire was smothered. Meanwhile Ernő had done the same, but without the blanket. The poor kid kept using his body as a rolling pin, trying to put out the flames.

The sound of falling bombs indicated that by now all planes had flown far beyond the ghetto, and it was safe for us to stand up and move around. My lady's face, hands and legs were badly burnt, but, although unable to move, she was very much alive. Ernő's lady was less fortunate. Her whole body was brown, not red, covered by ashes in place of clothes. Although she was still breathing, we knew she would not survive.

Why, we'll never know — things happened so irrationally in those days — but within minutes the ambulance drove by, picked up the women and drove out of the ghetto. We returned "home" without the glass, but at least unharmed and with a dozen or so blankets. Everyone came to greet us with happy tears; we had become their personal heroes. They made a bed for each of us from several crates, topped with the thickest mattresses. Feeling pleased about our accomplishments, enjoying being admired and wanted, in the momentary lack of imminent danger we relaxed and quickly fell asleep.

I woke up around dawn, itching all over. Although I scratched my head and body, the itching would not stop. I tossed and turned and tried, but could not go back to sleep. Looking around, I noticed that others were doing the same.

I whispered to Ernő, "Are you awake?"

"Yap," he said.

"Do you itch all over, like I do?"

"Yah, it's maddening! Believe it's lice."

We quietly got up and walked upstairs. By now the sun had risen and it was light enough for us to actually see the little pediculi crawling on our coats.

Ernő parted my hair and exclaimed, "It's full of lice! And they have already laid their nits!"

Feeling upset and helpless, we returned to the cellar. The people were gradually getting up. I asked one of the old tenants if he had noticed lice there before. He said with a chuckle, "My child, everyone in the ghetto is infested with them! We don't even notice them any more!"

"Isn't there a way to get rid of them?" asked Ernő.

"Yes," the old gentleman said, "you can burn *all* the furniture, shave your body and head, and boil *all* your clothes. And make sure that *everyone* else does the same!"

Under the direction of our Red Cross lady, we made a big fire in our potbelly stove, sectioned off a corner of the cellar by hanging blankets, heated some water and made every child, one by one, get undressed and scrub from head to toe. Then, with the help of the older kids, we began to look for lice.

To our horror, every seam of every piece of clothing was full of those little devils. We squeezed the monsters to death one by one, but could not get rid of their freshly-laid eggs. Coats, suits, dresses could not be boiled and, as we lacked other garments, neither could they be burnt. But those parasites carry typhus, a dreadful disease! So, we taught each child how to find and kill the repugnant creatures, and set aside two one-hour periods of each future day to play the game we named "bug-hunt". Then we proceeded combing their hair. To put some humor into our misery, one girl suggested we have a contest: a piece of bread to the one who removes the most lice with one stroke of the comb. I won only once, with a count of 83.

After dinner one of the old ladies told me that if I were willing to tolerate the pain, pouring on my head some of the petroleum I had brought for the oil lamps would kill the lice. She forewarned me that in six days the eggs would hatch and the application would have to be repeated. Petroleum, she said, was not available; I was lucky to get it even once from the doctor, and the process was painful, since it burned the skin already full of scabs. I couldn't care less. Anything to get rid of that maddening itch!

I speedily grabbed the jug of unrefined gasoline, leaned over a bowl, poured some on and rubbed it in well. By the time I had done the same to Ernő, my skull was aching mercilessly. Joy superseded the pain, however, when we saw the dead little devils drop into the bowl by the hundreds. We smeared the seams of all our clothes with the petroleum, wiped our tears, ground our teeth to tolerate the burning pain, and stayed away from all fires and matches. I made up my mind to begin seeking new living quarters at sunrise.

I was, however, destined to carry out one more sad task before parting from the group. During early evening, our little friend with the chest injury took his last breath. We noticed it just before retiring. After the children's farewell cry, Ernő and I were chosen to be his pallbearers. We put his withered body into a large crate, and carried him through the dark, desolate streets to the tiny park. From half a block ahead we could see the man-high pile of corpses and hear the squeaks of the feasting rats.

No, that was not good enough for our little friend. With pieces of metal debris lying around the street we dug a hole near one of three trees, lowered the crate-casket, covered it with earth, cried a little, prayed a little, then speechlessly returned home. Wanting to be alone with our thoughts, we made believe we went right to sleep.

The next morning Ernő and I decided to examine living conditions in the area. We began with our building, going door to door. The entrance doors of apartments and offices were open, except for an occasional one room which Jews had been allowed to lock. One entrance door was locked, yet we heard voices from within. We knocked, but no one came to open it. Then we heard laughter, coming from the third floor. We followed the sound and knocked. A young boy opened the door. Lo and behold! He was one of the boys we knew from the Király Street orphanage.

The other six boys inside were also part of the old gang. They were all thrilled to see us and enjoyed immensely hearing about our escapades. Their lives had been quite uneventful. I asked about the other kids.

They said that after all the gentiles had been evacuated

and the ghetto was sealed on December 10, every Jew inside moved about freely. Order was kept by the few unarmed members of the Jewish police force. Organization, such as securing food or assigning living quarters to victims newly brought in, was the job of the Jewish Council. There were only occasional atrocities committed by German and Hungarian Nazis.

For a while each of our friends had roamed the streets, buildings and cellars, looking for loved ones. Some were lucky and moved in with them. The ones who found no one split into small groups and left to fare for themselves. These seven boys had been together ever since we left.

"Have you been seeing the others?" Ernő asked.

Jancsi replied that they had at times bumped into some of them, but that there were around 70,000 people in the 3 x 7 block ghetto, most of them living in cellars and hardly ever surfacing. Thus, accidental meetings were not very likely. Another boy said that many had died, including those who had remained in the house when a bomb hit the building a few days after we had left.

I wanted to know what they ate, why they were not residing in a cellar, how they spent their days, etc. A third boy answered that at first they ate only what they found while scavenging amongst the rubble. Then, when central kitchens were set up, they too had one guaranteed meal a day; the mud-bread and the garbage-soup brought in big barrels from house to house. As to why they did not live underground, he replied that they abhorred lice, felt hopelessly depressed and trapped down below, and disliked the company of the babies and old fogies who typically populated the cellars. Besides, they felt that possibly being buried alive by a collapsing building was worse than chancing injury upstairs.

According to Géza, their daily activities consisted of

reading the stacks of books they had gathered, or playing a large variety of games. For exercise and adventure they scavenged in the rubble after each bombing, and went occasionally to Síp Street to inquire about conditions and new arrivals to the ghetto. I interrupted, asking him to clarify his last statement. He said there was a functioning Jewish Committee that had some, although very limited, contact with the Nazis. They kept a list of the residents. However, since listing oneself or reporting relocation or someone's death was not compulsory, the roster was inaccurate and incomplete, but still worth checking periodically.

Compared to ourselves, the boys seemed apathetic and depressed. They claimed the prevailing opinion was that the Russians were close by, but that the Germans would annihilate all the Jews before retreating. As to the means, they figured either by poisoning the food or by bombing the ghetto.

Although their bleak outlook and general apathy depressed me, I figured it was still better to move in with them than to fare alone. They were not too happy having me, a girl, as part of their group, but after Ernő's assurance that I was very resourceful and far more help than hindrance, they accepted me.

Their physical setup was very simple. One large room, facing the courtyard. One big window, neatly boarded up. One huge office desk, two tables, seven comfortable chairs, and a neat little potbelly stove. Finally, a row of mattresses, touching each other, along the inside wall. We talked until it got dark, then, fully dressed as we were, we all dropped on the padded floor and went to sleep.

The fact that I was different, a female, did not occur to me nor to them. Living in such a state of constant fear, of both the bombings and the cruelties of the Nazis, our minds suppressed our feelings. Not only our sexual drives, but most

111

emotions and sensations. Feelings about the loss of our loved ones, pain caused by frostbite, infections, diseases, etc., we barely registered. The mind is very potent. It can intercept, alter or redirect far more neural impulses than we normally think, *if we will it with determination.* The stronger the will to survive, the better the chance of success. Those of us who lived through the Holocaust geared our nerves and senses to just one thing: physical survival. Giving in to secondary feelings or emotions, or becoming apathetic, signed one's death warrant. That is why so many of the weaker-willed perished.

CHAPTER 17: MY SECOND INGENIOUS ESCAPE

As the days went by I kept feeling more and more depressed. The boys took care of getting wood and keeping the fire burning; they did the nominal cleaning; they even went to the Center and relayed whatever news was available. I had nothing to do or to worry about, nothing to occupy my body or mind. I began to *feel,* and that was dangerous.

The only excitement in days was when the boys came home one afternoon with a cat. She was an alley cat; lost, starved, wandering in the rubble. With gleaming eyes and salivating mouths, the boys prepared boiling water to cook the little beast. All of a sudden I felt very sick. My mind and body could not reach a compromise. Yes, I was hungry like the others; yes, the body craved meat; especially the bodies of those who had had none for many months by now. But a pussycat? Perhaps someone's pet? And *that* cat? She had hardly enough meat on her to yield for each of us even one decent bite! Besides, she looked so pathetic and helpless — like we Jews in the hands of the Nazis.

I walked outside and roamed the streets while the boys skinned, cooked, and ate the poor animal. On the way back I felt a strong desire to stop at our cellar, to let the habitants know where we were staying, in case they needed our help. I stayed only a minute, for I was afraid of picking up lice, of which I had managed to rid myself by using petroleum, a painful price to pay. Upon my return I uttered no comment, just forced my mind to go blank and to fall asleep.

I awoke during the night and began to think. — I had to get out of that situation! Fast! As a matter of fact, I had to get out of the whole ghetto! Why not risk it? We were going to be annihilated anyway. Everyone was convinced of that. If I stayed, I would be poisoned or blown to bits by the bombs. If I tried to escape and was spotted, I would get shot. A quick and painless death, the best of the three. But if I were to succeed, I might survive! Yes, I should attempt to escape! — But how? Climbing the walls was far too risky. Windows facing outside the ghetto had been boarded up or filled with brick debris. Trying to break through, I would surely be heard and seen. Since I had not noticed the ambulance lately, I assumed the Wesselényi Street gate must have been closed. But the one at the Dohány Temple must still be in use. Food and supplies must be brought through there. — Yes. I shall simply walk out — via the Dohány gate.

The next day I felt great. I had a purpose and my mind was busy. I gathered all the boys and told them my decision. One quickly touched my forehead, thinking that I had typhus and was delirious from fever. Convinced of the absence of a high temperature, they thought my mind had snapped. After the initial shock they all listened and concluded that I was normal, but agreed unanimously that the chance of escape was infinitesimal and that my plan was suicidal.

I reminded the boys that it was *they* who had convinced me that here in the ghetto we would all be killed, thus the chance to survive either way was equally small. Further, that even if I changed my mind at the last minute, planning the escape and preparing for it would challenge our minds, give us something to do, and bring us out of our apathy. After all agreed that I had made a good point, that no one had anything to lose, each boy pledged his help with the details. Since my plan had not yet crystallized, I tabled the discussion, thanked them for their offer, and went about my daily routine of washing up and rinsing my underwear.

Since months ago my entire worldly wealth had consisted only of the following: one reversible in-between-seasons coat; a light wool dress; the Nazi shirt and skirt; two sets of underwear; one pair of heavy-duty nylon stockings; one pair of hand-knit cotton socks; a wool kerchief; one pair of medium-heeled women's shoes, now with great big holes in their soles, stuffed with rags and bits of old papers; and, of course, my little black diary.

Since we had left our hiding place on Thököly Road I had been wearing my entire wardrobe day and night, mainly for protection from the bitter winter cold, but also to keep it from being stolen, and to be at all times prepared for any immediate action necessitated by the circumstances.

While engrossed in my washing activities, the term "Red Cross" kept popping into my mind. It seemed to have no significance, so I ignored it. But the words were persistent, like flashing neon lights. Finally, I mentioned it to the boys. Géza laughed, saying, "Yah, you're gonna lead us out of here like the Red Cross ladies led us in." That was my clue — a scheme started to crystallize.

But all the boys were cowardly. None, not even Ernő

114

was willing to take the chance. I tried to convince them that I could come up with a really good story, and if we could walk through either gate, the guards would just order us to march right back in. However, the boys said my idea was full of "ifs" and to count them out. I felt disappointed and sad to lose my seasoned friend Ernő, but I was determined to chance an escape.

I retired into the neighboring empty apartment, not to be disturbed while reasoning out the pros and cons of every minute detail of my plan, and to prepare a list of necessary items. When finished, I gathered the boys and presented the scheme: I was to walk out as a Red Cross messenger, having been sent to bring medical supplies.

Necessary items were a piece of white cloth, a small basket for my arm, stationery, typewriter, ink, and an official-looking rubber stamp. Jancsi announced with great joy that he still had a few sheets which he had acquired from his former residence, the legal International Red Cross orphanage on Nagyfuvaros Street, and that he even had a fountain pen. The most important item, the stationery with the official letterhead being taken care of, gathering the rest seemed to be easy and fun.

The next day we all went scavenging. By mealtime we had located an old, torn sheet, a suitable basket, and a round rubber stamp. Yet to be found was a stamp pad and a typewriter. The latter became a problem. The boys insisted that any we could find in the rubble would not be functional. As we were pondering what to do, a brainstorm hit me. Maybe one of the locked-up office rooms in our building contained one! Stimulated by the challenge, motivated if for no other reason than to see the outcome of the hair-raising scheme, we began functioning as a team.

The first door was a cinch. Like a master criminal, one of the boys picked the lock in seconds with a piece of debris. We entered. There was an old desk, a coat hanger, a wastebasket, and papers covering the floor. Oh well, let's try another!

The next double door was even easier. Géza slipped a playing card between the wings and pushed back the extending tongue of the lock. The wings parted. Ugh! This place was even worse. Bookkeepers' files were piled on the floor knee-deep.

Not yet discouraged, we continued. The next office door had a glass insert. We saw nothing but a huge drafting table and rolls of paper lying around. No good; let's try still another.

Working our way from top to downstairs, skipping through empty apartments without locked doors, we reached the second floor. Ah! Here we struck gold, we thought. The first entrance hall had elegant wallpaper, a chandelier, and old magazines scattered around. Pityu and Géza worked on the lock feverishly. Our tense anticipation ended in a real letdown when the open door revealed nothing but a dentist's chair.

By now the sun had set and we were bushed. It was a healthy exhaustion, even the boys agreed. We talked for a while. Some were a bit discouraged, but all planned to continue the next day.

I slept that night very well, but awakened before the others. My mind began to wander. — There was an iron-barred gate next to the Dohány Temple. Pityu could spring that lock in seconds, without being noticed. Beyond I had seen no wall. Thus, the guards must be just outside that gate, within or in front of the nearby buildings on the right side of the street. From there they could observe the gate and the bar-fence of the temple's little garden-cemetery. No, I couldn't sneak by without being seen. I would have to walk up to the guards with a good story and act. Yes. That would be no problem. I had managed such before. There must be both German and Hungarian guards, as usual. I might be able to bluff the latter, but Germans always have the final say. My "Deutsch" seemed insufficient. But! If a dispatch order were worded in fluent and grammatically correct German, I could bluff the Arrow Cross guard while the SS examined the paper. If I acted like a dumb little kid, bitter about having been sent to help Jews, perhaps they wouldn't even ask for other identification. If so, I still had my doctored-up workbook. Yes. Everything could work out fine.

The next morning we attacked the last likely place, the big office that occupied half of the floor. I closed my eyes and called upon the Almighty. Beyond the foyer we encountered a big, thick, double door. Besides the built-in lock it had a heavy chain around the handles, reinforced with a formidable huge padlock. Jancsi and Géza stared at it, then threw their hands up. Not a chance; they couldn't even begin. But I was determined and insistent, and nagged the boys to try. They poked at it with every bit of tool-like debris they could find, but to no avail.

Heads hanging low, they were about to walk out when I had another brainstorm. Suppose there was a fire and someone was inside. What would firemen do? Break the door down with their shoulders! But these poor, little, half-starved skeletons were no firemen. All of them, simultaneously, ran against the door, but bounced back like rubber balls. They tried again and again, but it was "bigger than all of us."

While the boys were swinging like bouncing-bags, I snooped around. I came across an open storage room, with some broken tools lying around. I picked up a rusty old axe and hatchet — probably once used to sliver wood for the ceramic stove — and ran to the boys with my precious find. They happily stopped bouncing and began to chop the door down.

While two of them were gnawing away at the barricade, Ernő left and returned, dragging a huge beam. Putting it on their shoulders, five boys went charging against the door. Boom, bang, crash! Not yet, but there was hope! Two more charges and the wing had a man-sized opening.

We crawled in, one by one, and drooled over the multitude of treasures. The room had everything. It had been a notary public's office, and when the ghetto was established, the Nazis probably did not consider the old records and stuff worthwhile to relocate. We found fascinating ancient books and documents; paper and all sorts of writing instruments; official round stamps and pads by the dozen; and yes, we found a working typewriter.

After our daily meal we all pitched in and composed an official-sounding note. Only then did I spring the news that it had to be in German. Back to the notary's office for a dictionary! We translated, criticized, changed the wording, read and re-read it; still it didn't sound good. Finally, Géza had a thought. There was a young man living in the caretaker's apartment. The man was crippled and sick, but very intelligent. Maybe he could help.

We went over. I recognized the apartment to be the one from where I had heard voices before, when no one had opened the door. Géza knocked on the window, stated his name and that he was a neighbor. An old lady came to let us in. The man, seemingly in his late twenties, was in a wheelchair. The small window had been completely boarded in, and the room was dark and tiny, but warm. They had an oil lamp, enabling the man to read.

They were very cordial and seemed happy to have us — young, cheerful, relatively clean kids — as neighbors and visitors. We learned that the lady and her husband had been the caretakers for years, but during the October purge the husband was taken away. Their son's legs had been paralyzed since birth. He had a good education, including a teaching credential in languages. He had not been teaching, though, for he had become ill with tuberculosis just before the German occupation. Géza interrupted by offering to bring them wood and coal daily, to bring them books and better furniture from the rubble, and to help them in any way they wished. Both expressed their deepest gratitude, then asked what they could do for us.

We told them a little about ourselves, how our small group had been faring, and finally about my escape plot. The motherly lady became terrified, begging me to abandon my plan. They both felt there was no way a Jew could have the upper hand with the Nazis, and that we should only keep our spirits up until our near-future liberation. They felt the SS would not harm people in the ghetto, just simply abandon us as they retreated.

Be that as it may, I wanted to escape right away. The young man, with his thorough knowledge of German, had no difficulty composing my note. Géza remained talking while I ran back to our abode with the news and for the stationery, up to the office to type it, then back to our neighbors for an adult's signature. Anxious to finish the document, we returned home without delay. Meanwhile, the boys had been hard at work doctoring up a circular stamp. They had managed to carve the rubber so it showed a big cross in the center and blurry writing around the rim of the circle. They had selected a moist, dark red pad, and seconds later my document looked perfectly official. Satisfied with our accomplishments, we all slept well that night.

January 7, 1945, was D day for me. I borrowed some tools from our neighbors, cut two pieces from the old sheet, then folded and sewed them together so as to form an armband and a nurse's cap. Lacking anything else suitable, I pricked my fingers and with the blood I drew two neat crosses, one on each of the items. Having pinned them on, I was ready for the big event.

The boys and neighbors enjoyed the dress rehearsal, but everyone once more attempted to talk me out of trying to escape, as they all felt sure that I had no chance to succeed. After saying good-bye and wishing my neighbors the best, I returned to our abode, washed my face and fixed my hair neatly, got dressed again, then gathered the boys and gave them the instructions. At dusk we left the house and soundlessly proceeded to the designated exit. The boys were moved to tears. They had gotten attached to me and now felt that this last walk to the gate was my funeral march.

It was just light enough for Jancsi to manipulate the lock, yet dark enough for my props to be a bit blurry, when we reached the huge iron gate. Jancsi and I were to go ahead, and he was to slip a tool in the lock inconspicuously while my body and hands on the handle blocked his figure from view. The boys' eyes were wet, and Ernő was quietly sobbing as we said good-bye. They hid just around the corner of the nearest building, ready to jump if help was needed. Heart in mouth, choking on my tears, but with head up high and confident, I firmly walked to the "gallows".

At the exit no one was in sight. I put my hands on the gate's handle and, before Jancsi had a chance to work on it, the heavy door opened. I motioned him to retreat. Without turning back I walked slowly through.

No wall beyond, no guards ahead; something did not seem right! Traffic in the distance seemed normal; we could not yet have been liberated. Where were the guards? How should I act? This, I was not prepared for! Calling upon the Lord to guide me, eagle-eyed but in a casual manner, skipping and humming like young children often do, I proceeded forward.

Being alert like a leopard about to descend on her prey,

I soon spotted two men standing under the archway of the fourth house, about a hundred yards from the ghetto gate. They had not noticed me yet. I had the upper hand. Increasing the volume of my hum and the speed of my skipping, as soon as I caught their attention, I aimed directly toward them. Raising my right arm and yelling "Heil Hitler, Kitartás Éljen Szálasi" in a typical Nazi fashion, I began cursing the Jews.

The guards did not know what to make of it. Not giving them a chance to think, I pulled my dispatch order from my basket and handed it to the German while rattling my story to the Hungarian. He shook his head and raised his eyebrows, then asked me to repeat what I had said, but much slower. Like a typical anti-Semitic child, with a bit of incoherency, I mumbled, "Those God d . . . Jews, I don't know why we even keep them alive; they should be shot, let alone given medication! . . . anyway, the boss of my orphanage sent me to bring some medicines for those half-Jew kids who were taken to the ghetto a couple of weeks ago. Well, I had to do it. Dr. Szappanos is an important man, and if he says I gotta go, I go!" I mumbled some more popular phrases like "infesting my pure Aryan blood," "scum of the earth" and "schmutzige schwein", in two languages to make music to the ears of both of them. Then, having given enough time to read but not to scrutinize, I turned to the SS and held out my hand for my paper.

The Arrow Cross man translated what I had said — including the swear words — quite accurately. The intonation of his voice implied that he believed my story. The dispatch order, written in "hoch Deutsch" (classical German, used by the highly educated) verified my story, making the whole affair quite plausible. The SS ordered the Hungarian to request additional papers to prove my identity to the bearer of the note. I dug into my pocket like a tomboy would, and produced from some childish-looking junk my doctored-up workbook. By now it was dark enough outside to make the forgery inconspicuous. Both guards having been satisfied, the German touched his hat in salute and motioned me to go.

"Heavenly Father, is there a limit to your love and omnipotence? You hear and shield even a little speck like me!" With these thoughts I walked ahead, leaving the ghetto-prison behind.

Ghetto scene after an air raid.

House across the street from the Dohány Temple, where I met with my father the last time, and where the guards stood when I escaped from the ghetto the second time. (The ghetto gate connected the temple yard to the fourth building east of this one.)

CHAPTER 18: MY COMPASSIONATE SERGEANT

After I turned the corner and disappeared from sight, under a nearby archway I changed the Red Cross accessories to the Nazi armband and insignia, mulled the situation over for a while, then decided to go back to the Red Cross house from which we had been taken into the ghetto on Christmas day.

Assuming that the place was empty, but being cautious, I knocked on the entrance door. To my unexpected horror, the tiny lookout window opened and a machine gun was stuck into my face. I shriveled when a husky voice asked in Hungarian, "Who goes there?" I mumbled the name on my workbook and, needing to think of something instantaneously, I asked for Mr. and Mrs. Bolgár, the first name that came to my mind. To my utter amazement the door was flung open, and I was asked to come in. In the hallway stood a giant of a man, in a Hungarian soldier's uniform. He led me into a big room on the ground floor, where twelve other soldiers were sitting around a large dining room table.

The highest ranking, a well-built, middle-aged sergeant

stood up and asked what I wanted. Having to play everything by ear and fast, I said I came to visit the old couple, friends of my family. The sergeant asked for my identifications. With shaking hands I handed him my workbook. In the bright light of a large hurricane lamp I was sure he would spot the forgery. He thumbed through the pages, looked me up and down, then returned my book without comment.

Now what? A little braver, I asked for the Bolgárs again. Without answering, the sergeant motioned me to sit down with him beside a small table in the far corner, then requested that I tell him about myself. I was totally baffled! What in heaven's name did he have in mind? What were he and his soldiers doing here? Who else was in the house? What did he think about me? I had to know the answers to all these to avoid signing my own death warrant.

Meanwhile his searching eyes kept looking me over, while I did the same. His expression was pleasant and warm, not like that of a Nazi, nor of a desiring male, not even like that of the other soldiers. He looked at me more like a father would look at his child.

Seeing that I was not about to start blabbering, he told one of his soldiers to bring us some food. Within seconds, thick slices of ham, cheese and bacon, accompanied by white bread, real butter and delicious-smelling cups of coffee were put before us. I relaxed a bit and acted as if I were not hungry. He prodded me to eat, so I nonchalantly began to sip the coffee. The cat-and-mouse game was on. He fixed a sandwich for himself and asked where I lived. I knew he noticed the address on the first page of my workbook, so the question was either to trap me or just to lead into a conversation. — What if the house had been demolished in a recent air raid and he was aware of it? What would he do if he caught me lying? — I answered curtly that my address was stated in the workbook and, without looking at him, busied myself with a sandwich. His next question was about my occupation. Petrified, since I didn't even know if schools were still in session, I answered simply that I was a student. "In which school?" he continued. I said curtly that I used to go to a private school far away, in the Carpathian mountains, but because of the war my parents wanted me near them. This fall, because of the frequent bombings, I went nowhere; my father had been tutoring me.

His expression indicated that he had accepted a stale-mate. He finished his coffee and sandwich, leaned back, lit a cigarette, and waited for me to make a move. I decided to play his game. I began to eat my sandwich very, very slowly, and asked for another cup of coffee. He got up, brought another for each of us, sat down again and waited for my next move. Shaking inside, yet challenged by this game of wits and reading minds, I almost relished just sitting there and waiting to see who could discover the other's hidden truth first. An hour must have passed. We had finished our second sandwich and fourth cup of coffee, scrutinizing each other without further words. I thought I was ahead, but my saying or doing nothing for so long had cost me the game.

The sergeant figured out that a normal 14-year-old child, with parents and a home, would not just sit there until so late in the evening. Therefore he assumed that I had not been telling the truth. Finally he smiled and said, "My child, whoever you are, you must need a place to sleep." The fact that I did not answer convinced him that he was on the right track and that I was a Jewess looking for a hiding place. He took my hand and gently led me down to the cellar.

Lo and behold! There were the three-level bunk beds, another fifteen or so children, and who else but Mr. and Mrs. Bolgár! We flew into each other's arms, cried, and leaving my compassionate sergeant behind, we sat down to talk.

After I related what I had been doing, Mr. Bolgár told

me their story. This building was originally a hotel-like structure, with one-and two-room suites. The original owners had abruptly left the country and the building had stood there abandoned. They had heard about it from a friend who used to work for the Red Cross. After my mother and I had disappeared from the star-house in November, the Bolgárs had decided to go into hiding in this house. They knew of some children whose parents had been taken away. Their friend knew how the Red Cross functioned, so being old and by now without loved ones, the three had decided to dedicate the rest of their lives to attempting to save Jewish children. With the remainder of their hidden valuables, they had purchased supplies on the black market and set up the illegal orphanage. Through word of mouth, children kept hearing about the place and kept coming.

Mrs. Bolgár continued by saying that they had been hiding in the first floor suites, where we had stayed on Christmas Eve. When the bomb had hit the building it had left a hole in the kitchenette wall, which they had boarded up so that it could be used as an exit to a large cavity formed by the fallen debris. When the Nazis came on Christmas, that was where they had hidden. After we were taken away, they had moved into the cellar. Children kept showing up, as Ernő and I had done before. They housed the two oldest boys in the suite upstairs and moved with the little ones into the cellar. Mr. Bolgár finished by telling me that three days ago the soldiers came snooping around. His wife had told the sergeant that they had all lived in a nearby orphanage that was bombed recently, so when they found this place empty, they had moved in. The sergeant said, "We could all co-exist," and without further questions or comments he had left. They had heard but had not seen any of the soldiers. Thus, think what they wished, neither party knew anything about the other. Not even each other's names. At that point I was too tired to think, so I dropped into the nearest empty bed and promptly fell asleep.

The next day I spent getting to know everybody. After we had some warm, black liquid for breakfast, I was introduced to the children in the cellar. They were all young, between three and ten years of age. Next I went up to our old suite. There I met one of the boys who was about twelve years old, and a new girl who had crept in during the night through the rubble. Éva said she was twelve and a half and had been hidden by Christians, but their home was bombed and the family had perished. Since she had visited a friend here before, she knew about the hole in the kitchen wall and that's how she had gotten in last night.

The Bolgárs had left in that room a table and two chairs, and straw mattresses all over the floor. The rest of the things — potbelly stove, furniture, games and books — they had moved to the cellar. I staked my place near the kitchen door, told my new friends I'd see them later, and then went down to the ground floor to find out what I could about the soldiers.

The sergeant seemed happy to see me. They were just about to have dinner, so he asked me to join. I gladly accepted. He had one of his soldiers serve the two of us at the little corner table, and we chatted about trivialities while eating the delicious cold cuts. After the meal we sipped our coffee and talked further. We discussed art, music, Hungary's past history — everything, but all impersonal. He seemed far too intelligent to be only a sergeant. And he fascinated me.

I was just about to ask some personal and direct questions when he shocked me by saying: "I'd like you to come to my home." Nope! That curious I was not! He must have read my mind, for he quickly added, "And meet my wife." True or false, I deemed it best to make a polite but hasty exit, using sleepiness as an excuse.

I went upstairs, talked to the kids for a while, then, when it got dark, I lay down and soon fell asleep, coat and all, as usual. During the night I was awakened by something that sounded like tank or cannon fire. I listened for a while, thinking, could the Front be that close? Possible, but I could not be sure. Everyone else was asleep; I returned to slumberland.

Upon awakening the next morning, I felt terribly itchy. Right away I knew what it was. I woke the boy next to me and asked if he had lice. He giggled and said, "Everybody does! We are all full of the little beasties!" I went into the bitterly cold bathroom and got completely undressed. Sure enough, my clothes were full of them. I ran down to my sergeant and asked for some petroleum. He knew why immediately, and chuckled as he poured some into an empty can, then said: "My dear, it is of no use. The mattresses and chairs are full of them, and we cannot afford to burn everything, including all our clothes. Believe me, we have tried everything. You have two choices: stay here and get used to the lice, or come to live in my clean home, as I offered yesterday."

Not wanting to pursue the conversation, I grabbed the liquid and swiftly ran upstairs. My head and body skin raw and aching, I spent the rest of that day lying in my corner, sobbing.

A sudden disturbance awakened me about midnight. Something big was crawling around in the kitchen. One of the boys flung the window open, trying to see in the moonlight what it was. I watched him tiptoe into the kitchen, heard some whispering noises, then a few seconds later felt an ice-cold thing land on top of my body. I was just about to scream from fright when the "ice-block" spoke and said, "Save me! I'm frozen to death!"

Assured that it was a friend, not foe, Eva and I rolled

the body between ourselves, covered him with all the blankets in the room, and began to rub his chest and arms gently. The window closed by now to block the gush of cold air, we could not see, but felt that the boy had only underpants on. We felt no broken bones or open wounds, but his moans indicated that our rubbing caused him pain. Éva and I unbuttoned our clothes and cuddled him tightly, trying to warm him with our own body heat. The older boy, the one who found him, was kneeling at his head, breathing warm air into his mouth. For a long time he just lay there, without uttering a sound.

In the still of the night, cannon shots were clearly audible. One round seemed to come from the left, the other from the right of us. I wondered how long before we would be hit, if we should not move down to the cellar. But would it be safer there? Would a direct hit have enough destructive power to make the whole house cave in on us? I had no desire to be trapped under rubble! When in the rubble-cleaning force, I had witnessed the agonized suffering of many, pinned down by stones and beams for hours, even days, barely alive when we had dug them out. And what about those we did not find? And those whom the rubble had buried alive? No! Not the cellar! Maybe I *should* go away with the sergeant? Maybe he did have a wife and indeed just wanted to save me?! But why should he? Something was fishy about him. . . .

My thoughts were suddenly interrupted by a thundering blast. The impact forced our window open, revealing a light that turned the distant sky red. It looked like the burst of a giant firecracker – terrifying, but beautiful. The lack of small secondary explosions convinced me that it was no bomb, no flying debris about to hit us, so I relaxed and watched the gorgeous view. A tenth of the city was flooded by light! I could see the top of the parliament, the basilica, the castle and the fort, even the Citadelle in Buda.

Suddenly, the body beside me began vibrating. A good sign! I had not been sure whether he was still alive. I hit his chest with my fists, forcing him to breathe. He let out a roaring moan. Thank God! We had saved him!

The boy stopped breathing into his mouth. In the eerie glow of the shimmering light outside I could see our patient's face. I stared, rubbed my eyes, and looked again. It was Rizsa! The boy in the Király Street orphanage, whose ears had gotten infected from my scratches. Gee, I had felt so guilty then for causing him pain. Now I made up for it by being instrumental in saving his life. But I had scratched him because he was trying to get fresh with me! Gosh, had I known it was Rizsa, I would not have cuddled up to his body. — Oh, I would have. This was different, this was therapy, not sex. — I realized then that I would have stopped at nothing short of dying to save another Jew's life.

Covering as much of his body as I could with my own, I kissed his cheek and whispered, "Rizsa, this is Györgyi. Remember me? Relax! You're among friends. I promise to take care of you!"

Gradually his convulsions began to subside and his breathing became more regular. Finally he said: "I'll be all right now. Just keep me warm. I love you."

Upon awakening the next morning, I watched him for a while. He seemed to be in a deep and healthy slumber. Éva remained at his side while I went to eat breakfast and to tell the Bolgárs about him. After they assured me that we had acted wisely, I had Éva relieved so she, too, could eat. Then I quietly stole outside, through and onto the top of the rubble, to evaluate the war's progress. Standing a flight high I could see the whole Andrássy Road, covered with freshly fallen snow and not a soul in sight. The stillness was interrupted only by the distant sound of tank and machine gun fire, coming from a few miles northeast of us, beyond the Városliget (Townpark). Content that we would soon be liberated, I crawled back through the hole.

Rizsa was just waking. Reaching for my hand and smiling, he said, "Thanks for saving my life!" I stroked his head, sent a boy for the Bolgárs and for some food, put another blanket on my friend, and asked him to tell how he had been faring.

Rizsa related that he had hidden well when the Nazis took the children from Király Street into the ghetto. He had stayed there in peace and comfort for a while, until a bomb had fallen nearby and had damaged the building. He had lived in the rubble while the food supply lasted, then he went to Újpest, a suburb, where he was hidden by a Christian friend. Someone must have found out and reported it, because one evening Gestapo men came and took them to an Arrow Cross headquarters. Stripped to their underwear, they were locked up in a dark cellar with many other people, who had been beaten and tortured before their arrival. The survivors were taken out after sunset and marched along the Danube River. They heard extensive cannon fire and saw many retreating German trucks and tanks. Soon a car stopped and its occupants gave the guards some orders. After the victims were lined up along the river bank, with stretched-out arms, their wrists tied with ropes to one another, the executioners mowed them down with submachine gun fire. All forty of them had gone tumbling into the river.

"Were you shot, too? And how come you didn't die?" asked one of the boys.

Rizsa raised his eyebrows, stared into vacant space, then said, "Some mysterious force must have watched over me, because while falling I noticed the rope around my right wrist dangling. Since I felt very much alive and my right arm was free, I used it as a wing, balancing myself to assure a vertical impact. Once under water, I managed to free myself from the dead man next to me. I did not come up for air, for those who were still alive and surfaced were shot at once with pistols. I held my breath and swam with the current. By the time I finally surfaced between the floating ice-blocks, the river had carried me downstream quite a distance. Totally numb from cold and fear, I chanced to climb out on the dark and deserted river bank. Crawling in the snow on my hands and knees, along the sides of buildings, in side streets and alleys, having heard about this place from Ernő, I came here. The rest you know."

It was then I noticed the wound near his shoulder. A bullet intended for his heart or brain — the usual method of that type of execution — had missed and pierced instead through the flesh of his upper arm. That is why he had moaned last night when we were rubbing him. But the blood had clotted and the wound seemed to be healing. That and the severe rope burns on his wrist seemed less of a concern than his hot forehead, which indicated a very high temperature. We wrapped blankets around him tightly and helped him down to the cellar, which was heated by the iron stove and lit by oil lamps. For lack of medicines, keeping him warm and applying cold compresses to his forehead was all we could do. It was up to God, whom we beseeched.

When dusk descended, I paid a visit to my sergeant. After supper he took me aside again, to our private little table, and initiated a serious talk. He informed me that the Russians were closing in on the city, and it looked as though they would proceed down Andrássy Road. He estimated that within the week our house would be caught in the cross fire. More ominous, however, was the information that one of his soldiers suspected that the old couple and the children were possibly Jews, and had reported that to the local police. If the report was relayed to the Nazis, we would surely be exterminated.

Wow! And I had thought that we no longer had to worry about the Nazis! It was time to lay our cards on the table. I admitted being Jewish, but said I was not willing to be anyone's mistress, which was why I had refused his offer. At that point he pulled out a picture of an attractive lady and a child. He said they were his family, living in a private home in Buda. My expression must have revealed my distrust, for he continued, saying that his wife was currently hiding eight Jewish children. I tried to change the subject, but he seemed insistent. After a brief hesitation, he confessed that he and four of the soldiers were uncircumcized Jews. No one but themselves knew this fact. And no one else was to know!

I pledged my secrecy, but wanted to know why they were not fighting at the Front. He said they had recently defected, and that fact was also to be kept top secret. Now was I convinced and ready to go? I said I needed time to digest all he had told me and that I would let him know my decision on the following day. Expressing my gratitude, I left.

The next morning, Rizsa's fever was still very high. Also, the Bolgárs had completely run out of food. After washing and brushing the straw out of my hair, I went to see my sergeant again. This time *I* asked him to our private nook, for I had favors to ask. We needed food for the children. From whence they came no one knew, but by now our group numbered twenty-seven. My friend promptly rose, took me to his source of supply, packed a box with milk, egg and potato powder, herb tea, dried lentils and peas, some lard, sugar and bacon, and handed the box to me. Encouraged by his compassion and generosity, I told him about Rizsa. He diagnosed the case as probably being double pneumonia, gave me some medication, and said that if the boy's system was strong enough to survive, we should see improvement within two days. Before parting I said that as soon as Rizsa's fever broke — if his offer still stood — I would go with him to his home. Although he felt it was dangerous to wait, we agreed to the compromise.

Everyone in the cellar was absolutely thrilled about my acquisitions. Rizsa was still burning with fever when we gave him some hot tea and medicine. The little ones were so sweet, talking in whispers and walking on tiptoes, lest they awaken or disturb him. Having mulled it over, I decided to tell Mr. and Mrs. Bolgár what the sergeant had said with respect to the progress of the war and our having been reported. My words hit them like a brick. Moving the whole group was far too dangerous. Besides, where to? Seeing them so worried about the children made me regret that I had even mentioned the topic. Leaving them pondering, I went through the back yard, to the street, to verify how close the Front was.

At the horizon, the Townpark looked like an enormous anthill. Machine gun fire, even pistol shots, were clearly audible. My friend spoke the truth; even his timing seemed to be correct. Within days the Hungarian and German forces would surely be retreating, right along our street. Not having yet seen foot soldiers fight, I could not visualize how it would affect us. My logic told me to go with the sergeant right away; my heart said stay with Rizsa; my intuition assured me not to worry, the Lord was watching over me and would protect me.

As the day went on, the sound of shooting and retreating machinery became louder and louder. Before nightfall, through the upstairs window I could even see what looked like soldiers running across the street and into a building at the end of Andrássy Road. I went downstairs quickly, following Éva and the boys.

Our basement was enormous and, although not paneled,

was divided into sections with huge wooden planks. The enclosed large area on the right of the staircase was still empty. The farthest big room on the left had a tiny window, facing the yard, and was occupied by the children. One small enclosure before it was where the Bolgárs slept, another was the improvised kitchen, and between the two was the toilette. On the other side of the narrow, tunnel-like corridor, which led to all these rooms, were eight- by eight-foot bins, where tenants had stored wood, coal, or any of their belongings.

The soldiers were also moving to the cellar, carrying their supplies to the room on the right. The little ones were petrified, for they had never actually seen our soldiers. They were not allowed to open the window, nor to go beyond the end of the corridor. To put the children at ease, I brought my sergeant to them. He explained that he and his soldiers were friends, here to protect them. He also said that there might be some loud shooting soon, but not to worry, for he and his men would not let anyone harm them.

After we ate and tucked the children in, the Bolgárs and I sat down to talk. Hearing that the Front was only miles away, they said there was nothing else to do but to remain very quiet and to pray. We moved a bunk bed for Rizsa, Éva and myself into the Bolgárs' room, not to awaken the children in case he needed attention during the night; then we all retired.

The next day, January 12, 1945, the sound of small arms fire increased rapidly. We lit only one lamp in the small room and kept the little ones in bed. Everyone in the cellar was very, very quiet. From then on we did not run the water to wash, nor even to flush the toilette. We feared what the Nazi soldiers might do if they found us.

Rizsa's condition had remained unchanged. He was still barely conscious and ran a high fever. His throat and eardrums were hurting badly, and the pain in his chest was quite severe. I played some quiet verbal games with the children, trying to keep them, and my own mind, occupied.

It was just before dusk when we heard a sudden bang and crash upstairs, followed by a series of ear-piercing rapid fire. No one moved or let out a sound. Everyone was petrified. We heard the whistle of bullets flying back and forth across the street, some missing, some hitting, some ricocheting off the outside wall upstairs. Then silence. Then another rally. Silence and rounds of machine-gun fire alternating for a while, then commotion and the sound of falling bricks from upstairs, then footsteps in the back yard, then silence again. The frequency and intensity of the battle sounds did not diminish with the approach of dusk, but the center of the battle seemed to have passed us by.

During the night Rizsa awakened me, asking for water. I brought him some. After gulping down a pitcherful of water he sat up, for the first time, and said his pains had subsided and he felt almost well. I touched his forehead. Thank God, he was no longer feverish!

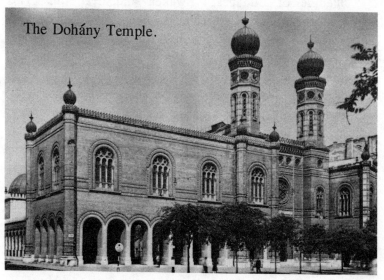

The Dohány Temple.

CHAPTER 19: THIS IS LIBERATION?

I was awakened by a tap on my shoulder. Opening my eyes, in the light of a match I saw my sergeant standing beside me, holding his finger to his mouth indicating "hush", then motioning for me to follow him. Feeling our way in the dark, on tiptoe we went up the stairs, up another flight, through the hole in the kitchen, then onto the top of the rubble.

It was dawn. The moon was setting and the sun rising far in the horizon. The guns were silent. I felt tranquil. We stood there, motionless as the city began to awaken. Far in the distance, in the Városliget, a truck began to move. Someone was talking through a loudspeaker. As the truck got nearer, the brisk wind carried the sound toward us, and we could understand the words:

"People of Budapest! Awaken and hear this: The Russian Army is here. We came to liberate you! We bring *democracy*, freedom and equality for all! The Liberation Front is the People's Army! Do not resist but welcome us! We bring communist solidarity — peace and freedom for all!"

I couldn't bear my happiness! I wanted to scream with joy! The sergeant put his arm around me, his hand over my mouth, and gently led me back into the house. He sat me down on the staircase and whispered that the war was not yet over. The Germans and Hungarians had pulled back during the night, about a tenth of a mile, but the Russians had not yet reached our house. They would come, being just as afraid of the civilians as the people were of them. We should be very quiet and try not to move. If the Russian soldiers did find us in the cellar, we should all step into clear sight, be silent, hold our hands above our heads, and do exactly as we are told.

He asked me not to awaken anyone, that there was still plenty of time. Since I said I could not go back to sleep, being too excited and happy, he tiptoed to the supplies, brought me some candy, and told me to return to my room.

By then the Bolgárs were awake. I called them into the kitchen, lit a candle and related all I had seen and heard. Instead of being excited and happy like myself, they both looked worried. Then Mr. Bolgár uttered the same concerned admonitions. I listened for the second time, but the words still did not penetrate. All I felt was happiness. The culmination of our hopes and desires! We had been praying to live to see this day for so long! For me, the war was over. Nothing could hurt me any more!

As the children started to stir, the couple awakened them all and gathered them closely. Mrs. Bolgár reiterated the instructions, almost verbatim. She then ordered everyone to return to bed and to try very hard to go back to sleep. I crawled in with the children and mutely followed her command.

It was Saturday, January 13, 1945, about 10:00 a.m. when suddenly the board of the little window came crashing down. Instantly a Russian soldier jumped in and pointed a machine gun at us. Seconds later, three more soldiers followed the same procedure.

I wanted to fling myself into their arms, to hug and kiss them, but the guns discouraged me. Shouting "Davai! Davai!" (Get going!) while nudging us with their guns, they ordered us all to raise our arms and line up at the foot of the stairs. The poor little ones, obviously scared to death, without a murmur followed our example. By the time we all got there, Mr. Bolgár had put a coat on Rizsa and had leaned him against the rail. Our soldiers were there too, hands up high above their heads, guns on the ground in front of their feet.

The four Russians still kept pointing their weapons at us while the five who had come through the entrance door grabbed our soldiers' guns and, with Herculean strength, snapped them in halves over their own knees. They ran their hands along the bodies of the Bolgárs and us children, and, having found no hidden weapons, allowed us to lower our arms and return to the big room.

As we were leaving, my sergeant smiled and called out, "Now all of you be good! Do as you are told! I'll be back to visit you later!"

Via the word "davai" and the sign language of their waving guns, our four new guards made us all sit on the beds along the walls of the big cellar room, motionless and soundless. Hungry, cold and frightened, we sat like that for several hours.

My mind wondered — what did my sergeant mean by "I'll be back later?" He was now the enemy. Would he not be taken prisoner? Why were they keeping us like that? Was it not obvious that we were no foes? That we were totally harmless? And why so long? What were they waiting for?

Finally a three-year-old burst into tears and cried out, "I gotta make a doody! Can't hold it longer! I just gotta!" He slipped off the edge of his bed and toddled toward Mrs. Bolgár. One of the soldiers, sitting backward on a chair in the middle of the room and still pointing his gun at us, barked out some words and motioned the little boy to return to his place quickly. Éva yelled, "Mess in your pants!" And total silence enveloped us again.

Good Lord! Why didn't he let the child go? Even if they did not understand Hungarian, it should have been obvious that people, especially children, have basic physical needs. And why didn't he let the babe at least sit beside Mrs. Bolgár? This is liberation? — I started to have doubts about our Messianic liberators.

And thus started the new era, replacing National Social-ism (Naziism) with International Socialism (Communism).

CHAPTER 20: IVAN THE UNTERRIBLE

The sun was still up, its weakening rays shining through the empty frame of the little window, when we heard the outside door open, followed by footsteps down the corridor. Lo and behold! It was my sergeant and four of his men. In civilian clothes! Son of a gun, he *was* telling me the truth! They must have proved somehow that they were Jewish, so the Russians let them go. But we were Jewish, too! How could we prove it?

My friend walked straight to one of our guards — the smallest and youngest one — showed him some papers and said a few words in Russian. Then that guard said something to the others, upon which they all put their guns on their shoulders and indicated that we could talk and move around. One of them, by moving to the foot of the stairs and pointing his gun appropriately, informed us that the Bolgárs' room, the kitchen and the toilette were all to be within limits.

While the Hungarian men began to talk to the children, my ex-sergeant called me out to the corridor and proceeded with his explanation. They were not only Jewish but for several years members of the Communist Underground. He was now assigned to assist the setting up of the first Party headquarters, here on Andrássy Road, as soon as the Front moved beyond the parliament, a few more miles west of its current position.

He eulogized communism: how well everyone was to be treated, without discrimination and oppression, how the new government would take care of the old, the poor, the sick, and so on. He ended by saying that I was a very smart and intelligent young lady and would be a great asset to organize the Party's new youth movement. Telling me his full name, Zoltán Kádár, for the first time, he and his men parted by saying, "See you later."

Meanwhile, under the watchful eyes of one of the guards, the Bolgárs had concocted some food and had cleaned up and fed the children. Rizsa, not feverish any more, had received some clothes from one of the bigger boys and was sitting among us. The three guards, with guns on their shoulders, were sitting silently but watchfully, in three different corners of our room. My stomach was churning. Filled with conflicting emotions, I was very restless and tense. I wanted to run away — even into danger — just out of this cage! Knowing that an attempt to escape at that moment would have cost my life, I did the next best thing. I walked over to the young guard Mr. Kádár had talked to, and greeted him in English. He looked up at me with his great blue eyes and responded in English, "How do you do." In sign language, I asked his permission to pull up a chair and sit down beside him. He motioned "yes." Continuing in my very broken English, and using body movements, I told him my name and asked how long we would have to stay there like that. In English no better than mine, aided by his hands, he said, "Until our relief arrives." To my question as to when that would be, he replied, "After it gets dark and all the shooting has stopped."

Wow! We could communicate! That was fun! Without moving, I translated my news to the others. The kids were still shivering from fright and the penetrating cold. I turned back to my guard and asked permission to start the fire. He got up, said his name was Ivan, went to the stove, started a fire for us, then came back and sat down again.

As the room got warmer, the kids began to thaw out, relax, and gather in little groups to play. Meanwhile, I scrutinized my new friend. He was only slightly bigger than I, at most 5'4" and 130 lbs., and just a teen-ager. With thick blond hair, big blue eyes, soft hands and long fingers, and a well-proportioned build, he looked very handsome.

Curious about his intelligence, I threw him a curve. Recalling the Latin song typically sung at the graduation exercises of all college preparatory students, I began to hum, then quietly sing "Glaudeamus igitur". He joined in with the second line, "Iuvenes dum sumus". Both of us wearing big grins, we finished the verse together. Feeling very much at ease with him and being fascinated and curious, I asked in German where he had learned English and Latin. He replied in broken but understandable German: in the gymnazium he had attended in Moscow.

I was sitting there feeling just absolutely great when several Russian soldiers came shouting, singing, and tramping down our corridor. Mrs. Bolgár immediately ordered each child to bed, then Éva and me to come at once into her room. As I was about to exit, Ivan, who by now was standing at attention, called out in English, "See you tomorrow!"

In the light of a candle, Mrs. Bolgár looked frightened and very worried. She said the newly arrived soldiers were terribly drunk and who knows what they might do during the night. She firmly told us not to ask any questions, just follow her commands. She ordered us to grab four straw mattresses and some blankets, and to drag them into the large storage bin across the corridor. We had to lay two of the sacks next to each other, on the coal-covered ground. After we lay down on them, she threw a blanket and another mattress on top of each of us. While we were still speechless from amazement, she left and seconds later returned with two of the littlest boys. After they climbed on top of us and she had tucked them in tightly, she bent down to check if our heads were turned sideways so we could breathe. After telling us to be absolutely silent and not to move, no matter what, until daylight, she tiptoed out and closed the plank-door behind herself.

Alone with our thoughts, we lay there like corpses. Each second seemed an eternity. The new set of soldiers were howling, shouting, and tramping back and forth in the corridor. In the light of the two huge oil lamps they had hung, through the cracks of our enclosure, we could see up to about their waists. I counted eight different sets of legs having walked by before two soldiers stopped right in front of our bin. One was a private, the other some sort of an officer. They were shouting at each other, obviously arguing about something. Then we heard noises like someone being punched and falling against the wall next to us, then a pistol shot, then a clunk as the officer collapsed. A long while later we heard someone drag the body away. Finally it was quiet, except for the loud snores of soldiers near the stairs. The only occasional footsteps implied that we were guarded by no more than two or three.

I was lying awake, regurgitating the recent events, when I heard singing and footsteps coming down the stairs and corridor. These soldiers, carrying a flashlight, looked into every opening. Reaching our bin, one shoved the plank-door in and two of them entered. They shined the light at our heap; then one began to laugh. The other bent down and playfully tickled one of the boys. Terrified, the toddler began crying. Apologetically the soldier sat down beside him, of course, right on top of Éva. The other staggered around, stroked the other boy, then plunked himself down, right on me. The foul smell of liquor, vomit, and filthy bodies turned my stomach, but I didn't dare move. They might have found us had they been less drunk; as it was, they played with the babies for a few minutes, gave them little packets of margarine and lumps of sugar, and finally left.

I took a deep breath and thanked the Almighty. Although still puzzled and fearful of whatever Mrs. Bolgár had anticipated, exhausted from the fluctuation of my emotions during the last eighteen hours, I finally dozed off.

I was awakened this time by Éva poking me in the ribs, telling the boys and me to tuck ourselves in tightly. Listening alertly, I heard another wave of drunken soldiers' howls, followed by several sets of footsteps. They bypassed us — Thank God! — stopping in the big room. Next I heard the bloodcurdling screams of the children. In the beams of the flashlights, I could see five sets of boots, each dragging a screaming, struggling little girl.

When silence finally descended, I was alone again with my thoughts. No longer puzzled about what Mrs. Bolgár had anticipated, telling myself that what I thought could not be true, I forced myself to go back to sleep.

The rays of the rising sun glittering through the cracks awakened me. Everything was peaceful; everyone was still asleep. I barely had a chance to collect my thoughts when I heard sobbing and the sound of tiny footsteps, descending the staircase and down the corridor. I took a chance and crawled out to look.

The four little girls I had seen being dragged out during the night were returning, pulling the fifth one's body behind them. Ignoring the possible danger, I jumped to my feet and ran to them, lifted the little body into my arms and brought them all into the Bolgárs' room. The commotion awakened the vigilant couple, and the sight of us made them jump to their feet. The wife grabbed a blanket, wrapped the child in my arms into it, put her on the tiny table, told the other four to get into her husband's bed, then sent me to boil some water. By the time I returned from the kitchen Éva and Rizsa were there also. Mrs. Bolgár sent Rizsa to cuddle and quiet the whimpering little girls, then she unwrapped the child on the table.

Her little body was black and blue, her abdomen and legs covered with blood. She was still breathing, but in a coma. Mrs. Bolgár hurriedly washed the blood off. The flesh next to her groin was torn, her organs protruding. Mrs. Bolgár gently readjusted her tiny body, applied some ointment and gauze, placed her thighs tightly against each other, wrapped her in the blanket, and put her to bed. Once again we prayed.

She then put each of the other girls on the examination table, starting with the *oldest, less than 11 years of age.* They were discolored and bloody also, but their flesh was not quite so badly torn. In tearful anguish the couple and I cleaned them, gave each some of my sergeant's candy and a sleeping pill he had given us for Rizsa, then put them all in the Bolgárs' bed to rest.

We looked at each other and shook our heads. Finally Éva said somberly, *"Is this liberation? What we have been praying for?"*

We had barely finished when the new guards arrived. Ivan poked his head in and greeted me with a warm "Hello!" I was in no mood to converse, but since he was the only communication link with our new oppressors, I waved to him to come in and pointed at the little girls. Ivan hung his head, as if he knew exactly what had happened. He motioned me to wait, that he would be right back.

As I stared at those children, I felt very dirty. Not just physically — from the straw, the coal and the lice — but also inside, as if my blood, brain cells and nerves needed cleansing too. More than anything else I wanted a bath, wishing to purify body and soul.

Aiming for the upstairs bathroom, I ran to the end of the corridor. Not a chance. The armed guard blocked the foot of the staircase. I burst out crying; I was bitter and angry! I was hateful. For the first time in my life I wanted to kill. The emotion frightened me, yet I could not suppress it. Barbarians! Worse than animals!

Mrs. Bolgár left the side of the little girl and came over to calm me. She just kissed and hugged me, for there were no appropriate words to say.

Ivan arrived soon with an army first aid kit and his personal gear. He gave us all his food and his only blanket, then just stood there, looking compassionate and sad, wanting desperately to help. For the others, maybe; but for the little *nine-year-old,* help was too late. Never recovering from the coma, she bled to death.

Ivan escorted the old couple, Éva and myself — the funeral procession — carrying the child to the yard. We dug a hole under the snow, placed the tiny body inside, covered it with muddy earth, and ended the ceremony with Mr. Bolgár's recitation of a psalm. As we were returning, I saw a body lying in the snow. It was that of a Russian soldier, an officer with a bullet hole in his heart. I recognized the pants and boots, as they looked to me from under the mattress in the bin the previous night. Strange — I felt no compassion for him. No more than for a dead Nazi.

During the afternoon the four children awakened and told their story. Twelve drunken soldiers had attempted to rape each. I couldn't bear looking at the girls. I had an insatiable urge to run, just run, anywhere, just away from it all! But I knew that escape — mental or physical — was not even remotely possible.

One vigilant guard was still at the staircase. In the big room Ivan and the other soldiers were no longer holding their guns; they were playing with the kids. When I entered, Ivan motioned me to sit down beside him. Reluctantly I did. As the day before, with hands and feet and in three languages, we began to talk. He asked me to inform the Bolgárs that within a day or so the orphanage was scheduled to receive food. Further, that the purpose of the soldiers' presence was not to keep us prisoners, but to defend the Front, to prevent, if needed, the Germans from returning to our house. He said that the western part of Andrássy Road was still within the front-line zone, and might not be completely occupied by them for another day or two.

As dusk approached, Ivan said he wanted me to sleep in the upstairs suite. Being afraid of his intentions, I said positively "No!" Although he tried to convince me that he only wanted to protect me, I thought of the little girls and kept reiterating, "No, no, no!" He must have understood my thoughts, for suddenly he indicated that I could take some of the children with me. He said that since he would be off duty, he could stay right at the entrance of our sleeping quarters, to "bang, bang away" with his gun any other soldiers who might want to come in.

I ran to the Bolgárs to ask their opinion. Having considered the matter, they agreed that it might be safer than the cellar, provided Éva, Rizsa, and the three twelve-year-old boys go along. After an early supper, before it got dark, taking along some necessary items, Ivan escorted the six of us upstairs and left.

It was eightish when my Russian friend returned. He brought for us a flashlight, several blankets, bread, margarine, and a large box of sugar cubes. Acting fatherly, he changed our sleeping arrangement. He put Éva in the furthest corner, next to her the three boys, me in the inner corner, Rizsa to block the kitchen door, positioning himself across the front entrance. We munched ourselves to sleep while Ivan sat beside his lantern and read, holding his submachine gun in his lap, in readiness.

Again the familiar singing and shouting awakened us during the night. Someone kicked and tried to push the front door in. Ivan jumped to his feet, grabbed his gun and yelled out a few harsh words. When the response was another shove on the door, he let loose with a round of fire, aiming at the floor. His point clearly made, he sat down again with a big sigh, listening to the sound of the departing footsteps dying out in the still of the night. Thus ended the second day of our "liberation".

Ivan was gone by the time we awakened. Although the water was ice cold, it was still a pleasure to wash in the bathroom, from head to toe. My clothes and hair were full of lice, but by now I was used to them. Besides, each Russian soldier was a walking louse-farm! While the four boys took advantage of the bathroom also, Éva and I watched the war's progress from our window.

Our first view of the outside was shocking. Dismembered bodies lay all over the street. Dozens of dead soldiers, of all three nationalities, were clearly visible. At the far eastern horizon we observed Russian military equipment; at the western end of our sight, German heavy artillery. In between, no more than a couple of hundred yards west of us, bullets were still whistling back and forth across Andrássy Road. Germans and Hungarians on the south side of the street, Russians on the north, the occupation-retreat game moved a house at a time.

Convinced that we were best off where we were, at least for a while, Éva and I returned to the cellar. The only guard was lounging in the big room on the right of the staircase, staring at the ceiling and smoking a foul-smelling cigarette. We greeted him politely, but he didn't seem to hear us, nor even to care.

The children had eaten by then, from what we still had on hand, besides the black bread, margarine and sugar that were being supplied daily by the Russians from then on. The Bolgárs were thrilled to see us and to hear how nice my soldier-friend had been.

No sooner had I finished the account than Ivan appeared. He told me to inform everyone that they were free to go, if they desired, but only northeast, toward the strongly reinforced area of the Townpark and beyond. Overhearing this, Mr. Bolgár insisted that I not mention it to anyone; the children were much safer here. Ivan had acquired some army-type sleeping bags and a battery-operated heating unit, and he asked me to come and help him fix our room upstairs. He helped me clean up the place and plug up the bullet holes in the wall and window, after which we sat down to talk. I told him a little about my past, and he proceeded to do the same.

We were lounging on top of the mattresses and sleeping bags, pleasantly warm and comfortable, alone in the room. Unexpectedly he rolled toward me, put his arm around me and attempted to kiss me. I instantly pushed him away and slapped his face. He moved a few feet away, looked at me strangely, and asked how old I was. I said 14½. He then wanted to know if there was something physically wrong with me. I answered, "No. Why?" Without responding, he asked if I found him repulsive. Being as puzzled as he, I replied that, to the contrary, I found him rather attractive. His next question was blunt and outright. Had I never had sex before? I was glad the lighting was not too bright, for I knew I blushed as I said, "Of course not!"

He shook his head in disapproval and commented, "Strange Westerners! At home, as soon as a girl becomes of age, she has a boyfriend and sex. Having babies with or without wedlock is patriotic. It is good for the country. We need manpower!" Since his comment obviously did not alter my conviction, he said he would respect my wishes and we should remain friends. I was delighted to shake hands on it. He looked at me for a long time, then asked if he could confide in me, if I would promise to keep his secret. When I assured him that I would, with the assistance of two dictionaries (Russian-English and Russian-German), he told me the following:

His grand- and great-grandparents had been factory owners. When the Bolsheviks came to power, they killed the old generation and took away all the family's wealth. His grandparents had to become assembly workers in their own factory. Because of his capitalist background, his father was not allowed to go to a university. Ivan himself was blackballed also. He said his family had another strike against them. They had been, and still were, devout Catholics. Since people were not allowed to receive religious education, someone had reported his father for having hired an ex-priest to tutor him in Bible studies. For this his dad had served a jail sentence.

When the war broke out, his parents had a serious talk with him. They suggested that before it ended, he should enlist. Then, since emigration from Russia was impossible, as soon as he was on Western soil, he should defect. So, although he was only 15½ years of age, he had managed to be accepted in the army a few months ago. He and several of his buddies planned to learn Hungarian, practice speaking English and German, and as soon as the opportunity arose, defect.

I was filled with conflicting emotions. We Jews, for so many years had been praying for communist liberation. My intelligent sergeant friend Kádár had eulogized it. Even my brilliant father believed that Social Democratism — similar in concept to International Socialism, i.e., Communism — thought it was the most humane and desirable political philosophy; yet Ivan and his friends, who really knew from first-hand experience, were willing to risk their lives in war, at such a tender age, to escape from it!

As evening was approaching, Ivan said he was about to get off duty, and after he checked in with his superiors, he would return to guard us again during the night. In a short while my friends came upstairs, getting ready to sleep. I talked with Rizsa for a while. He claimed he felt much better and was anxious to leave, to try to locate his friends and loved ones. He planned to leave the next day, searching first in the eastern section of the city. Éva wished to remain. She knew her entire immediate family had been eliminated by the Nazis. She planned to stay with the Bolgárs as long as she could. The other three boys were also completely orphaned, and wanted to stay until the war progressed beyond both Pest and Buda.

After dusk Ivan returned. He had received a package from home, with all sorts of smoked meats and mouth-watering home-baked pastries, which he generously shared with all of us. Repeating the previous night's physical arrangements, after consuming the last succulent morsel of our heaven-sent manna, we happily drifted off to sleep.

The next morning, January 16, Ivan arrived with pencil, notebook, and a huge Russian-Hungarian dictionary under his arm. He offered to be a diligent student if I would spend the day teaching him my mother tongue. He also brought along a large variety of foods. We spent the entire day pursuing my favorite activities — eating and tutoring.

After dusk, as usual, Ivan went to check his next day's schedule. Upon returning, his head was hanging and his eyes were wet. He said that during the day the International Ghetto (safe-houses) had been liberated, and that his troop was leaving the next morning, going to the Front, to storm the main ghetto.* He wrote down my prewar address and promised to write, and to contact me if he survived.

Both of us feeling emotional about his news, instead of going to sleep, we talked until sunrise. Ivan asserted that most of the Russian people hated communism, but would not dare speak out against it. Any derogatory remark against the government was punished by a severe jail sentence at best. If small groups of people were discovered and even only suspected of expressing dissatisfaction with government policies or activities, they were picked up and taken away during the night, never to be seen or heard from again. He said they were thought to be taken to labor camps in Siberia, from which no one ever returned.

Ivan claimed to be amazed by the modern facilities Hungarians seemed to possess. He said, contrary to what Russians were taught and told, our farmhouses were elegant and our villagers lived in luxury. Russian farmers lived in shacks, without running water, inside toilettes, or electricity. At home only the Party members could afford the kind of apartments he saw predominant in our cities. He went on and on, concluding with the assertion that to escape from Russia was worth the risk involved in defection. When the sun rose we kissed each other on the cheek as we said good-bye, and then he left. Later I prayed for him often, but I never saw or heard from Ivan again.

I thought again of what Comrade Kádár had said about communism, what my dad believed, and of Ivan's words. The conflict disturbed me greatly. I felt confused and very tense. Although scared, I felt a compulsion to see the outside world, and thus ventured out for a walk. My stomach kept churning as I kept stepping on a dismembered arm, leg, trunk, or skull, hidden from sight by the freshly fallen snow.

---

* Without further Nazi atrocities, the ghetto was freed by the Russians during the night of January 17-18, 1945.

A few blocks west of our house I saw the hammer and sickle flag sticking out of a ground floor window. I entered. The Communist Party house was manned mainly by Russians, having only one interpreter. I asked to see my friend Comrade Kádár. No one there knew where he could be located. Then I asked if they would give food and supplies for the children in the orphanage. The answer was: "Not yet. Except for those children and adults who join the Party, who receive special treatment and various privileges." Having nothing to lose and everything to gain, I filled out an application. I was at once handed a package. It contained some powdered food items, canned stew and hash, sugar, and a pack of vile-smelling cigarettes.

I walked a few more blocks, until I saw some Russian heavy artillery at the end of Andrássy Road. Knowing the layout of the city, I estimated that using side streets I could get to the residence of Mr. Duka, Dad's Christian client and friend, who had hidden many of our valuables. I returned to the orphanage, gave an account of the situation in our vicinity, took a last look at every nook and crevice of the house that had provided me with so many deeply emotional experiences, and then began to say good-bye.

Parting was painful. The Bolgárs, Rizsa, Éva, the three boys, even the little kids had become a part of me, of my very existence. Not only did I realize how much I would miss each of them, but I suddenly had to face my total loneliness. I had been aware for a long time that sooner or later it would have to be faced, but the full impact of it did not occur until that moment. For the first time I began to feel like an orphan.

Mr. and Mrs. Bolgár tried to talk me out of leaving. They reasoned that the Front was too close for safe movement. What if the Dukas had moved? Besides, why the rush? My answer was that I felt a desperate urge to let a friend know that I was still alive, and then as soon as possible to get back to my prewar home, in case my parents or uncle had somehow survived and were looking for me.

Rizsa was also saying good-bye, for he said he felt the same way as I did. The Bolgárs understood. And so, with tears drenching my face, I set out on my ten-mile journey.

CHAPTER 21: JOURNEY INTO HELL

As I walked westward along the deserted Andrássy Road, turning southeast on a side street, I soon spotted the first Russian heavy artillery. From then on my path had to zigzag, to remain behind the Russian front line. Finally I reached the oft-frequented Eastern Train Station. Although I had been hearing the roars of cannon fire, I was not prepared for the frightening scene that faced me as I approached the intersection of the several miles long, arrow-straight Rákoczi Road. I was only a hundred or so yards behind a huge flamethrower, a mechanical dragon that kept spitting fire with thundering roars. Both sides of the road were enveloped in forty-to-fifty-foot-tall devastating flames, as far west as the eyes could see.

Oh, Lord! Those helpless people in the cellars — what a horrible way to die! How benevolent You have been to me!

I covered my eyes and proceeded, zigzagging southward. The streets were still void of all living beings, except for that one cluster of soldiers beside the flame-breathing dragon and myself. The night wind was bone-chilling. The cardboard-stuffed soles of my shoes allowed the icy snow to seep in, causing my frostbitten feet, legs and hands excruciating pain.

My destination was still a few miles away when the darkness of a starless sky fell upon the city. I decided to spend the night in the cellar of a nearby house.

Like a blind man, I felt my way around. I descended the staircase and walked through a long, tunnel-like corridor. Just around the bend I saw the faint flickering light of a candle. It came from a large room-like cavity, without a door. Inside was an old woman, lying on a mattress. She seemed puzzled to see me. I introduced myself and explained the reason for my presence. In response to my questions, the lady said that a day or two before heavy artillery fire had destroyed the major portion of the building, that all the people in the main section of the cellar-shelter were buried alive when the house collapsed, and that she was very badly hurt and could not move. I offered my help, even to stay and take care of her as long as necessary.

Tears filled her eyes as she responded, "My child, my life is like the flickering light of this candle. I have but minutes left on this earth. I am grateful to Jesus who must have guided you here, to warm my dying soul with your kind offer. Take this gold wedding ring as a token of my gratitude. I pray the Lord to keep guiding and protecting you." She handed me the ring, folded her hands in prayer, and closed her eyes. She said and breathed no more.

Only moments passed before the lonely candle also took its last breath. I remained sitting in the dark, on the damp ground, until I dozed off.

Loud footsteps and the familiar reveling of drunken soldiers awakened me. I jumped to my feet and began to run. Not knowing the layout, unable to see in the total darkness, after having bumped into several obstacles, my way was blocked by a large heap. I climbed higher than my height before reaching the top, then lay there motionless. I hardly breathed, due to both fright and the foul odor. The soldiers must have heard the noise I had made, for their footsteps were coming directly toward me. In the light of their lanterns my environment became visible: a heap of rubble, mixed with thousands of nibbling rats and dozens of deteriorating corpses. There lay a girl, covered with bloody dirt, but alive and breathing. I closed my eyes and remained motionless, trying to blend with my surroundings. The piercing beam of light moved, stopping on the face of the girl. She was a child, in her teens.

The soldiers laughed, exchanged comments, then one unbuttoned his clothes and dropped on top of the girl, angling his submachine gun into her ribs. The apeman must have been displeased, for he kept shouting and slapping the girl. He finally spat into her face and yielded her body to the next savage in line. The pattern of the first's behavior was repeated four more times. Then the last beast rose, spat at and kicked the poor child a few times, cussed, emptied his gun around her tender body, and finally staggered away. The combination of what I had experienced and the foul odor must have been too much for me to bear, rendering me unconscious. The protective mechanism of my brain must also have induced temporary amnesia, for the next thing I remember was walking along the desolate Üllői Road.

The sun had risen and the warm rays had begun to melt the snow on the sidewalk. The city was still deserted, though the cannon shots sounded many miles away. I felt numb all over. Although I could not remember what else had happened during the night, or when and how I had gotten out of the cellar, I did recall the evening's incidents vividly. My abdomen hurt severely, and the pain was overcome only by nausea and fear. Only the hope that my parents might be alive and soon returning gave me the impetus to continue to my first destination, to the Dukas on Mester Street.

It was late afternoon when I reached the residence of László Duka. The heavy throbbing of my heart eased up a bit upon observing that his two-story stone building had suffered only minor damage. I still feared not finding him alive or not in that location as I knocked on the door of his apartment. To my great relief, his wife Olga opened the door. I must have been a horrible sight, for she had to look twice before she recognized me. She welcomed me in and introduced me to the other residents.

Olga was about forty-five-years-old, and had known me since I was knee-high. She had been for many years my father's secretary. Only a year or so before the war broke out had she met László, my father's client. Mr. Duka had owned an ink factory. He was in love, and though Olga was Jewish and László a Protestant, in 1943 they got married.

In March of 1944, when the persecution of the Jews began, László hid Olga, her two sisters, brother-in-law, and their seven- and nine-year-old daughters in the cellar of his factory. Only a few days ago, after the Germans had withdrawn to northwest of Mester Street, did the whole family move out of their hiding place and into Mr. Duka's residence. Their home was in between and thus far removed from the downtown business and peripheral industrial section of the city. They had a three-room apartment, quite modern and nicely furnished. Olga's sister and her family, the Bergers, occupied the master bedroom; Mr. and Mrs. Duka, the den; and Olga's sister Magda and I were to share a sofa-bed in the living-dining room.

Although the Bergers showed immediate hostility, Mr. and Mrs. Duka warmly offered to share their home for as long as I wished to remain. Gratefully accepting it, I washed up superficially, ate supper with the family, then sat down with the Dukas for a long talk.

To satisfy their curiosity, I gave them a rough outline

of what had happened to me and my family during the past year. I was anxious to know if they still had my parents' valuables, but since during our long conversation they made no reference to it, I felt it was not the time to ask. It was nearly midnight when Olga handed me one of her pyjamas and suggested that we, too, retire.

I could hardly wait for the moment! Not only the anticipated joy of once again sleeping without my dresses and coat, and on a real mattress, but to be able to soak in a warm bath was to be an exhilarating experience. I fixed the bath and proceeded to scrub myself until raw, wishing to eliminate all the filth on my body and mind.

Shortly after breakfast the next day, the members of my new family, one after the other, began to itch. By late afternoon my bedmate, Magda, politely requested that I step into the bathroom with her, bringing along all my clothes, and then to undress. My face turned red, for I knew she was about to find out a secret I was most anxious to hide.

She looked at once at the seams of my dresses. She turned pale observing the swarming lice. With unwavering determination she asserted that at once all my clothes had to be burned. I would not have minded, except that I had none other to wear. Although I begged her not to tell the others, she said it was too late for that. She promptly gathered the family, announced her finding, and proposed actions she felt the situation called for.

Although Magda and the Dukas seemed somewhat compassionate, the Bergers kept insisting that I was an unwelcome stranger to the family, that I had no right to eat from their meager supply of food, and that I should be thrown out at once. I felt hurt beyond words. Amid flowing tears I kept saying that I was so very sorry, I did not harm them on purpose, that I would do anything to alleviate the situation, etc. While my dresses were put aside to be burned and my underwear was being boiled, even the Berger children kept calling me filthy trash and the like. No one spoke up on my behalf. Finally, in desperation I grabbed and put on my dresses and coat, announced that I was leaving, and, turning to Mr. Duka, demanded that he hand over to me all the valuables my parents had given him to hide. That changed the Bergers' tune! I was no longer poverty-stricken trash, but a lonely, helpless child who could possibly be fleeced from significant wealth! Mr. Duka said he would not hear of my departure, demanded that the Bergers apologize, then took me into his room for a private talk.

He said the jewelry was safe, but he intended to keep both the items and me until my parents' return. I was too deeply hurt to agree to it. I said I had fared all right until then and would continue to manage somehow. He kept reasoning that the area of my old home was still in German hands, that food was not available at any price, that the house we used to live in might already be in ruins, that I was still a child and needed adults to take care of me. But I was too emotional to reason. I felt that the future could hold nothing worse than the past had already dealt out to me.

Seeing that I was determined to leave, Mr. Duka pulled out his ace. From his vault he produced a postcard and handed it to me. It was addressed to him, postmarked in Hegyeshalom on December 23, 1944, and written to pass possible censuring. I could not control the flood of my tears as I read the following: "My dear friends. Some of us reached the plateau (Hegyeshalom means heap of mountains) on foot. We're digging in for the storm. If our return is delayed, take care of Györgyi." The card was not signed, but the handwriting was unmistakably my mother's.* Those words meant more to me than anything anyone had or could have said. Of course I stayed!

While each member of the families sprayed their clothes and hair with a horrible-smelling fumigator, I poured petroleum all over my head, dresses and coat, and said my final "good-bye" to pediculi. Although shivering from the lack of fire in the stoves (the above chemicals being highly combustible) and the bitterly cold air gushing in through the open windows, we all sat down at the round dining table for a peace conference. Mr. Duka laid down the law. Since all of them were Jews, they all owed their lives to him. He was still their sole supporter. I was now a new member of the family, and was to be treated as such. Anyone who acted or spoke cruelly was to be evicted at once. I could see the hatred in the eyes of the Bergers, but the words had been spoken. For the rest of that day, and during the next, we all co-existed without any incident. But only until midnight.

I had been used to sleeping very lightly, being prepared to jump and run at the first sight or sound implying trouble. Thus, I was the first to be awakened by the sound of heavy footsteps coming along the corridor, leading to our apartment. Without a moment's loss I dropped onto the floor and rolled myself into the large Persian rug on the far side of our open sofa bed.

No sooner had I accomplished the feat than I heard boots kicking the outside door, then a few loud remarks,

---

* During the first weeks of December 20,000 able-bodied men and women were taken from safe-houses (in addition to the 40,000 others) and marched on foot to Hegyeshalom, a town near the Austrian border. Those who survived the approximately 110 km. march with at most seven hours' rest, one meal a day and frequent Nazi cruelties, were to dig ditches. Those still alive in March, 1945, ended up in the Mauthausen Concentration Camp.

followed by gunshots fired into the lock. I could not see, so I can recall only the image I had constructed from the auditory inputs. Three Russian soldiers had entered. The first grabbed Magda, the second found Olga, and the last had to be satisfied with dear Mrs. Berger. The ladies of course screamed, and the husbands uttered a few futile protests, but after several shots were fired into the floor and furniture, only the ladies' sobs and the soldiers' grunts and exclamations could be heard. Ten minutes or so must have passed when I heard footsteps again, this time, thank God, fading outward. Partly from fear and partly empathizing with Magda's emotional trauma, I unrolled the rug and remained on the floor for the rest of the night.

The next day no one spoke a word in front of me about the incident, but everyone kept looking at me with much more compassion. These people had lived in isolation; till then they knew little about the horrors many like me had endured.

Although our night visitors had vanished without a trace, they had left souvenirs behind: full-grown and well-fed little representatives of two of the three species of pediculi, crawling happily all over the beds. This time I was in the driver's seat! But not being childish or vindictive, without a comment I went for the fumigator and assisted with the delousing procedures.

The days and weeks that followed were relatively uneventful. The news media were far from functioning, and people were too scared to walk on the streets. We ate only once a day from our rapidly diminishing food supply, and spent most of our time thinking, talking or reading.

I never met any of the neighbors, except the two women living in one of the ground-floor apartments. I went to the cellar once to bring up some coal, just as they were entering the house. They wore heavy makeup and were richly dressed. Curious about the outside world, I introduced myself and asked about the progress of the war. They said that, although there were still scattered combats in the outskirts of Buda, the entire eastern side of the Danube, i.e., Pest, had been "liberated" by the "glorious Red Army".

To my further questions they responded that pedestrian traffic had in a limited way begun, that a few service-type stores had already opened, and that the red-light district of the city was in full swing and spreading. They concluded by saying that if I wished food, money, beautiful clothes, or jewelry, just to drop into their apartment any evening. They would gladly introduce me to Russian officers, who would give me anything I wished. Returning to our apartment, I thought: how long before I, too, would have to sell my flesh to prevent starvation?

Five weeks or so after I had arrived, toward the end of February, 1945, the Dukas ran out of food. After a long powwow it was decided that the family should split up, Magda and the Bergers returning to their respective homes and attempting to re-establish their prewar existence. Since only Mr. Duka kept insisting on my staying, I decided to leave on that same day.

This brought up the problem connected with the jewelry. I wanted to take it all with me, while Olga insisted that they should keep everything until my parents' return. She was clearly stabbing me in the back, for she well knew that only jewelry would buy food on the black market. At first I thought that for some unknown reason she hated me and wished me to perish. Then I realized she was motivated by pure selfishness, hoping that my parents would never return, thus she could keep everything.

Feeling utterly helpless, I proposed a compromise. I said I knew my parents would want them to keep a few of the precious objects to express their appreciation to them for having safeguarded the valuables during those perilous times, plus additional ones, as repayment for feeding and lodging me all these weeks. However, the rest I needed for sheer subsistence.

Mr. Duka might have settled, but Olga was not willing. Having reasoned, cried, and begged to no avail, I asked Mr. Duka to give me at least the bar of soap which contained my tiny baby ring. Not knowing the real contents of the soap, my mother's two-karat diamond ring, neither objected to my receiving it.

Feeling very satisified with the situation's outcome, Olga packed a little suitcase with my second set of underwear, the pyjamas and the old dress they had given me, a couple of days' worth of food, and the soap, which she presented as their farewell gift. Early that afternoon, having politely thanked them for everything, I began the journey to my prewar home.

CHAPTER 23: THIEVES IN THE DAY

It was late February and the streets were no longer covered with snow, nor were they entirely deserted. Streetcars and buses were not yet functioning, nor were the shops along my path open, but a few pedestrians did pass me by. I was deep in thought while walking along Mester Street. — Was my old home still standing? Who lived there now? Would they let me move in? What would I find from our prewar possessions, and in the room we had locked? What will I do? How will I live?

Suddenly my thoughts were interrupted by the screeching of brakes, followed by the click of the cocking of a gun, then the loud command, "Davai!" My heart pounded like a drum as I turned my head and saw beside me a Russian soldier on a bicycle, pointing a submachine gun at my suitcase. Oh, no! Not my entire worldly possessions! I pleaded and begged, in every language I knew, but the beast laughed, grabbed the suitcase out of my clutching hands, and happily cycled away. Not only the few pieces of clothes and the morsels of precious food, but the soap containing my mother's diamond ring was gone forever. I sat on the curb and cried until no tears were left. When the sun began to descend, fearing to be on the streets in the dark, I started to run toward my destination.

It was dusk when I reached 31 Ráday Street. To my pleasant surprise, except for missing windowpanes and cosmetic damage, the building stood intact. I walked up a flight, down the corridor, and with my heart in my throat I knocked on the door of our old apartment. A robust, middle-aged woman opened it and asked what I wanted. Introducing myself, I told her that I was the prewar occupant of the flat and wished to reclaim my family's possessions.

She looked a bit suspicious and disturbed, but invited me in. The few remaining tears began to trickle down my cheeks as I sighted our old furniture where and as we had left it. The woman's expression mellowed as she led me into the kitchen and scrutinized me in the light of a powerful oil lamp. Her husband and thirty-year-old son were sitting beside the table. I introduced myself again, gave a brief summary of the events having affected me and my family during the past year, and told them of my intention to move back.

Mr. Keresztesi listened carefully, then leaned back in his chair, puffed on his awful-smelling pipe, and said unemotionally, "Young lady — the war has hurt everybody. Some of *our* loved ones have also been killed. Our house was demolished by a bomb. We, too, have nothing and have nowhere to go. Since the apartment and furniture have been assigned to us legally, we shall not turn them over to you. However, we would not object to your moving into one of the rooms."

Before agreeing, I asked to see the entire flat. Everything was intact. The bedroom on the far left, furnished as we had left it, plus some old beds; next to it the dining room, with a big empty space from where we had taken the buffet to the star-house; on its right the living room, where the piano and even the contents of the vitrin (china cabinet) were untouched. The waiting room was also as it always had been. Even the lock on my father's office had not been tampered with. I said I wanted to move into the bedroom. However, due to the layout, it was most inconvenient to relocate the furniture, and as I expected, Mr. Keresztesi objected. Then I proposed a compromise: until my parents' return, why couldn't we live like one family? I would move into my father's office, a room they never used anyway, leave everything else as it was convenient for them, and in return they would provide me with one meal a day, sharing whatever they had. Mrs. Keresztesi jumped eagerly at my proposal, offering to share more than just the food, wishing to treat me as a relative. The men, seeing her and my enthusiasm, sealed the deal by shaking hands and hugging me. After Mr. Keresztesi sawed the lock off the door, I collapsed on the leather couch, with shoes and coat on, being totally exhausted from the events of the day, and at once fell asleep.

It was noonish when I awakened the next day. I looked around. The room contained my father's enormous, glass-doored bookcase; the matching, hand-carved ebony desk and chair; the couch and two leather barrel chairs; and the five-foot-tall, empty safe. In one of the corners I found a potato sack, containing a down-filled comforter, two pillows, and one of mother's hostess gowns. In the desk drawers I found paper, writing instruments, old letters, some of my schoolwork and textbooks, my briefcase, and, to my greatest joy, my "emlék könyv" (autograph book and memoire) and a few old photographs.

My first three objectives were to clean the place, board up the window, and make the built-in stove functional. The first I accomplished without difficulty. The second had to wait for Mr. Keresztesi's return. He and his son János had begun working in a mill. The processed grain was confiscated by the Russians, but the workers were paid with (and stole) wheat and corn; non-purchasable, yet greatly needed commodities. So, after we all ate our supper of corn soup and bread with vegetable oil, the two men managed to find some boards and fixed my window. Building a fire in the stove, however, was out of the question. Coal was not readily available; besides, chimneys had not been cleaned during the war and were completely blocked by soot and debris. Even without heat the night was tolerable, though, since spring was approaching, the window was sealed, and I had a comforter.

The next day I began looking for loved ones and clothes. Since the Front by now was far west of Budapest, except for pillaging soldiers, it was safe to walk on the streets. First I journeyed to the ghetto area. I was happy to see that it had not been demolished, nor had the people been annihilated. Much of the rubble had been cleaned away, and residents no longer dwelled in cellars. The house I had resided in near Wesselényi Street was in ruins, and so was Blau Grandmother's home. But Blum Grandmama's wartime residence still stood erect.

Tearfully I walked inside, up the flight of stairs, and into the unlocked apartment. It was empty. All the furniture was gone. In Grandmother's room stood only a large box. In it was a dress and a coat of hers, old papers and letters, and some badly-worn bed linen. I grabbed the box and began to walk toward the staircase. A neighbor spotted me, ran out and hugged me, then insisted that I come in for a chat. Over a cup of ersatz coffee we reminisced about old times. When she heard about my fate and noticed Grandmother's clothes in the box, she insisted that I let her alter them for me. I gratefully agreed and promised to return soon.

On my way home I stopped at the Dohány Temple. The altar had been robbed and the whole place was desolate. With heavy heart, I returned to my apartment.

The following day I continued my search. Hoping to find friends, I went to my old house on Andrássy Road, but to my dismay the building was deserted. On my way home I passed my third cousin's cleaning store. It was in partial ruins, but I saw a faint light far in the rear. I stepped over the rubble and walked toward the storage room. Sure enough, Lili was lying on a cot, with her mother, Aunt Etta, sitting beside her. Seeing me made both of them very happy. After I gave them an account of the events during the past year, Aunt Etta summarized their story. She (over seventy) had lived since the star-house era with Lili (an old maid, in her late forties) on Dob Street, later part of the ghetto. After "liberation" they found only the ruins of their prewar house. Since the Dob Street apartment was also demolished, they had moved into their store. But the facilities there were intolerable. The front of the store was too big to board in, and the storage room was extremely small. Besides, it had no window for ventilation, nor door for privacy.

Etta went on to say that Lili was very sick, bedridden with cancer of the lungs. She begged me to let them move into my apartment, in exchange for a potbelly stove, heating material, and a meal per day for me. I was not too enthusiastic to share my only room with an old and a sick woman, but I felt sorry for them, and the meal-a-day sounded good. So, I stayed with Lili while Aunt Etta managed to round up a wheel-cart, upon which we put the stove, the two cots and Lili, together with their meager belongings. So did I come home with my new family.

The Keresztesis were quite upset about my new arrangement, showing their displeasure by reducing the variety and quantity of my meals. Aunt Etta spent the daylight hours scavenging, digging under rubble for things she could trade. She exchanged the acquired costume jewelry and shiny bric-a-brac with Russian soldiers for canned goods, margarine, black bread or lard, while usable housewares and clothing she traded with other scavengers for dried peas or lentils, rice, tea, candles and soap. Each day the poor soul returned with some edibles, and as much coal and wood as she could carry.

I used to go out daily also, attempting to locate friends and checking the list posted at the entrance of the Dohány Temple, signed by Jews personally, listing those reported to be alive or confirmed to be dead. At home I frequently had long talks with and attended to Lili, who was constantly in great pain, by then too sick even to read or go to the toilette.

Days passed by uneventfully, until one afternoon when three Russian soldiers banged on the door of our apartment and announced that they wanted sleeping quarters for a day or two. Mrs. Keresztesi negotiated with them in broken Russian. After they departed, she informed me that the soldiers would return later and occupy the living room and bedroom. She, her husband, and son planned to sleep in our big dining room, on the floor on mattresses, so that I and mine would not be affected. I expressed my gratitude for her consideration and returned to Lili.

At dusk our house guests arrived. No sooner did they reach the inner rooms than I heard several rounds of gunshots, followed by loud cursings. We were petrified. Aunt

Etta locked our door, blew out the candle and lay down beside Lili, while I stretched out fully dressed on the floor behind my sofa. I must have dozed off, for the next thing I recall was the commotion and someone downstairs yelling "Fire! Fire!" Aunt Etta went out, but returned shortly, saying it was nothing serious and everything was under control. We could all go back to sleep.

First thing next morning, as usual, I went to the bathroom to wash. My face turned red as I opened the door, seeing one of the soldiers urinating into our elegant sink. I ran back to my room and did not venture out until afternoon, when I heard the soldiers leaving. Amidst tears, Mrs. Keresztesi showed me the damage and gave me an account of the events.

One of the Russians, with a curious look on his face, turned the knob on a radio her husband was fixing to operate with an old truck battery. Since broadcasting in Budapest had not yet been re-established, the radio projected some weird noises. That scared the soldier so that he promptly "killed" the roaring monster with a bullet. Next, the Russians tried to open the wardrobe. Since it was locked, the logical choice was to shoot it open. Lastly, the image the third soldier saw in the mirror must have displeased him, for the fate of the looking glass was the same as that of the radio.

Mrs. Keresztesi continued by saying that she awakened during the night feeling warm and smelling something burning. When the Russians ran out of the bedroom half-dressed, she dashed in to see. Right near the entrance she noticed a washbowl full of feces. These soldiers, not ever having been in a city apartment with West European (to them ultramodern) facilities, took two huge metal bowls from the kitchen and, instead of searching for the toilette, a separate room opening from the dark and cold hallway, they excreted into one. The other steel container, since the tile stove spit

168

out smoke and ashes, had to suffice to provide heat. Thus, they started a fire in the bowl. Of course the hot coal eventually melted the metal, and burned a hole in the floor and through the ceiling of the ground floor apartment below. Fortunately, the fire was noticed at once and was controlled without anyone being injured.

While the tenants were busily attending to the fire, the drunken soldiers kept demanding vodka. As no one could produce any, they began searching in drawers and cabinets. Their scavenging stopped at the medicine cabinet, where one discovered a bottle of alcohol, which they greedily consumed to the last delicious drop, as they did with Mrs. Keresztesi's precious cologne. Before leaving in the afternoon, they registered their dissatisfaction and asserted that they would not return. — "Amen," said Mrs. K. and I.

Many days passed without incident, until finally Aunt Etta failed to find sufficient commodities to trade for edibles and for medicine for Lili. I let them stay, but could not provide the necessities. Aunt Etta's last big business deal was the acquisition of half a loaf of bread in exchange for the gold wedding band the dying lady had given me in the cellar.

I did not eat from the bread, and I even shared my bowl of corn soup, but it was not enough to prevent Lili from turning into a living corpse. Finally, upon awakening one morning, we found that she was not breathing. Neither of us cried — we thanked the Lord for having relieved her from further hopeless suffering. Only after Etta found someone to remove the body, did she admit that Lili had tuberculosis besides incurable lung cancer.

The next day Aunt Etta told me she was leaving. She said she had found someone who needed to be cared for in exchange for food. But she would not tell me the name or address. I think she went to wherever Lili was taken, to lie down and to die. She had no one and nothing to live for.

I never heard from or saw her again.

I felt sad losing them both — they were good, compass-ionate people, and besides, my only so-far-found relatives — but unselfishly I had to admit that both were better off going to their repose. From a materialistic point of view, their departure was greatly advantageous to me. I could air and clean the room I no longer had to share, and since the Keresztesis were pleased to have them gone, they fed me better than poor Aunt Etta did.

CHAPTER 24: SIX WRISTWATCHES FROM A GRANDFATHER CLOCK

Time crept along without change or significant incident. By April the war was nearing its end. With the Front now on German soil, the people of Budapest slowly began to live again. The Russians reopened factories, converting them to the manufacture of war supplies and necessities for their own use. Small service-type shops began to open, the owners bartering for skilled labor.

One morning an old lady knocked on our door, wanting to see my father. I told her what had happened to him, that he might never return. She then said she was in trouble, and she needed someone to defend her. If my father, who had been her attorney for twenty years, could not do it, she would settle for the next best thing — his child, me! She was very old (in her eighties) and seemed desperate, so I listened to her story.

"I have an old, run-down apartment house, with many very poor tenants," she said. "I mind my own business and know very little about most. Two of the women sharing a one-room flat have recently been arrested and charged with having had leading positions in the Nazi Party," she continued. "A man just brought me this summons, to appear in the police station tomorrow, to defend myself against an accusation of harboring and aiding war criminals. Now, what shall I do?"

When I said I couldn't help her, that I was a child and she needed a lawyer, she began to cry. She said she had nobody to turn to, and begged me to go to court with her. She insisted that I could at least testify that she did not sympathize with the Nazis, proven by the fact that she had for many years a Jewish lawyer. I felt sorry for the poor soul and promised to do as she asked.

The following day I went to her house. It was a dilapidated shack, where no Nazi big shot would even have thought of residing. Next I went to the local police station, to check the arrested women's files. The records showed that they had both been employed by the Nazis, but only as cleaning women. Armed with the information, next day I took my old lady to the improvised local "people's court". Communist Party members were officiating. I presented myself as a key witness and spokesman for an unjustly accused civilian. The accusers were not present, so after hearing my short defense speech and seeing the women's work record and the pathetic-looking old lady, the comrade in charge dismissed the case. The next day the old lady appeared at our door, dragging an enormous bundle containing flour, sugar, rice, tea, lard, jam, salami, and other delicacies, "a token," in her words, "to express my gratitude for your brilliant performance." I cried from happiness. Manna from heaven!

The day after I consumed the last delectable morsel (I could no longer even look at another bowl of corn soup!), on my way to the Dohány Temple I bumped into an old acquaintance who knew the address of the Szilárds. I promptly turned around and went to visit the elderly couple. They were overjoyed to see me and asked me to join them for dinner. Since they had been in the grocery business all their lives, they had the connections to acquire all the foods imaginable. During the conversation I asked about the valuables my parents had given them to hide. They claimed two suitcases had been destroyed by a bomb, and the third had been taken by a Russian soldier who robbed them. True or false, I acted as if I believed it. They appreciated my attitude, enjoyed my company, and invited me to visit again.

During the weeks that followed I visited the Szilárds two or three times a week, about dinner or suppertime, and filled my tummy like a camel, to prevent hunger pains during the in-between days. I also watched diligently the rapidly-growing temple list, but my loved ones' names did not appear.

One sunny afternoon I noticed a young man running along the street, wearing only his underpants. It seemed strange, but I paid little attention. The next day I observed a similar event. During the following weeks I saw several more men, and two women, in similar lack of attire. Finally, when I perceived the third lady running along a deserted side street wearing only a slip and crying, I could not resist stopping her to inquire. While weeping and cursing, she asserted: "A Russian female soldier stopped me with a pointed submachine gun, and in very broken Hungarian ordered me to relinquish all my clothes!"

I loaned her my coat and walked her home while she kept reiterating that such activity had become a common practice of the many defecting Russian soldiers. She claimed that lately several females had applied for jobs in her laundry shop — women who did not speak or understand Hungarian or German, and had no identification. Even in her building, two robust young men had moved into the old shelter area in the cellar. They scavenged and held up local residents to acquire whatever they wished, communicating via a few Hungarian words with a heavy Russian accent.

Suddenly I remembered Ivan and wondered what proportion of our "liberators" had similar intentions. I hated the Russians for their crudeness and brutality, yet I could not stop feeling sorry for them. How much these defecting soldiers were willing to risk in order to avoid returning to their homeland, the "communist paradise"!

On one of my excursions to locate acquaintances, I passed our old jeweler's store and noticed that the door was open. I entered. To my pleasant surprise, the old man's crippled son, Izidor, was sitting in his wheelchair behind the counter. He said his family had been killed, but Christian friends had hidden and taken care of him during the war, and now he planned to earn a living repairing jewelry. We exchanged addresses and promised to keep in touch.

Two days later, on my way to the temple, I saw Izi wheeling his chair down Ráday Street, coming toward my house. I ran to him and saw his eyes all red and full of tears. He blurted out with a stutter that two soldiers had come to his store, carrying a huge grandfather's clock. They handed it to him and, in broken Hungarian, commanded him to make six wristwatches out of it, claiming it was surely big enough for six small chronometers. Izi was terrified. He knew the soldiers would return and shoot him if he could not produce the items. I tried to console him, advising him to wait in his store for someone to bring such a timepiece to be repaired. Upon my visit the next day, I found the store ransacked, the furnishings smashed, and behind the counter poor Izi's dead body stretched out on the floor. – Oh, Lord! How much more can we take from our "liberators"? Haven't we suffered enough yet?

173

Soon after the above incident, a neighbor mentioned the rumor that educational institutions were soon to resume functioning. I ran all the way to Práter Street, to my old school. The main building of Zrinyi Ilona Leány Gymnázium stood erect, having suffered only cosmetic damages. Nothing was posted on the entrance, and the school grounds were desolate. I walked around the yard and began to reminisce. As I was about to leave the school site, a voice from behind called out my name. Turning around, I had to look twice to recognize my old schoolmate.

Jutka had been a beautiful girl, with long, golden hair and azure blue eyes, tall and well proportioned, graceful and vibrant. Now she was skin and bones, hunchbacked, with mousy eyes deep in their sockets above protruding cheekbones. Her hair was short and gray, in spite of her tender age of sixteen. I was embarrassed to shower her with questions, so I asked if she would come to my home for a visit. She seemed pleased to accept my invitation, because, as she explained on the way, she had recently returned from the Ravensbrück Concentration Camp, had as yet found none of her relatives, and since her prewar home was in ruins, she was temporarily staying with an old neighbor. After eating some food Mrs. Keresztesi had graciously provided, we curled up on my couch and Jutka began to talk.

JUTKA'S STORY

"Since I didn't look Jewish, a few times I dared to go out without the star. Well, in May of 1944 I got caught. It was near the railroad station, where 100 or so others had already been rounded up. We were squeezed into a cattle car, with only one bucket of water and another to eliminate in. The train moved, on and off, for nearly three days. Each time we stopped some started to shout to let us out, to give us food, to get a doctor — of course, to no avail. Upon arrival, about a third of us were dead.

After all the living Jews poured out of the several

Elévülhet?

CONCENTRATION CAMPS IN GERMANY AND POLAND.

SS-EUROPA

TREBLINKA

MAJDANEK

OŚWIĘCIM (AUSCHWITZ)

ROGOŹNICA GROSS-ROSEN

OBRZYCE (OBRAWALDE)

RAVENSBRÜCK

SACHSENHAUSEN

TEREZIN (THERESIENSTADT)

SONNENSTEIN

MAUTHAUSEN

HARTHEIM

BERGEN-BELSEN

DORA-NORDHAUSEN

BUCHENWALD

FLOSSENBURG

DACHAU

ONE OF THE MANY CREMATORIUMS.

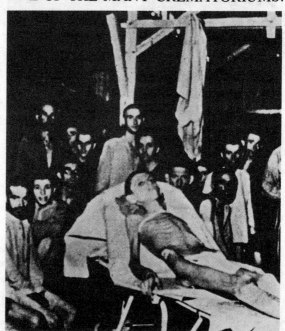

VICTIMS OF NAZI EXPERIMENTS
IN THE INFIRMARY IN BUCHENWALD.

Gas, instead of water, came out of the shower-heads.
Having been gassed — many still alive — the bodies
were thrown into the burning ovens.
(Pictures from an SS guard's photo album.)

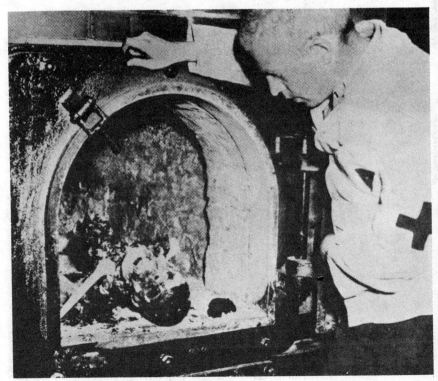

"MUSULMÁNOK" — THE SKIN-AND-BONE LIVING DEAD SLAVE-WORKERS AT VARIOUS CONCENTRATION CAMPS.

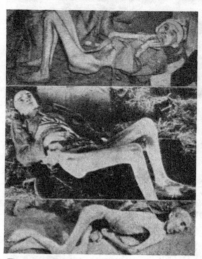

Bergen-Belsen
Ravensbrück
Nordhausen

Mauthausen

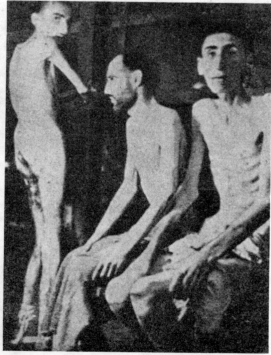

Birkenau

Dachau

wagons behind ours, we were separated from the men and the SS herded us away. Inside the camp we were ordered to strip, then to line up for inspection. As the SS men looked us over, an officer pulled me and another girl out of the line, saying to his partner, 'Send them to Dr. Rascher, for the animal-warmth experiment!' We were given some clothes, put into a sealed truck and driven away.

The next thing I recall was a big room, where Edit, a gorgeous girl of 21, and I were lying on a sort of wide operating table, with a man wedged between us, all of us without clothes. Men in white jackets attached electrodes to each of our organs, heart and brain. They introduced a shock wave, which made us wiggle our arms and body, while they recorded all our reactions. They kept replacing the warm-blooded man between us, again and again, until they brought one whose body was ice-cold. Soon two SS entered. The one addressed as Reichsführer (Himmler) pointed his Luger while the doctor ordered us to do all sorts of unspeakable things, to bring the man back to life. We failed.

Next I recall being given some rags and thrown into a sealed wagon. There were other girls like us there already. One said she had been in the cursed Hartheim Castle, where the guinea pig deportees had been subjected to some abominable experiments. She spoke of the male cell, whose prisoners had been injected with malaria, typhoid, pus, various poisons, etc., which produced extreme fever, blindness, imbecility, sterility, ulcerations, or gangrene. Those who survived the initial attack of the induced disease were then treated with experimental drugs, until they wasted away. The girl also said that the hermetically sealed hearse-truck we were riding in was equipped to gas its passengers, and was used regularly to eliminate invalids.

All still alive upon arrival in the dead of night, we were dumped and herded into an isolated barrack in the notorious women's camp in Birkenau. Our daily nourishment consisted of ersatz coffee, turnip soup, and a piece of bread. Our food was brought in, and the buckets to eliminate in were taken and emptied once a day. Our barrack's door was kept locked. Except for killing huge armies of fleas and lice, we had nothing to do.

One day male nurses came and took some of us to the 'cement block' (the surgical barrack). I was put on a gynecological table. My hands and ankles strapped, my head was forced down firmly while Dr. Clauberg stabbed my insides with an oversized syringe filled with something that smelled like lye. I remember screaming while my belly seemed to burst into flame, just before I passed out from the pain. I came to when already back in our barrack, throwing up and in agony. For weeks, those of us thus sterilized lay writhing in excruciating pain.

The male nurses came again, this time for Edit and those who had been left behind. The end result was the same but the method this time was X-ray. Their suffering was even more unendurable, for they developed extensive cancerous radiation burns, which kept filling up with pus. The SS must have softened, 'cause they finally allowed a Czechoslovakian deportee nurse to come in daily to change their paper bandages.

It was she who told us one day that there was another barrack like ours, occupied by boys, having been castrated also by 10 to 30 minutes of radiation. Some were immediately taken back to the Auschwitz men's camp to resume work, some had part of their burnt organ removed, or an arm or leg unsanitarily amputated, while the rest were taken for lab tests daily, until the rapidly spreading malignant ulcerations consumed their withered bodies.

She also told us that, according to rumor, my group would have to return for two more monthly injections, after which, to test the effectiveness of the drug, Clauberg planned to artifically inseminate us. Before our next shot Providence intervened, because due to the rapid advance of the Russians, we were evacuated and transferred by train to Ravensbrück.

In our huge barrack there were now women of all nationalities. Some had been there since 1942, some came later, and some, like us, were transferees from other camps. Most were mental and physical wrecks, starved, diseased, many the remnants of various abominable experiments. A few of the oldest residents had huge sores and enormous infected scars, where they had been injected with gangrene pus, then treated with experimental chemicals and/or operated on several times without anesthetics and under unsterile conditions by student trainees. There were also two cripples, each of whom had had a knee cap and a shoulder blade removed for transplant.

Although women from other barracks were taken to work in factories from morning till night, we only stood at

Concentration camps had a single purpose: to facilitate mass murder. They were staffed with *S.S.* sadists, who used a variety of means to accomplish their ends: machine guns, gas chambers, starvation, poison, brutality, disease, overwork.

Nazi regime profited even from murder. While the aged, the very young, and the infirm were killed on arrival, the strong were usually hired out as laborers in mines or factories, until they, too, became useless from hunger, neglect, and overwork. At Auschwitz, the most horrible of all the camps, where an estimated 3,000,000 perished, the great I.G. Farben chemical trust built a plant to take advantage of the cheap slave labor. With Germanic efficiency, the Nazis worked out the average profit to be expected from a slave laborer.

Nothing was wasted. Americans found all neatly sorted in Buchenwald warehouses: bales of women's hair, spectacles, dentures, clothing. A sight that especially infuriated them was a bin with thousands of pairs of babies' shoes.

Table of profits (or yield) per prisoner in concentration camps (established by SS)

Rental accounting

Average income from rental of prisoner, per day   RM (Reichsmark) 6.00

Deducation for nourishment, per day   RM 0.60

Average life expectancy: 9 months: 270 (days) by RM 5.30 = RM 1431.00

Minus amortization on clothing   RM 0.10

Profits from rational utilization of corpse:

1. Gold teeth	3. Articles of value
2. Clothing	4. Money

Minus costs of cremation   RM 2.00

Average net profit   RM 200.00

Total profit after 9 months   RM 1631.00

This estimate does not include profits from sale of bones and ashes.

THE "MORGUE" IN AUSCHWITZ.

attention, often in below-zero temperatures, for the many-hours-long daily inspection. Otherwise we were left to lick our wounds and vegetate. Each day dozens with diphtheria or typhus stumbled to the infirmary, never to be seen again. Others expired quietly. The stiff bodies were dumped near the latrines, and carried away eventually by the 'death crew'.

Five Poles had puffed-up bellies, looking like pregnant women ready to deliver. To my query one of them said they had come from Auschwitz, where they had been fed soup containing an antiovulation drug. She also admitted the reason why they looked well fed. Their barrack was not far from the 'morgue', where they could sneak nightly and feed on . . . "

My friend could not continue; neither did I wish to hear any more.

Jutka asked me if I would go with her the next day to a doctor, who, she had heard, had begun practicing. I gladly said "yes," and off we went. His waiting room was full of patients, so we simply sat in line. A short while later the doctor came out to call the next person in, and as he looked around, his eyes fell upon me. He hesitated for a moment, then called me by name. When I responded he came over and hugged me tightly, asked about my parents, then asserted proudly that he was the doctor who had delivered me. As he led Jutka into his office, he looked back and asked me to return later and have supper with him.

Once outside, my girlfriend seemed much relieved. The doctor had told her that by some miracle the damage to her uterus was not extremely severe, that she even had a chance of someday bearing children. I walked home with Jutka, chatted for a while, then returned to Dr. G.'s office.

After supper with him and his wife, the doctor and I sat down to reminisce. He told me that he was a schoolmate of my father, had attended my parents' wedding, and was later my mother's obstetrician and my pediatrician until 1932, when he moved to a distant suburb.

I was happy beyond words to have found him. I was so very lonesome and so very much in need of a wise, adult friend, who knew my background and my family, someone I could turn to for advice and help if needed.

Although not expressing but obviously thinking that I might never see my parents again, and judging me to be sufficiently mature, he answered in depth many of my questions about my parents' background, youth, health, and physical and emotional relationship. Most significant for me to learn was the fact that after three years of marriage, two years before my birth, my mother was pregnant. The baby, a boy, was stillborn. His name would have been György. Both my parents wanted another child, a boy, to replace him. That is why my name became Györgyi. There had been no chance for another child, for my father had meanwhile become impotent. It was such an emotional shock to him — a handsome man in his early forties — that he could not bear facing the facts, nor for anyone to know. To camouflage it he turned to playing cards nightly. My mother — a beautiful woman in her early thirties and a devoted wife — could not understand my father's changed behavior, and so my parents began to quarrel frequently. This drove my father further away from the house and into his shell, until by the time I was five years old, he had become an addicted card-gambler. My mother reconciled her marital emptiness by focusing all her love, and dedicating her entire existence, to me.

I went home but couldn't sleep that night. I felt so guilty for not having shown more overt love to my Dad, for being bratty at times, for not having sensed all this and tried to bring the two closer together. I thought of so many past incidents when, had I known these facts, I could have been instrumental in making them happier. — Of course my thoughts were illogical, but under those circumstances emotions dominated the rational. I begged the Lord to bring my parents back to me and pledged that I would "mother" them, as it seemed I had done to all my acquaintances during the past year.

CHAPTER 25: THE PETALS TORN OFF

During the next few weeks I continued to walk the streets, still searching for loved ones. As time went on the city became less deserted, shops began to open, and even a very limited variety of edibles gradually became available. Thus, slowly the need for money became evident.

I walked into dozens of stores asking for a job, but I was too young and had no special skills. Besides, there were hundreds of qualified adults seeking each available opportunity. So, I continued to eat the corn soup at home, drop in on the Szilárds and Dr. G. occasionally at mealtime, and stuff the hole in my shoes with fresh cardboard daily.

One day I noticed that my father's old barber shop had reopened. I went in and asked to be hired as an apprentice. The owner was happy to see me alive, but said he needed no helper. When I literally begged him to let me earn some money, he reached in his pocket and gave me some, to be repaid when my parents returned. I was grateful for the money, but even more welcome was a name he mentioned during our conversation, someone who supposedly was in the same labor camp as my father.

Overwhelmed with emotion, I ran to the cafe where he said the man used to hang out. With heart pounding, I entered, took a seat, and ordered a soda. Moments later two men came in and sat down in the booth behind me. While sipping my drink I overhead one say, "Isn't that Dr. Balla's daughter?" The other replied that he did not think so. Hoping to hear the truth, I deemed it wiser just to listen, without identifying myself.

The first continued, "What a pity! He was such a good man! He once defended me in court when I was broke, and he accepted no fee for his services. Even in the camp, he carried every sick man's load. . . . He was thrown overboard, you know."

The second man replied, "No, I didn't! What did he contract?"

"Cholera, of course! I had a touch of it too, but didn't report to the infirmary. I knew that those who got it were put aboard the ship, and when they got too weak to take care of themselves, they were thrown overboard. None swam out of the Danube, ever. At least not to my knowledge."

"And Balla was one of those?"

"Yeh, he got it sometime in December. He had no resistance; skin and bones by then. The river was icy . . . he didn't have a chance!"

Without a word I got up and left. I could not bear to hear any more. Once home and alone, I kept seeing the image of my father, feeling the pain of the disease, even the terror of gasping for air as he was drowning under the ice. I did not pray this time – I felt angry at my God.

It was days before I went outside again. The motivating force was the news brought home by Mr. Keresztesi, that schools were soon to be reopened. I pressed the black suit made from my grandmother's old clothes and went to Práter Street. The news was posted on the gate: "School will resume functioning on May 1, 1945." I went inside. The completely new administrative staff informed me that, according to the new policy, Jewish children would be admitted to their appropriate grades, but were expected to study simultaneously on their own the material covered by the gentiles during the beginning of the school year. If they could pass the year's comprehensive final examination, they would be promoted as the others. This suited me fine. I promptly enrolled. While descending the staircase I began to think: Where would I get the money for books and supplies? And for candles, to study at night?

The Lord must still have been watching over me, for as I exited the building, I bumped into Marika Goldgruber, my old classmate. She insisted that I come to her house, say "hello" to her mother, have something to eat, and chat about old times. I gladly went. Although we had not been very close before, I was now desperately in need of friends. We exchanged stories about the way we had fared during the war, our concerns about the current situation, and expectations for the future. Then Marika abruptly changed the topic and said she really worried about passing the comprehensive test without having been taught. This was a great opportunity for me to help and be helped! I promptly suggested that I would gladly come over daily to study with her, if she would allow me to use her books. She was pleased about the deal and, relieved of our anxieties, we parted until the opening day.

Once in school I had little time to visit or look for survivors, nor even to ponder much about my loneliness. During the six-day school week I studied with Marika each day until it got dark. Then I went home, ate, got up at sunrise, and went over to Marika's house to do my current homework while she got dressed. After breakfast with her family, Marika and I then went to school together. Only on Sundays did I have the chance to trace down leads about the whereabouts of relatives and old friends, and to check the list at the Dohány Temple.

Finally, one day in May I read the name of Uncle Lacó among those liberated from Austro-German labor and concentration camps. I flew to Grandmother's prewar apartment, but those living there had heard nothing from or about him as yet. Feeling overwhelmed by anxiety and restlessness, I decided I deserved the luxury of stopping in a nearby coffee shop for a cold drink. My eyes filled this time with joyous tears, when the lady who served me was none other than Mrs. Viltschek!

Dropping the tray, she flew into my arms. She said she had escaped while marching cross-country to a labor camp, and had been in hiding until the Front had moved beyond Budapest. Also, that Erika was well and still at the farm, but she knew nothing yet about her husband or Bandi. With hope in our hearts, we parted temporarily.

That week I went to the temple on Friday. Services had recently been resumed, and members of the Hungarian Zionist Federation* had managed to secure and serve refreshments. It felt good to pray again in the house of the Lord, and to meet a great many young girls and boys orphaned like myself. I felt understood and wanted among them, and promised to return to the lecture on Sunday.

The speaker was a young man named Tomi, who talked about life in Palestine. He and his family had moved there in 1938, when he was seventeen. His father was a teacher and they lived in a kibbutz. He had gone to a university, majoring in political science, and belonged to the Hanoar Hazioni (Youth of Zion). He returned to Hungary to organize plu-

---

* The Zionists were the only organized group in Budapest who actively helped the Jews during the war. They smuggled some out and into Palestine; they forged foreign safe-papers; they secured money from the American Joint Distribution Committee (A.J.D.C.) with which they literally bought back important individuals and entire transports from the Germans; they even physically rescued Jewish hostages.

gas (groups) and aliyot (immigrations).

He emphasized the need for a Jewish homeland, a country that could, and would in the future, prevent the slaughter of our people. He said that especially *we,* who had lost everything and almost everyone, must work for and fight if necessary to establish Israel. He concluded by suggesting that we form a congenial group, with his help requisition a house and some land where we would live, study and work collectively, and prepare for our eventual emigration to Palestine. It all sounded good, really good, to all of us. Waves of warmth, compassion and hope radiated from and to each of us. Right then and there we pledged allegiance to each other and to our common goal of building Israel.

During the coming weeks I kept hoping and watching the Red Cross lists, but no news came about Mother, Father, relatives, or Bandi. I studied hard and got good grades in school, but they meant little to me. By June everybody had found all or at least some of their loved ones; even the Zionist Youth's membership began to dwindle as soon as World War II was over in Europe and people began returning from concentration and labor camps. I still had no income, no job outlook, no means to support myself in a society that slowly began to normalize itself. I was forced to plan my future, alone.

One Sunday I managed to locate Uncle Jenő Halász. I had no love for him, for he deserved none. I recalled that my aunt had committed suicide, via a gas pipe, when Jenő got into legal trouble for having forged someone's signature. He had often been unfaithful to her and untrustworthy to his associates and friends. After her death in 1933 he had continued to forsake his responsibilities, even that of a father. My cousin Pista, who was barely eleven at that time, had to go to different relatives each day after school and for supper. Pista was bordering on genius, but without the proper upbringing, he grew up to be very conceited and ill-mannered. He maintained straight A's scholastically with no more than twenty minutes of daily study, but his arrogance used to get him into trouble constantly. And it was always *my* father who had to bail him out. My parents wanted to adopt and rear him, but Jenő's ego would not permit it. In spite of these memories I still wanted to see him, hoping that the horrors of the war had changed him, wishing that he would treat me like my parents had treated his son.

Upon my knock he opened the door and welcomed me in. Having introduced a middle-aged lady as his wife Helen, we all sat down to talk. The apartment was very nicely furnished, decorated with lace curtains, paintings, crystal and objects of fine porcelain — nicer than any Jewish home I had seen since the war. They listened to my status report intently, but at the end, instead of offering help, Jenő attempted to convince me how helpless and poverty-stricken they were.

Not wishing to hear his phoney excuses, I rose to leave. But he detained me, having noticed an opportunity not to be missed. Jenő asserted that I should reclaim all the jewelry from the Dukas, the apartment with all its contents from the Keresztesis, and the rightful ownership of the apartment house my mother had in Újpest. He said my mother would be grateful, not having to be concerned with such unpleasant chores upon her return.

I was momentarily stunned. I had not thought along those lines before. I just then realized that I had been living in a sort of limbo, hoping that in time everything would return to normal, as it was before the war. Although I knew it in my mind, in my heart I had not yet accepted the fact that my father would never return; perhaps not even my mother, nor Uncle Lacó. I was not ready to take my place as an adult in that hard and cruel world. I wanted desperately to remain a child; to be loved, wanted and cared for. Let the Dukas, Szilárds, Keresztesis, the tenants, and all the others keep what they wanted; just let them like me! I had had enough of hatred and fighting! No, no more! Not even for what rightfully belonged to me.

Jenő saw through me and instantly read my thoughts. He promptly offered to be my legal guardian — of course, only until my parents' return — and to take care of all those unpleasant matters. He said he owed that much to my family. Striking while the iron was hot, he sent Helen for one of their friends, conveniently an attorney, who soon appeared with the appropriate authorization papers for me to sign.

I returned home in a daze. Did I do the right thing? What would Jenő do? How would the people involved react? What was I going to eat? The Szilárds and Keresztesis would surely stop feeding me! And if I would sell everything, how long would it sustain me? And when Mother returned, what would both of us live on? She was such a meek and helpless person, I would have to take care of her. But how? — I had to stop thinking; my anguish was unbearable. It was not a difficult feat by then, for I had become a highly experienced expert in suppressing mental and physical pain, coercing myself to fall asleep instantly.

Uncle Jenő came to me the next Sunday, reporting that he had begun unpleasant negotiations with the Dukas. When I asserted that I did not want to be involved, he began to take inventory of my family's properties in the apartment. After he had left, the Keresztesis behaved exactly as I had expected. They felt insulted by his boorish attitude, and said they had taken good care of, and would have returned, every item to me or my mother. However, if that man was about to start legal litigations, they would fight me and him in court.

Feeling helpless and very depressed, I went to the temple. I said a quick prayer, looked at the list, then went upstairs to the recreation room. Upon sighting me, a girl named Ági rushed to the door and, while babbling exuberantly, dragged me to a group deeply in conversation. Observing my bewilderment, Tomi explained that the ten or so youngsters around him were all totally orphaned, having no means to sustain themselves. They knew their families had been annihilated and wished to start a new life in Palestine. While waiting for the chance to go to the Jewish homeland, they had decided to form the core of a kibbutz, to live and work collectively. Would I like to join? My mood was just right to answer "Yes!", but my logical mind needed more details.

Tomi summarized the plan. First, as an organized group, we would requisitiion a large empty house with a garden. Being children, the Red Cross and the American Joint Distribution Committee (A.J.D.C.)* would supply us with food and clothing, at least the bare necessities. Each of us would go to school independently, but share everything else equally. This meant both the chores and what we had possessed or acquired. Further, we would have total freedom of movement, even to move out of the kibbutz if for any reason we so desired.

Wow, that sounded great! Yes, of course I wanted to join! Tomi said we should all look for a suitable house and two ladies to move in with us as housemothers, while he would take care of the official steps.

Our second meeting on the following Sunday was

---

* Hungarian Jews owe much to the A.J.D.C. Their $2,250,000 financed the various life-saving activities of Raoul Wallenberg, the Swedish emissary who started the issuance of safe-papers (protective passports) and the safe-houses, i.e., the "International Ghetto," saving over 35,000 Jews. A.J.D.C. also contributed a substantial part of the money the Zionists had at their disposal. Further, for nearly two years after the war, they helped needy Jews financially.

attended by fourteen children, between the ages of 13 and 16, and two of their mothers. From the list of suggested dwellings we chose to requisition a house on Andrássy Road, near where I was "liberated". It had formerly belonged to a Nazi, who had recently been arrested. Péter's mother, Mrs. Bárdos, and Tomi had seen the house during the week, and thought it to be the most suitable. Since it needed some furniture, we all pledged eagerly whatever we had, and authorized Tomi to proceed with legalities. By the next Friday everything was all set. Sunday the movers picked up each of us with our belongings, and took us to our new home.

119 Andrássy Road was very nice and clean, and hardly damaged by the war. We furnished the huge upstairs room with a wardrobe and nine beds for the girls, the smaller one with five beds for the boys, the den downstairs for the mothers, and the huge old living room with my furniture, as our dining and recreation area. The Keresztesis did not object to my taking the exquisite dining room furniture, since I left everything else behind, they no longer had to feed me, and they regained their privacy.

I was relatively happy in my new home. We were all intelligent, well-brought-up children, all lonely and wanting to be loved, willing to share and build for a common future. The mothers were patient and compassionate, true surrogates to all of us. We cheerfully carried out our rotating chores of cleaning, washing, ironing, improving the premises, and caring for our vegetable garden. We helped each other with our homework, and learned Hebrew and Jewish history from Tomi in the evenings. Only on week-ends did we part, when each of us usually went visiting old friends.

One Sunday in June I returned to Grandmother's pre-war apartment. The resident family informed me that Magda, Uncle Lacó's wife, had also been there inquiring. I was thrilled to hear that she was alive and promptly followed the lead to her new residence. I found her and her aged mother living in real poverty, in one room of an almost totally destroyed building. I begged Magda to move in with us, but her mother needed her constant care, so we exchanged addresses and promised to notify each other as soon as word came about Lacó.

Next week-end I revisited Ilus Mama, Mrs. Viltschek. She had not yet heard about her husband nor about Bandi, but Erika had sent word that she was anxious to come home. Mrs. Viltschek also longed to be reunited with her daughter, but she lived in a tiny room and had barely enough food to sustain herself. The news about my new group and home thrilled her, for if Erika could join, she could live nearby, be provided for, and I could watch over her like a big sister. Once home, I pleaded with the group until all accepted my recommendation, and so in early July Erika joined our group.

Very, very slowly, life in the capital began to normalize. Five months after "liberation" electric power was finally restored, streetcars began to roll, and about a tenth of the prewar businesses began to operate. Very few consumer outlets opened, for there was almost nothing to sell. Although most factories were by now in full operation, they had all been "nationalized" (confiscated by the Temporary Communist Government) and were all under the command of the occupation forces. In plain words, in the past the Germans, and now the Russians, took everything the poor Hungarians produced.

The last weeks of July we all spent studying day and night. The finals were difficult and we had missed a great deal. Yet all of us in the kibbutz managed to pass; I, in the ninth grade, with all A's and B's. Our joy was dampened, however, when Tomi called a conference. He said we all needed to learn a trade. Further, that those of us who had completed the eighth or a higher grade should plan to look for an apprenticeship. This shattered my dreams. Since I was knee-high I had wanted to be a professional, with a doctor's degree. No, I was not ready to give up my dream!

The next day I visited my friend Dr. G., to ask his advice. He suggested that I try to be accepted in one of three college-preparatory, vocation-oriented high schools, my first choice to be the highest rated Bólyai Textile Precollege. After registering in my old school, Zrinyi, just to ensure my continued education, I rushed over to Bólyai.

The information I received there was not very encouraging. First, the student body was predominantly composed of boys, preparing to be textile chemists and engineers. Next, the curriculum was very hard and demanding: regular gymnazium subjects from 8:00 to 1:00, lectures and laboratory pertinent to textiles from 2:00 to 5:00 p.m. Finally, for the seven anticipated openings, there were already over 400 applicants. The choice, I was told, was to be based on the scores on a very long and comprehensive test battery. My friends at home — even Tomi — encouraged me to take the test, but cautioned me not to raise my hopes and to keep looking for apprenticeship opportunities, like all the other members of the kibbutz.

After a week-end of rest and prayer, I took the beastly examinations. When I had finished, intellectually exhausted but emotionally tense and physically restless, instead of going straight home, my sixth sense directed me to Magda. I found her looking like a zombie, crying hysterically. It took a while for her to compose herself sufficiently to tell me the horrible news. She had had a visitor, a man who claimed he had been in the labor camp with Dr. Arató (Uncle Lacó). During the winter a group of them were taken to Dunzkirchen, near the Mauthausen Concentration Camp. By God's miracles some of them had survived and were liberated by the Americans on April 30, 1945. As soon as the quarantine was lifted and leaving was possible, he, Uncle Lacó, and two others set out on their roughly 150-mile journey, from Germany to home. They had no money, no clothes, no food. They were all suffering from malnutrition, disease, and the effects of torture. They traveled on foot, slept in the meadows, and ate the fruits and vegetables they found along the road. On May 5 Lacó keeled over, collapsed and breathed no more. The three buried him at the roadside, somewhere near the Austro-Hungarian border.

Magda and I tried to console each other, but no words could soothe our pain. At home my friends attempted every means to cheer me up, but to no avail. Learning about the death of a loved one seemed to hit me harder and harder each time. I felt like a flower, whose petals were being torn off, one by one.

The next day Tomi came with delightful news. Each of us was scheduled to spend a two-week vacation in a resort cottage on the shores of Lake Balaton. I was to leave within a week, near the middle of August. Although the others were jumping with joy, I was not eager to go. I wished to be in the city to find out if I were to be accepted in Bólyai, and in case Mother or Bandi returned. But Tomi insisted that I needed to get away from it all for a while, and assured me that someone would bring news daily. When the time came I went to the moshava (Zionists' summer camp) with the others.

During the first few days we had a wonderful time. We sang and danced, swam and rowed, hiked and played sports, just as I did in my childhood — seemingly decades ago! Then one day one of the boys attached a long board to the end of the pier and suggested that we slide down on it into the deep water. We thought it was fun and kept doing it for a while, until after one of my turns we noticed the water around us turning red. It did not take long before I felt a pain in the sole of my left foot. By the time the boys had carried me to the cottage the blood was spurting from my foot, and I was barely conscious. Someone disinfected and bandaged my wound, and put me to bed.

The next day I began to run a high fever. All available medications seemed ineffective. On the third day I was put on a truck, and one of the rosh (leader) took me to the Rothschild hospital in Budapest. The doctors there determined that a rusty nail protruding from the slide had lacerated my foot deeply, and the germs of the polluted lake water caused an unusual infection of the blood, for which they had at that time no treatment. By then my foot had swollen to nearly twice its normal size, and five huge boils had appeared on my lower left leg. The doctors treated the boils with sulfur, gave me a bottle of aspirin and some sleeping pills, then sent me home to rest.

I spent the next few days mostly sleeping, to tune out the severe pain. On the sixth day the doctor came and lanced the boils, which gave me some relief. Better yet was the mail from Bólyai textile school, informing me that I had the fourth highest score and thus was accepted. I knew I would have to study day and night, but at least I would be college-bound while learning a trade and profession.

Seeing me awake and feeling somewhat better, my friends made the rounds visiting me the next day. One of the boys brought in my lunch, and began to tease me that the juice was made of passion fruit and contained a large dose of love potion. He warned me that if I drank it, I would not be able to resist the first boy who touched me. I laughed at him, ate and drank my lunch, then turned toward the wall and fell into a deep slumber.

I was awakened by someone leaning over me and kissing my cheek. Recalling my friend's teasing comments, I swiftly and powerfully slapped the person's face. Upon turning around, did I regret my action! Oh, did I! I had slapped none other than my dearly beloved Bandi. Amidst joyous tears he told me that he had journeyed home from the Dachau Concentration Camp, arriving in Budapest just that morning. He had first located his mother, who informed him that I was alive. Without resting or eating, dirty and ragged, he came at once to me.

That was the happiest moment of my life. Never before had I experienced such total joy. My eyes sparkled, my heart thumped, my blood boiled, my head felt weightless, and my body seemed in perfect health. I felt as if I were Snow White, holding the hand of my fairy tale prince.

Not wanting to part for even a short while, I got dressed, put a thickly padded bandage on my heel, topped it with a boy's slipper, and, with the aid of Bandi and the crutch, I wobbled with him back to his mother's house. We sat and talked for hours, hardly scratching the surface of all we had to say. It was nearly midnight when Bandi finally announced that he would move into the kibbutz, to be close to me at least until school started. And so, with Bandi near me, I spent the happiest few weeks since the start of the war.

During that time the two of us were inseparable. While my boils were keeping me tied to the house, we related to each other the happenings of the past year in detail.

After I brought him up to date, Bandi said, "Oh, how many times I wished I had listened to you! You begged me not to go with Jákob to the consulate on that dreadful October day . . . but I meant well. I thought I could secure safe-papers for all of us."

BANDI'S STORY

"We were walking down Aradi Street when we were stopped by a razzia. We might have gotten by, but the Arrow Cross boy recognized me. They took us to the notorious Gestapo Headquarters on Gyorskocsi Street. There, after a severe beating, they threw us into a jail cell.

One section of the jail housed a hundred or so active anti-Nazis and underground communists, the other held twenty-five hostages. Since we were neither of the above, the Germans selected the two of us for janitorial work. Although we slept in a cell, we were fed and treated much better than our unfortunate brethren.

In early December they took all of us prisoners, in cattle cars, to Hegyeshalom. From there we moved on foot across the border, into Austria. After a night in jail near Salzburg, we were taken to the infamous Dachau Concentration Camp. There we were separated from the hostages. After shaving our heads, stripping and disinfecting us, they gave us some old rags, including a jacket or coat displaying a big cross on the back, indicating political prisoners.

Our barrack had eight rooms, filled with triple-tiered, three-feet-wide wooden slabs called beds, bedecked with a straw or rag-filled sack. Three of us had to crowd into each narrow section to house the nearly 2,000 residents. While most of the 'muselmán'* had been working from sunrise to sunset in a nearby factory or the stone quarry, our group was temporarily allowed to vegetate.

A short while after our arrival I contracted typhus and, due to the extremely high fever, went to the infirmary. This barrack was much like the others, except there were only two bodies per bed. The variety of the diseases was innumerable, ranging from tuberculosis to experimentally-induced malaria. Most patients were untreated, even if suffering from several ailments. The sick, the dying and the dead shared the available spaces, not only on the slabs but on the floors and in the latrines.

A cup of ersatz coffee for breakfast, a half ladle of potato-peel soup for lunch, and a thin slice of sour bread at night was our only nourishment, and two daily aspirins our sole medication. All of us were afflicted with fleas, lice, meningitis and dysentery. By March, while I was still in the "hospital", I weighed only 90 pounds.

About mid-April several hundred of us were herded to the roll call square, were given blankets and some canned food, and were loaded onto trains. From Mittenwald we had to continue on foot. We marched for days, leaving a steady stream of dying and dead, at night sleeping in open fields

---

* Just skin and bone, living skeletons.

covered with the remains of thousands of bodies, or in nearby farmers' stables. Finally, one night we heard our few and old SS guards getting engaged in a gun battle. As soon as the cross fire subsided, Jákob and I crawled out of the stable. Seeing no one guarding us, we began running parallel to the shots. Eventually we reached the rapidly advancing American troops.

Soon the rest of our group was also liberated, and we were taken to the army base in Garmisch-Partenkirchen. There I checked into the hospital, just in time, for the next morning I was paralyzed from the waist down. It was August by the time I fully recuperated and was able to return home."

MY FIRST HOME
WITH THE
ZIONISTS.

CHAPTER 26: A SAD LITTLE BUNCH

By early September the first few boils on my foot had healed, and I was able to walk again. Bandi and I spent a few days visiting old friends and places, then decided to take a trip before school started.

Although it was more than half a year since Budapest had been "liberated", flour, sugar, meat, fat, and the like were still very hard to get. For example, a pair of solid gold cuff links was the black-market price of a large stick of hard salami. The townsfolk and farmers had food, but they lacked manufactured commodities, such as appliances, clothes, shoes, chemicals, and even first aid-type medicines. Money being hardly worth the cost of the paper, a large segment of society still secured most of their necessities through barter-trade.

Utilizing the few free days we had, Bandi and I set out on a trading expedition. We loaded our backpacks with small household tools, gadgets, patent medicines, yard goods and thread — items we had acquired with borrowed money and

I.O.U. notes — and at dawn on a lovely autumn morning we went to the railroad station. But getting on a train, any train, was not a simple matter! Most of our old trains and loco-motives had been taken by the Germans, and the newly manufactured ones were being shipped straight to Russia. Moreover, reconstruction of destroyed or damaged rails had as yet hardly begun.

Upon arriving we spotted a lonely six-car train, fully packed with passengers, standing on the farthest rail of the huge station. The more than twenty of us on the roof became bosom pals during the delay of an additional three hours, waiting for an oncoming train to clear the rails, before we reached the first suburb of the city.

Having traveled about 100 miles, we got off the train at the next day's sunrise. We knew not where we were, nor did we care. The farmers welcomed us with open arms and traded happily for each item we brought. Within a few hours our backpacks were stuffed with smoked hams, bacon, lard, salami, and various other goodies. We even had a dinner, the like of which we had not enjoyed for nearly two years. At dusk we were ready to return home. But by means of what? There was no train in sight, nor any scheduled for that day. Not until, at best, the day after the next! In desperation, we set out on foot.

Soon we noticed that our way along the rails ran parallel to Lake Balaton. We trotted along, hoping to soon reach a big town with trains from more than one direction. But it was not meant to be. Instead, in the bright light of a full moon and star-covered sky, the scenery began to look very familiar. Just as we were about to collapse from exhaustion, I spotted the Zionist camp where I had vacationed only a few weeks before. We turned off the road and nearly flew to the cottage with a burning light. Vacation time over, all the youth back in the city, the lonely guard was glad to let us stay for the night. Luck was with us, for the next day a truck came for the guard and the remaining equipment, and thus we got back to the capital without further misery.

Upon our return I was informed that Uncle Jenő had been impatiently looking for me. Although still exhausted from the trip, I went at once to see him. To my great joy none other than my cousin Pista opened the door. Since his father had informed him by then about how I had been faring, it was his turn to bring me up to date.

Pista narrated many gory episodes from the Nazi labor camp, and later when his unit was ordered to the Russian front to serve as human minesweepers. He said many men were anxious to step on a mine, a very speedy death, to prevent prolonging their suffering. The bitterly cold winter was bad enough, but underfed and underclothed, without treatment or medication for their ailments and wounds, mere existence was sheer torture.

He, on the other hand, claimed to be among the few real fortunates. Soon after he was assigned to that detail, he had safely crossed a mined field and was captured by the Russians. In the P.O.W. camp he was a diligent student of communism, and soon became a privileged prisoner. He had no bad comments about his own treatment (and refused to discuss that of the others), and since he had no chance to observe how the Russian civilians lived, his further comments were a pure eulogy of theoretical communism.

At first I sat there in amazement; then I presented a logical rebuttal in vain, and finally I began to sob. I had found, yet lost, my only blood relative! He had been brainwashed to total blindness of reality, to complete lack of logic and moral values. A man with his I.Q., a future leader in whatever field he chose, he was not only a great loss, but a detriment to a freedom-loving society.

Before parting I tried once more to alert him to the

state of affairs the "glorious Red Army" had inflicted upon our population, but Pista's only response was the parroting of communist slogans and promises for the future. He could not, or just refused, to see that the rate of recovery in the Iron Curtain countries was far below that of our Western neighbors, and that not only were we not helped, but we were still being fleeced by our "liberators". He laughed at my belief in God and my desire to help build a Jewish country, instead of taking advantage of the many personal gains I could have achieved by becoming an active Party leader. And so, with tears in my eyes, not wishing to encounter him again, I said farewell to my only blood relative.

By mid-September Bandi and Erika had moved out of the kibbutz. With their mother they patched up their prewar apartment and began to live again as a family. Erika went to school, Mrs. Viltschek kept working, and Bandi did both.

My grind also began. A new school, homework, household and gardening chores, plus Hebrew and Jewish history would have been hard enough, but since the kibbutz' inception so many new children had joined that in early October we had to move. Our new place at 39 Nürnberg Street was not nearly as nice, was less conveniently located, and most regrettably, our group was no longer congenial. Fourteen, even twenty could be homogeneous, but seventy in one house could not exist without conflict. The worst of it was the lack of privacy. Twelve youngsters in each small room, with beds end-to-end, having to share everything, including underwear, only one big room in which to eat, to play, and to study, was enough to drive us mad. To make things worse, our age-range was now from ten to seventeen, children from all walks of life, some very ill-mannered, some dishonest, many with weak body, character or mind, all lonely and war-torn . . . we were a sad little bunch.

I studied during the night into the wee hours of the

morning, and somehow managed to excel. Recognition came to me one day in October, when my mathematics teacher asked me to be his aide. The job involved correcting papers and tutoring. Though both paid very well, the honor meant more to me. Imagine, a sophomore girl, teaching math to a graduating boy! And correcting his tests! I was the talk of the school.

But two subjects gave me a great deal of trouble: history and government. Our history book was full of propagandized falsehoods. It painted Béla Kun, a communist dictator and murderer of thousands during the notorious Red regime after World War I, as a national hero! It eulogized rabble-rousers, jailbirds and criminals of the past, while discrediting with petty smears or outright lies some of our great patriots and diplomats. No! I couldn't swallow that! I knew my country's history. I was well versed in both, the so-called right wing's (what we studied and observed during the Nazi era) and the left wing's (my father's Social Democratic) views. I could also recognize the difference between a substantiated assertion and hearsay. On homework and tests I knew what the teachers and the system wanted me to assert, but my hands refused to obey. The topics on government and politics infuriated me even more. After studying The Communist Manifesto of Marx and Engels, I could not see how logical, intelligent, honest people could possibly believe communism to be desirable. *If* Marx indeed *believed* that communism could bring happiness to the masses, then he was at best a naive, unrealistic optimist. The Manifesto, the foundation of communism, cannot pass the test of common sense logic, and ignores the facts about man's basic nature. To illustrate:

1. Equalizing wealth. Taking from the "haves" and giving to the "have nots" sounds good, but in reality it is impractical and undesirable. First, all the wealth of the few, distributed among the multitude of poor would be an insignificant gain to the latter, and would soon be consumed. Yet, it would prevent the former from investing their surplus in new enterprises or research, to provide for more jobs or to find better ways of production, i.e., to benefit all. And what about *after* there was no more wealth to be taken away? Further, when the government owns and controls all production and everyone is paid a straight salary, the lack of the possibility of significant personal gains thwarts the incentive to excel or be creative, and thus hinders innovative growth. Also, limiting the acquisition and possession of worldly goods, combined with the "government taking care of everyone," induces men to lose their initiative and even their desire to work and produce. As a result, the government must force the population to work. The final consequence is quantitative and qualitative deterioration, and an unhappy and poor society.

2. Rule of the proletariat. Elevating the uneducated and unaccomplished "have nots" to ruling positions may appeal to the masses, but are they likely to make wiser choices and decisions than diplomats, specially trained men who are intellectually superior, who have spent many years studying the history, political and economic theories and structures of a multitude of past and present civilizations?

3. The end justifies the means. To falsify, to lie, to deprive, to forcibly take away, even to murder, are all justified and necessary according to Marx, in order to establish (and, as reality has proved, also to maintain) his communist utopia. Could even he himself believe that his doctrine would improve mankind or society?

I did not have to study my homework. I remembered every word the teacher read from our textbook, just because it infuriated me so. The theory that society can be divided into only two classes, the oppressors and the oppressed, constantly struggling against each other; the concept that the former always exploits the latter; the misery of every country's working class; the warning that the situation of the laboring classes would deteriorate catastrophically as capitalism progressed; the concept that the collapse of capitalism and the rise of socialism was "predetermined by nature," that the future could not be altered, was a collection of unfounded propagandistic lies! A simple observance of the status of the citizens of various countries and political philosophies rendered those assertions false and ridiculous.

Further, my common sense rebelled against accepting a philosophy constantly interspersed with irreconcilable contradictions. The communists defined the "oppressors" as the bourgeois and bourgeoisie, capitalist controllers of the means of social production, in general the employers of wage laborers; the "oppressed" as the proletariat, the wage earners who sold their labor to live. (The lower strata of the middle class — tradespeople, handicraftsmen and shopkeepers — according to Marx were all to sink gradually into the class of the proletariat.) According to this, doctors who employed nurses; professionals or small businessmen and the like, who employed secretaries or even errand or delivery boys; and farmers, who paid drivers of transport trucks — a few examples — would have to be classified simultaneously as both oppressors and oppressed! It just didn't make sense!

Still further, the communists claimed that in a bourgeois society only capital is independent, while the living person is dependent and has no individuality; that culture is a mere training to act as a machine; that bourgeois family ties are based on capital, on private gain. This implies that man is no better than a machine; that wives are mere instruments of production; that children are exploited by their parents; etc., etc., — a conglomeration of illogical contradictions, unfounded lies and rabble-rousing propaganda!

I recalled Ivan's comments ever so many times! I

thought of the many thousands of defecting Russian soldiers, risking their lives to escape from Marx's and Lenin's utopia.

As for the means of "liberating societies from the menace of capitalism," the communists advocate violence. We were told that communists, the world over, must support any and every revolutionary movement against the existing social and political order to achieve their primary aim, which is to gain control of every government of the world. They boldly assert that political power, properly so-called, is merely the organized power of one class for suppressing another, and that their ends can be attained only by forcible overthrow of all existing social institutions.

All these concepts I abhorred. The mere word "violence" made me shudder! Was the war not over? Was peace to be attained only after the whole world was conquered by the communists? Most disturbing to me, however, was our educators' frequent reference to our obligation to the "State". Teachers were constantly instilling the thoughts and reminding us that in the new social structure we were all beloved dependent children of the "State". "It" provided us with jobs, food and other necessities, took care of our health and all other needs from the cradle to the grave. In return, it was our *duty* to watch vigilantly and *report* anyone who spoke of dissatisfaction, even if we loved or were related to that person. Children in the schools were *never* taught to *respect* their *parents,* or the *beliefs* and *property* of others; *never* taught to value *honesty* and *integrity;* only to follow blindly the teachings and orders of Party leaders and the demands of that abstract entity, the "State".

In the beginning some of us attempted to argue with our teachers, but the firm reprimands and low grades were potently discouraging. Requests for clarification were either simply ignored, or followed by comments such as: "Your knowledge at present is too limited. You are advised to join the Party and attend supplemental lectures," or "Communism is a state of utopia, reachable only after man's mind and soul is purified. You must cleanse your mind of previous stupid religious teachings and oppressive bourgeois values, and help us to recondition everyone else's thinking, to prepare ourselves to conquer all decadent capitalistic tyrannies and establish worldwide glorious International Communism."

As time went on, each of us pulled more and more into his or her own shell. Although some of us studied together occasionally, we carefully avoided discussing anything remotely connected with history, government or politics, even during the elections, in fear of low grades and the chance of being kicked out of school as a "politically undesirable element."

In November, 1945, the first national election was held. Prior to it only the communist candidates campaigned outside their immediate location, for only they had money and access to vehicles to travel. Communist Party members were ordered to hang posters, distribute pamphlets, attend speeches, and participate in demonstrations and parades. Members of the Farmers, Smallholders, and other opposition parties, even the incumbent members of the Hungarian Provisional Government (civilians under the control of the Red Army), did not seem to have even a remote chance to be elected. Yet, when the votes were in, to the Red Army's dismay, the entire leftist block got only 40% of the votes, of which the Communist Party proper received a total of less than 16%!

Immediately after the election the communists began to weed out all of their Party's opponents, falsely accusing them of various crimes and participation in conspiracies. More important, the higher an office one held, the sooner was his turn to be jailed or to disappear. So frequent became unjustified arrests that people began to fear expressing any opinion, even to their immediate families.

CHAPTER 27: RULE OF THE NEW REGIME

By early December of 1945 I had begun entertaining the thought of leaving Hungary. Since there was still no news about my mother, and since the list of the survivors of labor and concentration camps secured and published by the International Red Cross and Tracing Service was relatively complete, I had to assume that Mother had also perished. Thus, if I would have left the kibbutz, I would have had to exist totally alone, without means to support myself, in a political milieu where my sheer survival was doubtful.

Living conditions in Budapest, nearly a year after "liberation", were still far from normal. Reconstruction of destroyed residences had not yet begun. Even most of the rubble was not cleared away, to remind us of our sufferings, and to imply that our primary obligation was to support and strengthen the "glorious liberation forces of the Red Army and their mother country."

Industrial and agricultural production had begun, but the fruits of the labor were shipped directly to Russia. Consequently, common necessities such as clothes, furniture, tools, appliances, ordinary housewares, even household chemicals, patent medicines and most food products were still scarce. And their lack of quantity was superseded only by their lack of quality and price. I recall paying 10,000 forints for a pair of wooden-soled shoes, and a few weeks later 50,000 forints for a half a loaf of bread. People stopped talking about currency in terms of numbers, referring to prices rather as blue, yellow or green money.

To top it all, the communist political philosophy made the majority of the people even more unhappy. Private ownership, the only real incentive for man to work hard and produce, was abolished. No income-producing land, house, business, or factory could be owned by individuals. Everyone worked for the State. (The attitude of people who work not for personal gain, but for the benefit of the State, a far-removed entity, plus foreign exploitation of the homeland's natural resources accounted — and still accounts — for the extremely poor quality of all types of production in all the communist-ruled countries in the world.)

Finally, the dictatorship began to control every phase of our existence. Job opportunities created by the expansion of certain industries depended on the choice of our puppet government, manned by communists dedicated to serve primarily the "glorious mother country", Russia. The type of vocational or professional training one could receive began to depend ever increasingly not on the individual's desire, ability or qualifications, but on the needs of the State. Religious beliefs were ridiculed, most churches, convents and monasteries were permanently closed, and all phases of religious training were banned.

As for mind control, AVH (secret police) members and informers were planted everywhere. Every worker and student had a "dossier", a confidential file to which anyone, except the individual, had access. Into it were recorded comments forthcoming willingly or through unpleasant and threatening interrogations of superiors, subordinates, or anyone who had contact with the individual. Derogatory remarks or dissatisfaction expressed about Party leaders, policies, communist philosophies or practices, or Russia, resulted in various means of punishments: demotion, forced relocation, jail sentence, mind-destroying drug therapy, "accidental" death, or traceless disappearance.

To illustrate: there was a boy in my government class who was appalled about the party line and frequently vocalized his criticisms. Although he had only A's thus far, he was expelled the fifth week of school, and blackballed so that subsequently he was rejected by every college-preparatory high school.

The fate of Gyuszi, a prewar cadet acquaintance of mine, was worse. As a commissioned air force officer, like all Hungarian military personnel, he came under the German High Command. As the Red armies had advanced, Gyuszi's unit had to pull back with the Germans. Just before the war ended, he became a P.O.W. of the advancing Americans. When he was repatriated, the communist regime marked his dossier "not above a driver of vehicles," forever limiting his future professional and financial achievements.

But even worse were the fates of my former neighbors. Dr. Gerő, his wife and young son had been hidden by Christians and thus had survived the Holocaust. As many other intellectuals did, the parents disapproved of communism. They had occasionally expressed such views as: "The people should select new leaders," "form a new party actively propagating individual freedoms," and "demand the removal of some appointed officials." Their son was a ten-year-old, disrespectful little brat, disliked by everyone. I knew he had joined the Communist Youth League, and often wondered how his parents must have felt. One day in December I went to visit them. The apartment was unlocked and empty. A neighbor told me that a few nights before three AVH men had come and had taken the parents away. The boy bragged that he was the one who had reported them. The next day the boy came home crying, saying that he must gather his things and move into a Party orphanage since, he was told, his parents would never return. No one ever heard from, nor saw, Dr. and Mrs. Gerő again.

Having studied the theories of Marx, Lenin, and Stalin, and having seen communism in practicum, I felt it worthwhile to risk my life to escape. Thus, near mid-December, I announced my intention to Tomi.

CHAPTER 28: HIGHWAY ROBBERY

I might have postponed my decision at least until we had heard whether other convoys had successfully crossed the border, had my relationship with Bandi been better. As it was, we hardly saw each other. I left for school before 8:00 a.m., got home close to 6:00, did my chores, ate, attended Hebrew and Jewish history class, and tutored until 11:00 p.m. I rarely finished my school homework before 1:00-1:30 a.m., and I was up again at 6:00 in the morning, six days a week. Bandi, meanwhile, attended eleventh grade classes, studied the tenth grade curriculum on his own, and worked several hours daily to earn some money to help support the family. We saw each other at most once in two or three weeks.

Meanwhile, the atmosphere in the kibbutz was very tense. New youngsters were coming in and old ones dropping out daily. Family members of many had returned from concentration camps, some changed their minds about wanting to go to Palestine, and some, of bad character, we managed to kick out. All of us wartorn, totally orphaned, wanted by no one, to various extents physically and emotionally sick, packed like sardines in our abode, poverty stricken — life was

206

barely tolerable. Mainly due to loneliness, we chose buddies and formed cliques. I did not feel close to any of the girls, and due to my deep love of Bandi, rejected courting approaches of the boys. Thus, in spite of my tender age, I gradually assumed the "mothering" role again. I helped the youngsters with their schoolwork, listened to their troubles, arbitrated their fights, settled girl-and-boyfriend problems, and attended to the sick. I was all: a big sister, a wise friend, counselor, negotiator, teacher, nurse, "to each his own." It was nice to be wanted, but it drained me. I hungered for parental love — to be liked for what I was, not just for what I could give. I needed to have a mother, not to be one.

To celebrate Chanukah, several of my old friends organized parties. I was invited to four, and was asked for a date by two of the kibbutz boys, all for the same Saturday night. I delayed commitment, hoping that Bandi would call. But he did not. In childish anger, on the morning of that special day I accepted *all* the invitations. Only when I was all dressed to go did the two boys find out that they were both dating me, simultaneously. They looked at each other as mortal enemies, as each took one of my arms.

But the battle was not fought, for as we were about to exit, who else but Bandi entered the front door. In his typical self-assured manner he announced, "I am glad you are ready. Let us go." I was positively furious. How dare he take me so much for granted! Suddenly I felt like a young lady. My female ego was hurt. And just to teach him a lesson, after a big fight I angrily told him to leave. When I began to cry, Péter Bárdos, one of the founding boys, who had for months been infatuated with me, grabbed this golden opportunity to console me. After crying on each other's shoulders for a while, we made a pact: as girl and boyfriend, we would be on the very next convoy to Palestine.

Near the end of December, Tomi informed us to get

ready to leave within three days. He told us no further details, for the mission was extremely dangerous. Immigration, yes, but emigration was not tolerated by the Reds! Péter, his mother Mrs. Bárdos, Ági (who was by now Tomi's fiancee) and myself were the only ones from our kibbutz to leave. And we were forewarned not to breathe a word about it! So, I used the meager time to visit old friends once more, not saying, but knowing within, that I would never see them again.

The three most difficult visits I left for the last. The first of these was Magda. I asked her, if I could get her out of the country, would she want to come to Palestine? Her answer was yes, but not while her mother was still alive. I said no more, but cried as I left.

Next I went to Jenő Halász. To him I had to tell the truth. Financial matters had to be settled. He had by then secured a large portion of our jewelry from the Dukas, plus three Persian rugs, handmade lace drapes, bolts of yard goods and other valuable items having been hidden by various ex-clients of Father. I had insisted that the furniture, safe, paintings, crystal, china, and antiques be inventoried and receipted, and to be left in our old apartment and cared for by the Keresztesis. Having never received a penny from my "dear" uncle-guardian, I asked for the rent money he had been collecting. Without being able to produce a single receipt, he claimed that all had been spent on legal fees, his expenditures in getting back items, and on some absolutely necessary repairs of my house in Újpest. I did not believe a word, but what could I do? So, on account he gave me some cash, just enough to purchase one pair of shoes, a backpack and a coat made out of an old army blanket, leaving me with about $10 in change. Their going-away gift to me was a used slip, a pair of panties from Helen, and four cartons of cheap cigarettes. Thus, leaving everything in Jenő's possession and/or in his charge, in case my mother should return, I said good-bye to my "dear" relatives.

Lastly, the night before our departure I went to the Viltscheks. To them I also had to tell the truth. Erika thought I was a fool. She felt the chance of a successful escape was very slim, and of reaching Palestine alive even less likely. Further, what future did I have there? Farming on a kibbutz? Or getting shot by the Arabs? She did not understand my mental and emotional state, so she could not empathize; she was still a child who had never really suffered.

Bandi's reaction, however, was quite different. Not being able to camouflage how deeply he felt, big drops of tears began rolling down his cheeks. He pleaded with me not to go. He begged me to move in with them and live as part of the family; he offered to support me, even to marry me if I so desired; and his mother, anything to keep me from leaving Hungary, backed up Bandi's every word. I was touched, deeply. They were the only two persons in the world who truly loved and wanted me, without anything in return.

I was tempted, but could not accept their offer. Either Bandi or I would have had to give up school for my support, which was a very high price for me to pay or accept; also, because I knew I could never be happy under communism, nor even survive for long. I knew I would be caught and eliminated for my "revolutionary" views sooner or later. So, after many tears, we reached the only possible compromise: Bandi promised that as soon as his family was financially stable, or in case his father returned, he would attempt to escape and come to me wherever I was. Thus, leaving my heart behind, I parted from the only loved one destiny had not deprived me of.

The following afternoon, all dressed and carrying only our backpacks, without revealing our destination to anyone at home, Péter, his mother, Ági and I left the kibbutz for-

209

ever. We joined Tomi and ninety-three other children at the train station. After Tomi led us to the farthest end of the platform, out of sight and hearing range of anyone, he briefed us as follows: "As you may know, during the past few days government officials have been negotiating about repatriation. I have well-forged documents for each of you, verifying that you were born in Austria. We will claim that we are returning to our homeland. The oldest of us will handle all necessary discussions; the rest of you are not to utter a word! Each of you twelve years or older will take charge of five or six younger ones, and see to it that no one converses until we are safely across the border. Until then we are all supposedly going to vacation in a camp for orphans, in the woods near the town of Hegyeshalom. Remember, our lives are at stake!"

Tomi paused for a moment, cleared his throat, then continued. "Now I shall tell each of you the place of your birth and when you were brought to Hungary according to your new identification papers, and for some of you a newly assigned name. Commit these indelibly to your memory. Hopefully no one will speak to you. But if an official does start asking questions, try to play mute, deaf or dumb. If you absolutely must respond, say as little as possible." When he finished giving each the information, Tomi called aside Péter, his mother, Ági, and myself. Since we were the oldest and we spoke German fairly well, we were instructed to put on a convincing act if he needed support at the border.

After a brief silent prayer all of us mounted the express train to Hegyeshalom, a small town about ten miles from the Austrian border. Our little wards ranged from 4 to 14 years of age, the majority being younger than 10. We let the children play until the locomotive arrived. As soon as the train pulled out of the station, we placed blankets on the benches and put the little ones to sleep. Péter and I talked for a while, then decided to take a nap, for we expected the latter part of our trip to be quite perilous.

The train had stopped and it was pitch dark outside when Tomi awakened the four of us. He held his finger to his mouth, indicating that we should not talk, then motioned us to follow him to the end of the car. He said the train had been standing for a half an hour or so, and we were to mind the sleeping children while he went to find out what was happening. Fretfully nervous, we waited impatiently for our guardian's return.

In the stillness of the evening we could hear Tomi's rushing footsteps, just as the train began to move. He said the station sign stated Győr, the only big city about halfway between Budapest and the border. He saw Russian soldiers taking a group of civilians off the train and marching them away at gunpoint.

Péter and his mother whispered a brief "thank you" prayer, but I did not join them. During the past few months I had lost nearly all my faith in God. I was angry at Him for taking all my loved ones away. Although by then I hardly cared whether I lived or died, I did fear being caught at the border, for the punishment of an attempted escape with forged papers was long-term imprisonment and severe torture. So, *my* prayer was not a simple "thanks", but a kind of demand, something like: "Lord, if you exist, you owe the protection of this small group of wee orphans to the millions you allowed to suffer and perish!"

As the train regained its normal speed, we returned to the still soundly-sleeping children. Being so close to real liberation, my mind began to wonder: — Suppose we were stopped near Hegyeshalom and the guards would not believe our story. What would they do with a bunch of children? They could not jail 5-and-6-year-olds! No, they would most likely take them back to the capital and put them into a

Party orphanage. But not Tomi, Ági, Péter, Mrs. Bárdos and me! We were the leaders; we would have to be severely punished! Would they brainwash us with drugs or make us "disappear", like so many I had heard of or knew? One was as bad as the other. . . . No! I would try to make a break. Then I would be shot; a quick and painless way to end my unhappy existence. — But what if we were to be successful? The danger was far from over! We knew the British blocked migrants from entering Palestine. There were millions of people waiting for the few thousand yearly quota. Even the Zionist leaders admitted that the overwhelming majority of the illegal immigrants never reached the shores of the Promised Land alive.

My head began to ache excruciatingly. I began to entertain thoughts of suicide. — Strange! I had lived through the real horrors of the Nazi era and the Russian "liberation", living with constant pain and fear, yet able to tune out the pain and wanting desperately to live. And now, when I was to leave all those horrors behind, when, if successfully crossing the last two barricades, I had a good chance to pursue a physically and spiritually rewarding life, *now* I considered suicide. — No, it was not so strange after all. Before I had hope, hope of being reunited with my loved ones and reestablishing the kind of life we had lived before the war. But now the hope was gone. Even the chance of ever seeing my mother or Bandi again seemed extremely remote.

The whimper of one of the children interrupted my thoughts. As I looked at those helpless little orphans, I knew I must not die. They needed a surrogate mother, and I was just right for the job. Maybe the Lord had preserved me to replace many, many of those mothers who had perished by torture or in the crematoriums.

Not knowing whence it came, in the stillness of the

night I heard a faint voice:"You must not die. Your mission is not yet finished. You were saved in order to help others. You will always find the strength and means to help. You must never forget the purpose of your existence, your duty to mankind."

Feeling relaxed and content, I must have dozed off, to be brought back to cruel reality by the shrieking halt of the locomotive. Tomi rose swiftly, shone his flashlight into the older children's faces and said firmly, "This is it. Remember your instructions. Our lives depend on it!"

The train had stopped in the station, but no one was as yet getting off. I looked out the window. Armed Russian and Hungarian soldiers were walking up and down along our five-car train. It was not long before a dozen or so soldiers entered our car, shining their flashlights into everyone's face. The teen-agers acted swiftly and maturely as some of the little ones were rudely awakened and shrieked out from fright. Tomi at once stepped up to the highest ranking Russian soldier and began his explanation in fluent German. The Russian stared at him stupidly for a while, then motioned for one of the Hungarian guards, the interpreter. As Tomi was about to continue, the guard ordered him to speak in the native language.

In an excellent imitation of very broken Hungarian, he responded that our mother tongue was Austrian, of the country to which we were all returning, substantiating his assertion by producing the pile of birth certificates. Examining them studiously and translating Tomi's every word, the guard seemed no less amazed than his superior. Without further comment Tomi presented a very official-looking document, written in all three languages, listing each of our names, stating that under the new Repatriation Agreement we were to be returned to Vienna, Austria.

The Russian scrutinized the document, then stated that

he had not received orders to allow anyone, except diplomats, to leave the country. Tomi then produced a bunch of newspaper clippings and argued that the orders must be on their way, the delay due to someone's inefficiency. He demanded that the soldiers verify it if they must, but allow us to get off the train and to continue our journey without delay.

The border guards were in a difficult position. If our story were true and they refused to let us leave, they would be punished by their superiors; if we lied and they let us escape, their punishment would be even worse. Their only reasonable choice was to hold us until verification. Since the train had to proceed back to the capital, we were ordered to get off and wait on the deserted but well-lit platform.

But Tomi's orders were different! Speaking in German — which by now he knew the soldiers did not understand — he instructed us to get the youngsters out through the windows and onto the covered truck that stood in a ditch, just beyond the tracks, on the dark side of the station. As soon as the Russian with his interpreter left to make a phone verification, and the rest of the soldiers got off to let us descend, the five of us started a noisy commotion near the exits, while the older ones quickly and quietly opened all the windows through which they began the evacuation. Meanwhile the truck had pulled alongside the train, and the Zionist leaders who came with it proceeded to transfer the children in deathly silence and with lightning speed.

Since the soldiers were ordered to guard us on the platform, none of them being smart enough nor brave enough to disobey, they waited patiently on the left for us to descend, while all of us got off safely on the right. Nothing was noticed until they smelled the burning rubber of our truck tires, as we sped out of the station. We "flew" on the road, straight as an arrow, avoiding the mines in the surrounding open fields. Just as we came within the range of the searchlights' beams, mounted on the guard-towers along the border, ready to smash through the barbed wires, a jeep full of Russian soldiers appeared from seemingly nowhere, only a few yards ahead of us on the road. Since they held their submachine guns ready to fire, our driver brought the truck to a screeching halt.

The four male and two female soldiers unlatched the back and jumped up into our truck. We huddled together, speechless and petrified. Separating us with the butts of their guns, the soldiers frisked each of us, one by one. They pulled off our rings and watches, ripped earrings out of the children's ears, took coats away from some, shoes from others, even entire backpacks from some of the older ones. From me they took a shiny tin lapel pin and my wallet. They did not shoot or hurt anyone, except the two children whose gold-crowned teeth one simply knocked out with the ring on his fist.

Having deprived us of as much as they could carry, the soldiers left our truck, got on their jeep, turned around and sped away. While the Zionist leaders kept consoling our sobbing little group, the driver put the gas pedal again to the floor, and with nearly supersonic speed crashed through the last barrier, into a land of freedom, leaving the Iron Curtain forever behind.

PART IV: GLIMPSE OF FREEDOM

CHAPTER 29: FROM PRISON TO PRISON

The Austrian border guards greeted us with big smiles and warm, welcoming words. Our driver stopped politely, but the guards took one swift look at the pathetic, crying children and waved us to move on, not wanting to see our papers nor even to hear any explanation. The moon and stars were fading, and the sun was about to lift its shiny head up far away in the horizon when we reached our destination, the non-demolished portion of the one-time Rothschild Hospital, in the outskirts of Vienna.

The hospital had been converted into a refugee reception center, and the Red Cross personnel awaited us with food, some clothing, and wall-to-wall rows of blanketed cots. After we ate and bathed, the social workers prepared a portfolio on everyone. (Having been conditioned to fear authority for so long, most of us parroted the data Tomi had told us to give, as it appeared in the documents the Zionists had provided for us.) After being "processed" (registered with detailed information), most of us did not even wait for supper, but simply collapsed from total emotional and physical fatigue.

The next day we underwent a superficial medical examination and received treatment for our most obvious ailments. Intensive care for many suffering from illnesses like scurvy (vitamin C deficiency), tuberculosis and blood disease — souvenirs of the living conditions during the war and of the rape-victims of the Russians — could not be treated in the newly improvised, understaffed and underequipped refugee reception center. But, however sick, we were happy, for we had at least successfully escaped from the communist "paradise."

216

On the third day we mounted our trucks again and were transported through the splendid scenery of the Austrian Alps to an old army camp on the Austro-German border. The camp's wooden structures were occupied now by various Zionist groups. Our little convoy needed only one barrack, as each big room was equipped with nothing other than a potbelly stove and thirty to forty bunkbeds. Tomi and Ági occupied the one-time guards' room at the entrance, while Mrs. Bárdos, Péter and I were assigned to different big rooms, to supervise the children. Since we arrived late at night, weary from the 150-mile mountain ride, we all dropped on the nearest bunk and rapidly sank into peaceful slumber.

The next day began with standing in the chow line for nearly an hour, then in line to be processed again, then in another line to receive a blanket, and in more and more lines for a metal plate, cup, eating utensils, soap, towel, etc. Some of the littlest ones went to sleep again without supper, too tired even to eat.

The following day Tomi and Ági moved to a distant barrack, and two young men from Munkács (a part of Hungary that was annexed to Czechoslovakia between World Wars I and II) moved into their room and took charge of us. Both were in their early twenties, well-dressed, conceited, uneducated and crude. They wasted no time informing us about the new rules and the daily schedule to be followed: 7:00 to 8:00 a.m., everyone to the latrine and to the washroom (five or more minutes' walk in the snow, in near-zero temperature); 8:00 to 9:00, breakfast; 9:00 to 10:00, cleaning the outside and inside of our barrack; 10:00 to 11:30, Hebrew studies; 12:00 to 1:30, dinner; 2:00 to 4:00, Jewish studies; 4:30 to 6:00, evening chow; 6:00 to 7:00, washroom and latrine; 7:30, lights out.

Grumpily we went along with our new leaders' orders for a few days, but meanwhile our tension was mounting.

217

There was a toilette in our barrack, adjoining their room. Why not let the little ones use it? Why did they make them walk in the bitter cold to the latrine? Why did they not secure enough wood to heat our rooms also? When were we to get some warm clothes and another blanket to cover the straw sacks in our cots? Were we forever going to live on powdered milk, eggs and potatoes, dried vegetables and meatless stews? Péter and I approached our leaders about these issues, but their response was: "All in good time."

As the days went on, I met a great many teen-agers in the mess hall. The camp housed nearly a thousand youths, most of them between twelve and sixteen years of age, plus a hundred or so in their twenties, who were kvutza rosh (group leaders), kitchen and infirmary workers, and general administrators. Except for a handful of UNRRA (United Nations' Relief and Rehabilitation Administration), Red Cross and occupation army personnel, plus Zionist organizers from Palestine, all of us were Jewish refugees from various countries behind the Iron Curtain, hoping to immigrate to Palestine.

We were all Zionists, but belonged to different factions of the movement; we to the Hanoar Hazioni, some to the Shomer Hatzair or Dror Habonim, others to the Betar denominations. We all believed in the need to establish an independent Jewish nation, but we differed in our convictions as to how it should be acquired and then governed.

We, the Hanoar Hazioni, followers of Zionism's Founding Father Theodore Herzl, believed that an independent Jewish state could be established via the help of the Big Powers, through negotiations, then governed democratically, somewhat like the free Western nations. The Drors and Shomers, forerunners of the Mapam, shared our beliefs as to the acquisition, but wanted to seat a socialistic government. The Betars, following the beliefs of Vladimir Jabotinsky, father of the Zionist Revisionist Movement (composed of many such men as later Prime Minister Menachim Begin), trained their members for defensive warfare. They held that Jews should not beg, but demand, freedom from British rule of Palestine, to fight if necessary to be able to bring survivors of the Holocaust to the biblical promised land, and to defend the future Israel's borders from anticipated Arab attacks. They propagated a free enterprise economic policy, and a republican form of government.

As I spent more time talking to members of the various groups, I began to identify most closely with the Betar philosophy. I found among my new acquaintances the intellectual stimulus which, having "mothered" the little ones all day long, I hungered for. Thus, after "lights-out", I began to sneak out nightly, to visit the nearby Betar barrack.

My new friends were illuminating, more than just politically. They enlightened me that each person entering the camp was to receive not one, but two blankets, candles and a flashlight, an entire set of clothes and toilet items, plus a weekly "CARE" package, consisting of cigarettes, chocolates, canned foods and milk, reading and writing items, notions, etc.

Sneaking back into my barrack about ten that night, I saw our two leaders carrying boxes out of our storeroom. I peeked in when they stepped out and was amazed to see what they had hoarded. Shelves after shelves stacked with blankets and canned goods, and racks upon racks of clothes! No wonder they wore fur-lined jackets, gold watches and diamond rings, while we hungered and shivered day and night! I was furious.

The next morning I discussed the matter with Mrs. Bárdos and Péter, and after breakfast we faced our kvutza rosh with our demands. They denied having received anything in our or the children's names, and, when I stated what

I had seen the night before, they claimed all was their own personal property, having acquired it on the black market.

I was angry beyond words. I wanted to report them to the authorities, but Péter did not want to start trouble. He and his mother felt that the two young men had more connections and influence than we did, and if angered, they could make our stay even more miserable. I pitied them, for they had been so conditioned to fear first Nazi then communist authority, that I wondered if they would ever learn to live like free men.

Getting no support from my own, I sought the advice of my new friends. They informed me that although it was indeed unfair not to issue the items to the children, such activity was commonly pursued, especially by the Shomer and Dror leaders. They sold the items on the German black market to raise the money for their underground activities, such as buying trucks to smuggle people out of countries, paying off border guards, hiring ships to smuggle people into Palestine, etc. They said that Betar leaders did not need to resort to such tactics, first because they had more independent donors, and second, they valued individual rights and properties more highly.

Having made up my mind to transfer membership to the Betar, I confronted our leaders with my demands. Each of us was to receive at once an additional blanket; whatever clothes we needed to keep warm; some of the toys, books and notions; all the canned milk and ready-to-eat food. With the remaining items — such as candies, coffee, tea, cigarettes, additional clothes and toilet items — the two could barter-trade as they wished, except what was needed to hire someone to chop enough wood to keep our fires going. The two objected at first, but when I threatened to expose them to the UNRRA and Red Cross personnel, reminding them that I had friends to testify to their deception, they at once

220

began the distribution. The next day I said good-bye to the children and old friends, and moved into the Betar barrack.

Just one day after I joined, my new leader announced that, to make room for a newly arriving group, most of us would be distributed to various refugee camps and kibbutzim in Germany. I was to go with four others to a small one near Landau.

Near midnight, after several hours of a very bumpy ride through mountain ridges and bad roads in our small truck, we arrived at the little farm. It was bad enough that my traveling companions were Polish, who spoke not a word of Hungarian or German, but all the members of the reception committee were also from Poland and Czechoslovakia, so there was no one I could communicate with. I felt very depressed over this fact, but the scrumptious homemade bread and butter and fresh milk, plus the delightfully soft bed with down pillows and comforter cheered me up a bit.

The entire group of nineteen gathered at the breakfast table the next morning. Fortunately there was a sickly-looking young woman who spoke enough German to translate for me. She said I had a choice of working in the fields, planting and raking, or in the stables, tending to and milking the cows. I asserted that I knew nothing about farming, nor had any desire to learn. That, as well as my inability to communicate with the members of the group, led the leader to decide that I should be transferred.

The next morning, just as the cuckoo clock struck seven, the truck arrived to take the fresh produce and me to another kibbutz. I bounced like a rubber ball among the milk cans and sacks of onions and potatoes as the converted jeep bumped across the meadows and uncultivated fields. The sun was high when we arrived in Ainring, near the Austro-German border, the old Air Force camp converted to a Displaced Persons' (D.P.) camp.

Yuku, the kvutza rosh, was waiting for us. He was a handsome, well-built and sharply dressed young man in his early twenties, from Transylvania (a part of Hungary that belonged to Rumania between World War I and World War II). He took me into the barrack, introduced me to two Hungarians, assigned me to the lower one of a two-level bunk bed, recorded my personal data in a huge black book, then issued the items to which each newcomer to any D.P. camp was entitled.

It would not be fair to say that I liked my new environment, but it was tolerable. Our barrack was a mixture of Zionists and other Jews. My room housed nearly thirty females, aged fifteen through forty, and the one across the corridor housed nearly fifty men of similar ages. The other two rooms were a little smaller, but quite the same.

Most of these people — and habitants of all the other refugee camps scattered in Germany — were survivors of labor and concentration camps, who did not return to their respective homelands, but waited for passage to various countries around the world. Nearly all were sole survivors of their immediate families; some had relatives on other continents, some had only friends in distant lands, yet many had nothing and no one to call their own. Almost everyone suffered from some ailment, the healthiest only from frostbite and malnutrition. Laughter was an unfamiliar sound, in contrast to the frequently heard cries and bickerings. Those poverty-stricken, physical and emotional wrecks — from different countries and backgrounds, filled with fear from the past and of the unknown future, thrown into such close proximity in those crude wooden barracks, having nothing else to do but sit around or stand in line for the washroom-latrine and the barely edible three daily meals — could hardly be expected to behave like normal members of society.

Here our days were not regimented; on the contrary, we

222

had nothing to do. For lack of sufficient membership, the Zionists were not yet organized. I became friends with only two boys: Putyu, a Hungarian doctor's son, the same age and completely orphaned as I, and Bubu, nearly seventeen, from the same town and a friend of our leader Yuku. While the latter two spent many hours trying to recruit, I went for long walks with Putyu, often to the airplane graveyard, playing hide-and-seek in the planes and scavenging imaginatively for usable objects. One of the precious finds was a shattered polyglass window, from which we carved rings for Bubu to trade for clothes or food.

Putyu and I had more than our age and business in common. Our prewar upbringing, moral values and political opinions were also similar. His hatred of the Russians was so intense and fierce that it almost frightened me. One day he blurted out his dark and repressed secret. He had lived with a farmer family during the war, in the eastern part of Hungary. When the Russian soldiers "liberated" the village, the nightmare began. First they ransacked and robbed every farmhouse; then, like pagans, they grabbed and carried off all the able-bodied females. Husbands and fathers who tried to resist were beaten, shot, even hanged in the town square.

The next division, the so-called Red Occupation Army, which, by the way, had many female soldiers, was even more barbaric. When drunk they went searching for victims for their orgies. For lack of civilians, farm animals often sufficed. For days people lived in cellars, but eventually the townsfolk had to surface. Young men, among them Putyu, were rounded up and herded to the town square. There, like cattle buyers, the soldiers picked and chose for their night's feast. Putyu, too, finally became their prisoner, and was subjected to unspeakable torment for nearly three weeks. When that division had to move on, they left their victims behind. The townsfolk treated their overt wounds, and hid them in cellars for many subsequent weeks.

It was months before Putyu was well enough to return to his birthplace. As soon as he found out that his whole family had been annihilated, he gathered what valuables his parents had hidden, and made contact and payment to the members of the anti-communist underground, who took him to Czechoslovakia. From there they went to the Austrian border, where during the night they were led across the mile-wide mined fields, under the barbed wires, into the tank of a fishing boat, up the Danube River, and safely to the Viennese Red Cross. From there he was sent to Ainring, where he was waiting for the chance to go to the U.S.A.

Putyu's story was not unique. Each one in the camp could have matched or topped it, but few of us ever spoke of the past. Our wounds were too fresh; we could not as yet bear to relive our pain and sorrow.

A few weeks after my arrival Yuku announced that Bubu, himself and I, the three Betars, were to move, to establish a group in another D.P. camp. The next day I said a very sad final good-bye to Putyu, and boarded the truck that came for us.

Except for its size, Pocking was very similar to Ainring. The barracks were the same and so were the people. Yuku and Bubu, as leaders, got a private room at the entrance, while I was assigned again to a huge room with nearly fifty beds. Here, too, the bunks were of two levels, equipped with straw-filled sacks for mattresses and pillows. I got an upper bunk this time, which I soon found to be an advantage, for it was warmer and airier than those below.

The next day we went through the processing procedures, as before, and got a new set of supplies. By now my backpack was overflowing with ragged clothes and shoes that did not fit, so among my barrack-mates I managed to trade the excess for a pair of decent shoes and some petty cash. My worldly possessions now consisted of: a nice light jacket, my old, badly-worn winter coat, two shabby dresses, a far too large but warm robe, two sets of underwear, two pairs of shoes, two towels, toilet items, some notions, three blankets, a flashlight, and my most treasured little diary.

Since Yuku and Bubu did not know anyone there, and since they wished to train me in the Betar philosophy, we spent much time together. I liked to go to their room, for it was built for two and connected to a tiny bathroom. It was warm and private, and we could talk until late at night without anyone demanding that we turn off the only light.

With the passage of each day, both boys paid more and more attention to me. Soon I realized that they were developing a crush on me. Bubu was nearly my age, shrewd and humorous, with a pleasant personality, but not physically attractive. Yuku was very handsome and impressive, a "lady killer", a leader in any environment, but he was conceited and not too scrupulous. In any case, I was not interested in boys. My heart belonged to Bandi, whom I still hoped would someday join me. Within a few weeks the situation became a problem. Both boys asked me to go steady, but what was the worst, they did it in front of each other. I knew that if I would reveal my feelings and deny both, I would lose the comfort of their room; yet if I chose either, the three of us could no longer be buddies. In any case, I had the most to lose. Shrewdly, I resolved my predicament by saying how much I liked them both, how hard it was to choose, and asked for more time to get to know them better. As they agreed, I decided to spend less time with them and seek friendship with others.

One evening, while on an errand to Betars in another barrack, I found myself in a strange position. The group was all Polish, speaking no Hungarian or German. I tried desperately to communicate by drawing pictures and using pantomime, but to no avail. Finally a young man jumped off a top bunk and asked if I were Hungarian. He could not translate, but stared at me for a moment, then asked if my first name were Györgyi. When I answered in the affirmative, he proceeded to ask some very personal questions, revealing that he knew my parents and father's relatives. Shivers ran down my spine as he identified himself as the ex-fiance of a deceased second cousin of mine!

Bandi Klein was eight years my senior, of average intelligence, by no means good looking, but not unpleasant. Although I did not recognize him, the mere fact that he knew me and my family made me feel toward him as though he were a long-lost brother. Needless to say, we saw each other daily from then on.

I also became friends with one of my roommates. Lenke was ten years my senior, and my complete opposite in most respects. She was calm, soft-spoken, timid and withdrawn, neither pretty nor agile. We complemented each other in those respects, and matched each other in intelligence and wit. She was also from Budapest, a child of a well-to-do and refined family. She was the only one with whom I could carry on an intellectual conversation, or discuss a variety of topics commonly referred to as woman-talk.

As the weather got warmer and the days longer, the camp came alive. I often dragged Lenke out of her cubbyhole to visit Bandi and others in nearby barracks, and rode the truck with Yuku and Bubu to meet with Betars in other camps.

Once I mustered enough courage to travel by train to Dachau, to see the remains of the old concentration camp and crematorium. I cried all the way back, thinking of the horrors my boyfriend Bandi had described, and of the tortures Uncle Lacó must have endured. As I sobbed silently, almost in rhythm with the monotonous chugging of the train and snoring of people around me, long repressed painful memories surfaced and filled my mind. I did not want to remember the past — it was so painful and futile — but this time I could not "tune it out" by constantly talking, or engaging in some useless activity just to keep busy. I even failed to force myself to go to sleep instantly. The best I could do was redirect my thoughts. What was my present state and outlook for the future?

I had lived by now for months in filthy refugee camps, hardly better than stables. The meals were only barely edible. My total worldly possessions were merely enough to protect myself from the elements. "Love", "share", "charity", had become empty phrases, for man's primal drive was self-survival, and we all needed so much and had nothing to give.

I tried to console myself by thinking it was only a temporary state, but I did not know the span of "temporary". Three months now in various camps, and I had not even heard of anyone who had left! . . . And when I would leave the continent, would I reach Eretz Israel alive? Or would the British sink our ship miles away from the shore, as we knew had happened to many aliyots carrying non-quota immigrants? . . . And if I did land in Palestine, could the Irgund and Betars smuggle us inland before the British soldiers gunned us down as illegal aliens? . . . And if by some miracle I would still be alive, then where? With what kind of people? Do what? Would I ever be able to go to college, become a professional, settle in a city and live a normal life? Would I ever see Bandi again, or meet someone else to love and be loved by? . . .

The train stopped and we got off. A few miles' walk across the fields and bumpy roads, through the barbed-wire fence, along the rows of barracks housing nearly 10,000 bodies resembling human beings, stop at the nauseating latrine, into my wooden structure stinking from the foul odor of filthy bodies, replace the outer clothing with the dirty but warm robe on tiptoes in the dark, up to the bunk, down on the straw sack, and off to the most joyous part of our existence — sleep!

CHAPTER 30: GOOD-BYE TO ZIONISM

By the end of March we had enough recruits to hold daily educational meetings. Young girls and boys came from other barracks to learn Hebrew, Jewish history, Zionist philosophy and Betar principles. We began to hold Friday night services also, followed by singing Palestinian folk songs and dancing the "hora". As our membership grew we acquired the entire barrack, and fixed up a section as our study and recreation room.

As I spent more and more time with the Zionists, Lenke and Bandi, who both hoped to immigrate to the U.S.A., drew closer to each other. Although Bandi flirted with everyone in skirts, he did like Lenke's intellect, patience, and compassionate mothering nature, and she needed a companion and the strength of a male. I praised each to the other, fostering their friendship, and was happy to see them almost daily in each other's company.

Although my situation was improving gradually, the rate was far too slow. I was desperately searching for a change. One evening early in April, Yuku came with news. He called me, Bubu, and two other boys to his room and told us that there was a well-functioning kibbutz in Dorfen, near the town of Mühldorf, whose members were working on a ranch and occupying the elegant home of a wealthy ex-Nazi, and had room for more Betars. He had found this out in Munich, in the Zionist central office, where he also heard that well organized groups such as that would be the first ones to emigrate. We needed to hear no more! All five of us were more than ready to go. Three days later I said a temporary "so-long" to Lenke and Bandi, good-bye to the rest of my acquaintances, stuffed my worldly possessions in my backpack and mounted the waiting truck.

During the long ride I got to know and like the other two boys. Pisti was tall, blond, rather good-looking, soft-spoken and intelligent, a bit shy but very pleasant. He was born in Debrecen, a city in the southeast part of Hungary, sixteen years before. Chehski was nearly nineteen, from Munkács, with a baby face, a quick wit, agile and fiery like me. He was not well educated, but had nimble fingers and was mechanically inclined. We were all so different, yet quite congenial.

Our mouths fell open when the truck pulled into the yard and we laid eyes upon the ranch-house. The glittering white structure was surrounded by an enormous garden of fruit trees with flowers in bloom, a paved patio connected by a serpentine path through the orchard to the gazebo, next to the huge, rectangular swimming pool. Our jaws dropped as we debarked and entered the house. The walls and floors of the hall, dining area and recreation room were made of marble, and the kitchen and bathrooms were completely lined with tiles. The four boys got their own room downstairs. Mine was upstairs, overlooking the pool, with built-in wall units and brass beds. The dressing-room walls were made of mirror, and my attached bathroom had even a marble sunken tub. I had never seen such elegance.

When bathed and settled, we were ready to meet the others at the dinner table. Our joy of the luxury turned to exuberance as we delighted in every morsel of the cuisine.

Homemade bread and butter, rack of lamb with wine and brandy sauce, freshly picked creamed vegetables, nutcake, strudel, and every imaginable fruit.

The people seemed nice, also. Healthy-looking and robust, ranging in age from thirty to fifty or so. But the letdown came when the thirty-seven at the table began to talk in Polish. As they saw that Pisti and I did not understand a word, the tongue was switched to Yiddish. It helped him a little, but not me. I understood only scattered words, those which were similar to my not-very-fluent German. I got depressed even more when I found communication with my roommates and leader almost impossible.

The next day I was assigned to help out at the stables. Among four middle-aged Poles, not knowing a rake from a shovel, I felt helpless and stupid. At the end of the day's work I cried on Pisti's shoulders, for he, too, seemed ill at ease. The second day I was sent to the cabbage and potato patches. There I felt equally useless and unwanted. The third day to the cornfields and then to the grapevines, then to the sheep and pigs, then to the chicken coop, back to the house for gardening — each day worse than the one before.

Meanwhile Yuku became the assistant leader, Bubu was put in charge of the horses, and Chehski the assistant cook. Like me, Pisti had made the rounds, ending up as a gardener.

Finally I found my place also. The members decided to have uniforms, but no one knew how to design and sew. Having always been handy with needles and yarn, I quickly sketched some attractive designs and passed them around the dinner table. Within minutes the discussion centered around which style to choose, leaving no doubt as to who would make them. Yuku traded some food for bolts of homespun wool and linen, a lamb for an old sewing machine, and chickens for notions and tools. I was in business. With Pisti's and

Chehski's help, I dyed the wool navy blue and the linen light blue, cut apart some old clothes to make a master pattern, and spent the following weeks as a designer-dressmaker.

Meanwhile we had a visit from our UNRRA* supervisors. The two American ladies were highly educated and intelligent, but except for their knowledge of a few phrases in French, they could converse only in English and German. Neither of them spoke a word of Polish or Yiddish. To my surprise and to their dismay, no one in the kibbutz except me spoke either of their tongues. Thus I became a double asset: dressmaker and, with Pisti's occasional assistance, official interpreter.

Early in May Mrs. Sager visited us again. After the official inquiries with respect to the health and welfare of the residents, we had a pleasant little talk. She wanted to know about my background, the fate of my family, my emotions and my future plans. She empathized with my desire to help build a Jewish country, but forewarned me that in Palestine I could only become a farmer or a soldier, the state having an abundance of college students and professionals. I filed away her comment without response and asked about her family and life.

---

* In 1945 the United Nations Relief and Rehabilitation Administration, UNRRA, was formed to assist the Allies' military authorities with the repatriation of deportees in labor and concentration camps. Although by the end of 1945 some seven million prisoners and slave workers had been repatriated, the welfare and relocation of the several millions who refused to return, and those who escaped to the free West from their Russian-occupied homelands, became an overwhelming problem to the UNRRA. As time went on, the flood of immigrants from the eastern communist countries swelled to such proportion that in June of 1946 the British, and in April of 1947 the Americans, denied further entrance to Displaced Persons' camps in their zones.

She said she was in her mid-twenties, a degreed social worker, childless but married to a prominent doctor in Long Island, New York. She spoke about the schools, the life, the opportunities in America, closing with an open invitation to visit her one day. I felt complimented and honored, but gave no second thought to our conversation until many weeks later.

During the month of May there was a strange electricity in the air. Kibbutz members began to gather in small groups and whisper, frequenting singly the rosh's office, and studying Hebrew every chance they had. We even had a Polish Betar move in and give us rifle training. We did not know, just felt, that our departure was nearing. I tried to find out what was happening from Yuku, but since he once tried to get fresh with me and I had slapped his face, he had found a Polish girlfriend and kept his distance from me. He claimed he knew nothing, even when Bubu approached him for information. But as time went on, it became obvious that at least some of us would soon leave for the Promised Land.

One morning the rosh said that several members would have to go to Munich, and asked Pisti and me to take their place for the day in the fields. We did not suspect anything, but when we returned, we found Yuku, his girlfriend and three other boys and all their belongings gone. The leader said they would return, but they never did.

Bubu, meanwhile, accepted my refusal to be his girlfriend and turned into my best buddy. He, Pisti, Chehski and I spent a lot of pleasant times swimming, riding, playing chess, or just exchanging opinions. Although I was learning Hebrew and Yiddish, conversing with the others was still difficult. But my friends stood beside me, and I did not feel too lonely.

A few weeks after Yuku had disappeared, the rosh came with a request similar to the one before: we were short-handed, some members did not feel well, and the vegetables were getting overripe. Would all four of us help out in the fields? This time we were not so eager, but gave him the benefit of the doubt. Sure enough, when we returned at the end of the day, we found four other members gone!

We tried to find and figure out what was happening, but without success. We had no access to a telephone, nor permission to travel; the leader even held our I.D.'s, without which we could not even go to the nearby town. We had written to the Zionist headquarters, but never received a reply. Bubu and I asked the rosh one Sunday to let us go to Mühldorf, only a few miles away, but he outright refused. My request to visit Lenke and Bandi, who by now were married and expecting a child, was also denied.

Some light upon the mystery was shed by Mrs. Sager's third visit in June. When I told her about the strange events, she replied that ships carrying Zionists had secretly left the shores of Greece; one even departed from the Frankfurt harbor. But according to the newspapers, one sank near Palestine, and although others reached the shores, the illegal entrants were captured by the British on the beaches.

As to why our leader treated the four of us as he did, the UNRRA lady had no comment. Watching my face, she could tell the news had upset me greatly. Putting her arm around my shoulders and hugging me affectionately, she made me a proposition: if I wished, she would try to help me immigrate to America. Mass emigration from Europe had not yet begun, but processing had started in isolated cases, where the refugees had close relatives in the U.S. Further, there was a proposal in Congress to sponsor 500 European orphans, waiting for U.S. visas in D.P. camps since 1945. – Wow! My head began to swim! – Since I obviously was in no condition to make a quick decision, Mrs. Sager wrote down her local address and told me to contact her if I decided to leave the

Zionists.

The following week Bubu pulled a fast one. He played very sick and demanded to be sent to a Munich hospital for tests and X-rays. At first he was denied, but finally he received his I.D.'s and was allowed to go. Wherever else, he also went to the Betar headquarters and returned with enlightening news.

Aliyah had indeed begun! Three hundred children had received British permits and were already in Palestine. Several smaller transports had also reached the shores, and with Irgund and Betar help, were taken safely inland. However, the process was very costly and dangerous, consequently slow.

Before leaving the offices he ran into an old friend. The man was surprised to see him because, he said, according to the records, Yuku and his four assistants from Pocking — that was the five of *us* — had been scheduled to leave on the same transport.

Oh, how unfair and underhanded, to send us to the fields so we would miss our transport! And to lie about it, twice! The news made us become disgusted with the leader, as a matter of fact, with the whole group.

Toward the end of June our kibbutz was filled with excitement. A Zionist convention was to take place in Fahrenwald, and each group was to send representatives. Whom would the rosh select to go?

I worked feverishly to complete the uniforms. Navy blue pants or skirts, white shorts and light-blue linen shirts or blouses, and Scottish caps were to be made for everyone. Shield-shaped insignias, uniquely representing our group, painted on white cloth, were to be attached to each shirt, blouse and cap. I even sewed and painted little flags and big banners. I barely finished everything the night before the rosh told me that I, too, was to go.

The trip was delightful, especially since my three buddies also came along. Two days later, upon our return, Chehski's roommate ran ahead of the others to greet us and exclaimed excitedly, "Where in the world have you been? You missed your transport again! The name of each of you was called by the driver of the truck. The rosh was searching for you feverishly!"

Oh, what a farce. He was the one who personally sent each of us away! That was the last straw.

We gathered in the garden after everyone was asleep and decided to run away. When I recalled Mrs. Sager's offer, the boys began to beg me to take them along. I agreed. We tiptoed back into the house, packed everything we owned in silence, and at nearly midnight we parted from the Zionists forever.

CHAPTER 31: A LOVELY AMERICAN LADY

The moon and stars were shining bright, the cool summer night's breeze whispered in our ears, and the air was filled with the aroma of freshly cut hay as we walked for miles and miles along the winding country road in silence. Once in Mühldorf, we tiptoed through alleyways like thieves, frightened to be picked up by a patrol for walking the streets at night, for being runaways, and especially without identification. By the time we zigzagged through the sleeping town, our energy was drained. Finally, next to the train station we spotted a shack with a window lit dimly, displaying a sign: "Gasthaus."

Our fear superseded by our exhaustion, we entered and asked for two rooms. The old man said there was only one empty room, with one huge clean bed. Since the rate was cheap and he didn't ask for I.D.'s, we promptly found the room suitable, locked ourselves in and, clothes and all, dropped off to sleep. At sunrise, while most in the town were still slumbering, we were again on our way.

It was about noon when we arrived in Dorfen, at the residence of Mrs. Sager. She and her friends were not at home, but when I told my name, the housekeeper let us in. She said Mrs. Sager was expecting me and that I was to be treated like a guest if and when I arrived. She drew a bath for us, served us lunch, then asked us to wait in the study.

Before sundown Mrs. Sager and her three co-workers arrived. Oh, was she surprised to see all four of us! With hands and feet and in two languages I told her our story, then began to plead for help for my friends. She was a beautiful lady, outside and within. "Of course I will help!" interrupted Mrs. Sager, as she gave me a big bear hug.

The next day she made some phone calls, provided us with a big brunch, packed us into her jeep and drove for about forty miles to and around the scenic Chiemsee, and finally to the Strand Hotel in Prien.

Oh, was that area beautiful! A small resort town hugging a silvery lake, in a valley, surrounded by the high-rising Tyrolean Alps. We could see a shining castle on an island isolated in the middle of the lake. The white sand sparkled like diamonds in the sunshine, the sailboat rocked gently at the end of the pier, while laughing youngsters in bathing suits ran in and out of the hotel. Inside, the place was immaculate. Huge and neatly furnished dining, living and recreation rooms downstairs, and a row of little all-white rooms with sinks, dressers and beds, under the slanting roof upstairs. The grown-ups were mild-mannered French, English and American administrators, the residents mostly youngsters in their teens. After introducing us to the two young men and lady in their

236

twenties, who were to be our counselors and interpreters, Mrs. Sager left us smiling in our new home.

Life was quite pleasant while staying at the Strand Hotel. We participated in various sports, went sailing, bathing, on nature walks, into the town of Prien, or to the Schloss Herrenchiemsee, the island castle. After supper we often gathered around the fireplace, played the piano or records and danced, or played various games.

Yet, although we enjoyed life at the resort, we felt mental anguish, not knowing how long this "vacation" was to last or what the future held for us. Although we were all waiting for passage to America, most of the others were better off than I, for they had relatives or at least close friends on the distant continent. If the bill in the U.S. Congress failed, I had no one to sponsor me and thus would never reach the "land of milk and honey." But I suppressed the thought; it was too soon to worry. I had just begun a well-deserved vacation.

By early August Bubu found Germans in Prien to trade with. He could get any service or skilled craft work, plus a variety of objects and notions for real coffee, tea, sardines, chocolates and cigarettes, items we received monthly in our UNRRA packages. If only for the fun of it, everyone began to trade. Some traded for paintings and portraits; some for cheap metal and plastic jewelry; others for homespun linen and yarn; the boys mainly for clothes to be altered. For me Bubu got part of a nylon parachute, from which a dressmaker made underwear and blouses, plus a new piece of washable and reversible canvas enough for a bicolored dress, and an M.P.'s uniform, which became an elegant suit. We all did business with the same tailor and his wife, not only because they were the best in town, but because we could communicate with them in English. They were polite and humble, for they were growing rich retrading the items we paid with.

237

But one day the wife made a mistake. She cut my dress incorrectly. Not intending to be the loser, I demanded cigarettes to replace the material. This made both of them furious. Not knowing I spoke their tongue, they began to curse me in German, calling me a filthy Jew-pig, wishing that all the Jews had been tortured to death in the camps or burnt in crematoria. (Those sweet, naive people, who claimed years later that they knew nothing about Nazi atrocities!) Their blunder was grave, for we reported them at once. The next day they were arrested, when the police went to their house to investigate our charges and found a stockpile of stolen goods in their home.

After the abrupt ending of Bubu's flourishing enterprise, everything returned to normal at the Strand Hotel. But unfortunately not for long.

About mid-August Mrs. Sager came to see us, bringing both good and bad news. The U.S. Congress had passed the bill to sponsor 500 specially selected children. They were to be wards of the government, completely financed and taken care of by state and charitable agencies, until they became twenty-one. To be qualified for consideration, these children were required to be: refugees from Iron Curtain countries; residents of Austrian or German D.P. camps since 1945; in good physical health; totally orphaned; and under sixteen years of age.

My three buddies could barely withhold their tears as Mrs. Sager enumerated the necessary qualifications. First the joy, and then the letdown. They were too old. Only I met all the requirements, but even I only until August 30, my sixteenth birthday. She had to turn every stone to get me processed within two weeks. Even though Mrs. Sager tried to hide her concern, her expression and the tears in her eyes at our departure revealed that she thought even my chance was almost nil.

Although since the end of the war my faith in God had been progressively diminishing, like a drowning man I again cried out to the Lord. "Heavenly Father, what will become of me now? Shall I go back to Hungary, to be reminded constantly of the horrors of the past, to live in constant fear of a cruel and oppressive government? Shall I rejoin the Zionists, to chance drowning in the ocean or dying as a soldier, or at best being a farmer, perhaps for the rest of my life? Shall I try to settle in Germany, a country that has caused all my suffering and whose people still despise the Jews? . . . Is there a place on earth where I am welcome? Where I can learn and work in peace, become an asset to society? I feel so helpless, lonely and rejected! Lord, I have no one but You. I am your child. Please accept me, love me, guide me, help and watch over me!"

As if the Lord had heard every word I said, as He had always stood beside me when I turned to Him in real need, three days before my birthday I was contacted by the CIA. The questioning took hours; I had to relive every detail of my past sixteen years. I knew not what the ordeal was for, nor how it affected my future, until the morning of my birthday.

I was out sailing when Pisti came running to the edge of the pier, motioning us to return at once. My escort pulled firmly on the strings of the sails, and we glided along the mirror-like surface of the crystal-clear water like low-flying seagulls. The gentle summer breeze carried my friend's voice as he yelled excitedly, "There is a long distance call for you!"

My heart thumped feverishly fast as I flew across the sandy beach, through the porch and den, to the office phone. In instant response to my "Hello" a chime-like voice announced, "Alles in ordnung, my dear Mirjam! We will celebrate your next birthday in New York!" Oh, that angel Mrs. Sager! (She had always called me by my middle name, Mirjam, for she could not pronounce Györgyi.) She had just found out that I was cleared by the CIA, the first step toward America!

Each day that followed seemed an eternity. I could no longer enjoy the lazy leisure; I wanted to fly to my new home and begin living again. Thoughts were chasing each other, images of my future self appearing in rapid succession, my body nearly bursting from the surge of excess energy. I had to find an outlet, something to occupy body and mind.

Lying awake one night, I had a vision. I was standing in the center of a large room, surrounded by people leaning over fast-clicking sewing machines, turning out exquisite garments. In the next room stood our handyman, Mr. Silber, surrounded by a variety of machine parts, teaching a class.

As an omen to help myself and others, my vision re-emerged with crystal clarity when I awakened the next morning. Not even waiting for breakfast, I charged into our administrative office and laid out my plan to the UNRRA lady. Considering that we were a large group of unproductive people, shabbily dressed in badly-fitting old handouts, bored from having nothing to do, I proposed to provide learning or useful and creative opportunities for them. At very little cost we could set up a wood or machine shop. Mr. Silber, a Rumanian refugee, a machinist by trade, who had been fixing every malfunctioning device on the premises, could surely teach a class. Participants would be occupied and stimulated, learn something useful, and help out with maintenance.

I also proposed a dressmaking shop. If no one else were available, I could teach how to cut, fit and sew a garment, but best of all, how to properly alter the clothes we had. All we needed was one sewing machine, easy to requisition or buy with cigarettes from the townsfolk. Before I had a chance to continue, the UNRRA lady exclaimed, "So it shall be!"

By mid-October I knew how each part of an automobile

functioned, how to locate and initiate repairs in sewing machines and appliances, even to fix lamps and radios. Each afternoon I spent hours in our sewing room, teaching, fitting, altering, or just repairing anyone's clothes.

One at a time, by November most of my friends had left. Some immigrated to other continents, and those who had no relatives abroad were transferred to various D.P. camps. They wrote me once or twice, but moved around so much that my replies never reached them. The only ones I could keep in touch with regularly were the Kleins. Having no benefactors, and Lenke being heavy with child, they were hopelessly stuck in Pocking. I would have visited them, but it meant hitchhiking nearly fifty miles to the nearest train station, which I was hesitant to do alone. Besides, I was afraid to leave Prien, in case the CIA or consulate wanted me.

My first friend to leave for the U.S. was Mrs. Sager. Overseas assignment completed, she was returning home. Reaffirming that my voyage was delayed only by the amount of paperwork involved, she repeated her invitation and said, "So long, for a while." I sobbed after she left, for that lady meant very much to me. She was the one who opened my eyes to the possibility of reaching my dreams and goals; the one who helped me cut the umbilical cord, to break away from the security of the Zionists; the only grown-up who had advised and helped me; finally, the only tie between the past, present and future.

Things began to move soon after Mrs. Sager's last visit. In early December the UNRRA jeep came to take two of us to the Funk Kaserne in Munich, a second stop collection center for near-future emigrants. Words could not describe the joy we felt! But a dark shadow descended upon us as soon as the jeep passed through the fences and gate.

The Funk Kaserne was originally a fortlike army camp, with huge, two-story stone structures, capable of housing over 10,000 people. Filthy and shabbily dressed refugees were rushing to and from buildings, some cursing and some crying, shivering as they splashed through the ankle-deep muddy slush. Guarded by M.P.'s and soldiers of different nationalities was the large edifice housing the administrative offices.

Here our driver turned us over to a D.P. interpreter, who helped us fill out a stack of official forms and secured for us various I.D.'s, tickets, passes, and the typical new-arrivals' package. Then he led us to a building nearly a mile away, up and down its dark, filthy stairs and corridors, and finally into a huge room. Here he handed us the "rules pamphlet" written in four languages, then left us to fend for ourselves.

Hella, a Hungarian girl of my age I had befriended in Prien, and I stood in the doorway, in tears, wanting only to escape. The room was filled with the typical two-level bunks with straw pillows and mattresses covered with greasy and smelly army blankets, one potbelly stove, and sixty females of all ages. A woman changing the diaper of a screaming infant yelled out to us in Yiddish, pointing to an empty bunk near the door. We had hardly lowered our backpacks when the shrill of sirens stirred up the beehive and, like stampeding animals, everyone at once tried to go through the door. Hella and I grabbed hands and followed the crowd.

Down the stairs, through the slush, around buildings,

across the yard, we finally reached the chow line. After we smelled and laid eyes on the horrible pig feed, we were convinced that it was not worth standing in line for nearly an hour in the dark, damp, bitterly cold winter night.

Once back, we went exploring. While the first floor of our building had several rooms just like ours, all housing men, the second floor was identical but habited by women. At the end of the long corridor was a huge enclosed cavity, equipped with a wall-to-wall basin below twenty faucets on one side, and doorless showers and toilettes on the other. The toilettes stunk, the showers were frozen, some of the faucets broken off — we had never seen a washroom quite that revolting.

Back in our room the people were getting ready for bed. For most that involved merely removing overcoats and shoes; for the rest, also replacing the outer garment with a filthy but warm robe. Only a very few compulsives took their turn heating a quart of water in a metal bowl on top of the stove, then sponging their bodies, part by part, behind a stretched-out blanket. About 9:00 p.m. the loosely hanging bulb in the center of the room was shut off and, except for the few who read with their flashlights, all went to sleep.

The next morning Hella and I woke up itching like crazy. Oh, we knew the cause well! Even the treatment! After brushing our teeth — the washroom was too cold and crowded for more extensive cleansing — and after the so-called food that was, in every respect, a replica of that served the previous night, we went to the infirmary for petroleum. The male nurse laughed at us and said in Yiddish, "You must be new! No one else bothers with such triviality. You can't keep yourselves free of lice around here!"

We did get and apply the petroleum, but just that one time. Three days later we were infested again.

During the day we had a chance to get acquainted with our roommates. Most were Polish, some Czech, some Rumanian, several Yugoslav, and only three Hungarian. Their ages ranged from two months to forty-five years, among them several mothers with their infants. Some had husbands in a downstairs room, but most were adults and alone. There were only three other teen-agers, just one of them Hungarian. Except for Hella and me, they all had relatives somewhere, to whom they were going. As for how long, some had been waiting there for months, others merely weeks.

A Hungarian girl became our primary source of information. She taught us how to succeed in Funk. "Lesson 1: check the administration building's bulletin board the first thing every morning. The alphabetical listing will reveal if you are scheduled for a hearing, exam or transport that day. Lesson 2: save your UNRRA packages; food and cigarettes are tradable for anything among the Germans. Lesson 3: get a pass and go to town periodically. It saves your sanity to get away from this hell at least occasionally. Lesson 4: if you want to travel to see friends, do it on week-ends when the offices are closed. Your name may appear only hours before your transport would leave for the harbor. Lesson 5: never volunteer information. When asked, say as little as you must; one wrong word can get you rejected. Lesson 6: never leave your possessions unwatched; people around here will steal anything."

Over a week had passed before Hella and I first saw our names on the bulletin board. We were scheduled for a physical. It took the whole day of standing in lines to get blood, tuberculosis and venereal disease tests, and to be seen by the doctor. The assembly-line exam was superficial, the doctors looking mainly for chronic and infectious diseases. The T.B. patch barely healed when we were scheduled for another physical, the exact replica of the first. Why? No one knew, nor did they care.

As Christmas was approaching and administrators began

to leave, I decided to visit my friends in Pocking. It was a long and tiring train ride, but worth it to get away from Funk. The Kleins were thrilled to see me, and I them, especially since Lenke had just delivered my prematurely born but healthy godson. They were all relatively well, in spite of the fact that conditions had not improved since I had left. The only change was the location of their living quarters: a smaller room shared by six couples. Somewhat rejuvenated, I returned to Funk right after the holidays.

The next few weeks were simply unbearable. It was an extremely cold winter. We could not secure enough wood to keep the fire going for more than a few hours a day, and even then the tiny stove's heat was negligible. We perched on our beds like sparrows in the snow, huddled around the stove or paced the floor, embracing ourselves with our arms, and wearing our kerchiefs and coats day and night. Often we did not even get out of bed, going hungry rather than standing in line for the inedible daily pig feed. The final blow came with the freezing of the water, causing the cracking of the sewer lines.

Meanwhile, most of us became infected with highly contagious scabies. We nearly went insane scratching not only our lice-infested heads and trunks, but the tender skin between our frostbitten, readily bleeding, scab-covered toes and fingers! Scabies was worse than lice, because the microscopic bugs survived for days without a host, on any object including doorknobs, and, since they burrowed themselves under the skin, they were hard to get rid of. Further, scabies delayed us from transport. Therefore, no one reported to the infirmary for treatment, not even if they had additional more serious and contagious diseases. Thus, various epidemics kept raging, without cure or control.

We pulled all sorts of tricks — like paying off the nurses, taking each other's place, faking fainting, etc. — while undergoing frequent compulsory tests and physicals, each the exact replica of the first we had. The local German druggists made a fortune treating us with herbal remedies and salves for chocolates and cigarettes.

A ray of sunshine entered my life when near the end of January I was scheduled for my final visit to the consulate. Worry kept me awake all night, since I knew that the selection of 500 from the tens of thousands of qualified children depended on the consul. My hands and body trembled as I entered the elegant office. The official motioned me to sit down. After scrutinizing my dossier, he asked some superficial questions. Seemingly pleased that we could communicate without an interpreter, he engaged me in light conversation for nearly an hour. Tears of joy flooded my eyes when he finally arose and asserted, "I am happy to grant your visa, my child. You will be an asset to your new country!"

My body went limp and a sigh of relief passed my lips as I exited the room. Still a little worried, before leaving the consulate, I asked one of the administrators two vital questions. First, could the consul have overlooked the fact that I had passed my sixteenth birthday five months before, and second, how much longer had I to wait for a voyage? The answer to the first was that since the CIA began the processing in time, my extra age was no deterrent. To my second question the clerk could not give an answer. Considering the tens of thousands of people already approved to go to their relatives in the U.S., he said it might take months before my turn.

Happy and sad, I returned to Funk. Hella greeted me with a letter in her hand. It was for me, from Mr. Silber and his wife. They wrote that they had left Prien, but the new D.P. camp was not too bad; the food was tolerable, the barracks and grounds were cleaner than in the other camps, and they had a private room. They begged me to come for a visit.

The timing of the letter was perfect. By then I had been walking around for weeks with a high fever, chest pains, cough and sore throat, bronchitis and pneumonia, plus who knows what else. A few more months under the abhorrent conditions in the Funk Kaserne would surely have put me in the grave! Therefore, it was not hard to decide to take the Silbers up on their invitation. Two days later I was in Pürten.

Not only was the camp in general a significant improvement over Funk, but via my friends' influence, I too became a privileged D.P. Since Mr. Silber worked as a member of the repair crew and the Mrs. in the kitchen, they had no trouble getting me a job, in the laundry. This meant an additional UNRRA package monthly, the contents of which we could trade for anything. But first, replacing my lice-infested clothes, taking large doses of penicillin and other medications for my various ailments, staying in bed in a clean and warm room, and being taken care of by friends, in ten days I felt well enough to work. Life again became tolerable.

One day, to my great joy, on my way home from the laundry I encountered several old acquaintances, girls and boys I had known in the Salzburg Betar kibbutz. They said they had been wandering from camp to camp, pursuing the same existence as in our first stop in Germany, still waiting to aliyah to Palestine. To continue bringing each other up to date, I promised to visit them the next evening.

From then on we frequently got together, knitting and sewing amidst pleasant company. As the weather got a little warmer, during the week-ends I often traveled: once to Salzburg, once to Prien, to Ainring, and to visit the Kleins in Pocking; stopping each time, of course, in Munich, to find out the progress of my emigration. So did I spend the month of February.

My first trip in March, however, ended in tears. I found out in the Funk Kaserne that I had been scheduled for the transport that had left only the day before. When was the next one? Nobody knew. Afraid of missing my chance to go to America, I returned to Pürten only for my belongings and to say good-bye to my friends. Then I moved back to my old place in the Funk.

After a mere two weeks of misery my name was finally on the bulletin board again. Several hundreds of us were leaving the next day for the coastal city of Bremerhaven. Trucks took us to the railroad station, where we were packed into — lo and behold — cattle cars! We sat and slept on the straw-covered floor all day and night, until we arrived at our destination on the following morning.

Our new accommodations were equivalent to those in the Funk. The crowded quarters, the filth and the mush called food, were hardly better than during the war. Only the knowledge that groups were boarding ships daily, leaving for various parts of the world, made our stay bearable.

Several days later, members of our transport began to be scheduled for physical examination. To our horror, more and more people came back rejected, due to newly acquired hepatitis, bronchitis, tuberculosis, viral pneumonia, pleurisy, scarlet fever, and of course scabies and venereal diseases — all contracted in, and souvenirs of, the infamous Funk Kaserne!

Some of these poor souls were sent to the returning trains at once, losing their chance to emigrate, perhaps forever. Others were sent to a local hospital, some kept in the infirmary, while the less infectious were given medications and told to report back to the doctor weekly.

Hella and I at once traded everything of value we had to secure salves and antibiotics. By the time my turn came up, I felt physically great. Even the mild case of newly-acquired scabies revealed only a few healing scabs. But this time my reaction to the tuberculosis vaccine was not entirely negative.

As the nurse examined the small pocket of pus on my

arm at the third-day check, she wrinkled her forehead. "I better let the doctor see that. Follow me please," she asserted.

Tears blurred my eyes as I entered the office. "Doctor, please, I feel in perfect health. Injected with live virus the ninth time in about a year, it is a wonder that I do not have a more violent reaction!"

"Nine times! That is outrageous!" exclaimed the doctor with horror. Observing my tears, considering that my whole future might be altered by his decision, he reviewed my file, shook his head, and decided that if the X-rays turned out negative, he would not stand in my way.

Feeling helpless and desperate, I turned to God again. He heard me, for within two days my name was posted on the bulletin board. On the morning of April 12, 1947, I boarded the *Marine Perch*, and by nightfall of that memorable day I had left Bremerhaven, and the shores of the European continent behind.

CHAPTER 33: VOYAGE TO AMERICA

Aboard ship, single men were quartered in a huge compartment below decks, couples and families with children were lodged in cabins on the lower deck, while single females were assigned to the upper level. The rooms had double bunks, but soft mattresses covered with white linen, a dresser with a mirror and a sink in each room, and everything was immaculately clean. We even had a steward to call on in need. And the lunch! Food fit for a king, served graciously on crystal and china, like at home before the war, seemingly a lifetime ago.

After I washed all my clothes and soaked in a hot bath, I visited Hella in the neighboring room. Her cabin was like mine, but instead of just eight, her abode was shared by sixteen young girls. Having met all her roommates, my friend and I went exploring.

The deck was lined with benches and lounges, interspersed here and there with little white tables and chairs. We leaned against the railing, filling our lungs with the clean salty air, and watching the shimmering surface of the ocean reflect the golden rays of the setting sun. Seagulls were hovering above, and some were riding the gentle waves as our ship slowly left the shores fading in the distance. As the sun retired on the far horizon, we too descended to the level below.

At the far end of the corridor we found the ship's boutique. Our eyes could not believe the beautiful merchandise we saw. Clothes, shoes and jewelry, the likes of which we had never seen. We quickly converted our marks, which totaled $3.71 between the two of us. There was one item we both wanted and could afford: sunglasses. Each of us bought a pair, then returned to our rooms just in time to clean up for supper.

The evening meal consisted of several courses, each more scrumptious than the one before. But supper time was not uneventful. As the waiters were hustling about with huge trays of succulent racks of lamb, suddenly the lights went out, the ship jerked, and people and food went flying from table to chairs to ceiling to floor. The passengers screamed, cried, cursed and shoved each other while attempting to escape from the room. Their behavior reminded me of the people's reaction to the first bombing of Budapest.

Unlike the passengers, the crew took the situation in stride, having been used to turbulence along the English Channel. They quickly appeared with flashlights and lanterns, and calmly guided the forty women to their quarters. The floor was mopped and the tables were reset by the time we returned to finish the feast. I went to sleep that night happier than I had been at any time during the past year.

The steward awakened us the next morning, asking if we wished breakfast. The question seemed strange, but I replied politely, "Of course!" Looking out the porthole I saw the sun high above and sailors hustling about. Then I noticed the horrible smell which filled our cabin. Diving out of my bed to "escape" from the room speedily, I noticed that all my companions were preoccupied with throwing up. Grabbing my coat, I ran over to Hella's cabin. She and her roommates were in the same condition. By then I realized that the ocean was playing ping-pong with our ship, and no one else had dared to get out of bed. I grabbed my clothes, dressed quickly in the bathroom, and up to the deck I went. The sight was positively fascinating. The whole crew was near the stern, watching some sailors trying to throw overboard an actively wiggling baby whale. I later found out, in addition to the normally rough waters of the corridor between Great Britain and the mainland, we had also encountered a storm.

I arrived at the empty dining room and found the tables beautifully set. As I was ready to leave, thinking that it was far past the time for breakfast, the cheerful face of our little steward appeared in the serving window of the kitchen. "Guten morgan, Fraulein," said he in broken German. He was thrilled to hear me say "good morning" in English, from which moment he hung around me like an affectionate little puppy.

"What do you wish for brunch and later for dinner?" he asked, bringing an enormous menu.

"When do you serve food?" I asked, looking around the empty room.

"Any time you wish, young lady, since you are our only

customer. It looks like we served our last meal last night, at least for the next few days."

Oh, what a luxury it was to have the chef prepare whatever I wished, and to be served by five waiters simultaneously! Poor Hella and her friends could not even hold down the ice cream and cookies, being too weak and sick even to get out of bed.

Our little steward became my sole companion. When not busy, he and I sat up on deck, played ping pong or cards in the recreation room, and danced to the jukebox. Twice he even took me to the movie shown for the crew. He helped me learn English while I taught him conversational German.

Time flew by quickly until ten o'clock on the morning of April 21, 1947, when our steward came running, calling all of us topside. All the passengers were there by then, or on their way, squinting their eyes to see the shining object on the horizon. By the time I wriggled to the rail, there she stood, bigger than life, in all her glory, the personification of our dreams, Her Majesty, the Statue of Liberty!

Joy and fear, hope and concern filled my heart, as at five o'clock that night I set foot on the "land of the free," the United States of America.

BOOK
TWO

AUTHOR, 1947
IN THE LAND OF MILK AND HONEY.

PART I: THE NEW LIFE

CHAPTER 1: MY SECOND LOVE

The neon lights of the city were dancing like ballerinas in the shimmering glitter of the bright stars, in front of the velvety curtain of the royal blue moonlit sky. The glossy surface of the ocean reflected our mirror image like an echo, as we, clutching our backpacks filled with all of our worldly possessions, slowly descended the gangway onto the pier.

The refugees were separated into groups according to their destination, then loaded into huge buses. Hella, myself, and forty or so other youngsters about our age were taken to a dilapidated brick building on Caldwell Avenue in the Bronx, serving now as the refugee orphans' reception station.

Observing the scenery along the way, Hella and I clutched each other's hands tighter and tighter, communicating nonverbally our ever-increasing disappointment. The shabbily dressed people reminded us too much of war-torn Europe. Only the hope that we were observing the worst kept us from jumping off the bus and becoming stowaways on the first ship destined to go back to the old continent.

Our new accommodation did not cheer us up. The three-story building had a huge dining and living room plus kitchen downstairs, and on the next floor a dark and narrow corridor, from which doors opened to the bedrooms assigned to the boys. The floor above was similarly constructed, each bedroom housing four to eight girls. At the farthest corner of each floor was an enormous bathroom with several toilettes, sinks and shower stalls, while the front rooms facing the street were occupied by two housemothers and three young male counselors. Everywhere in the building the wallpaper was old, filthy and peeling, the ceilings were damaged by water

1

stains from the leaking room, and the furniture was ancient and broken down. The housemothers fitted perfectly into the surroundings.

During the first few days we were kept busy by being bussed to a nearby hospital, and subjected to a multitude of tests and physical examinations. It was not until nearly a week later that we began to be allowed to leave upon request, to visit acquaintances. I promptly called my beloved Mrs. Sager, and cried from joy when she came for Hella and me, to take us to her house for a day's visit. On the way she drove us around Long Island. At home she talked about the opportunities we could expect to have in the future. She served us a scrumptious dinner, including the famous American banana-split, ending the day by taking us to Times Square and then to a show at the Radio City Music Hall. That trip reversed our initial disappointments about the U.S.A.

Once through with the medical examinations and the shopping trip, when our social workers purchased one total outfit for each of us, life at the center settled down to its dull routine. We spent most of our time eating, cleaning, playing various games, learning English and conversing with each other. We got one dollar per week pocket money to spend for candy, notions and whatnot, or bus fare if we went visiting, and since that amount was very meager, we mostly stayed at home.

As time went on, the predominantly teen-aged residents of the center began to be distributed to various agencies, scattered around in the U.S. Hella and I wanted very much to stay in New York, and Mrs. Sager even found a foster family who was willing and able to give a home to both of us, but the central office did not listen to individual pleas, so on the third of June nine of us were sent to Boston, Massachusetts.

Our new social workers took us from the train station to the Jewish Family and Children's Service's main office, from where, after several hours of waiting, we were returned to the train station and taken straight to Camp Kingswood in Maine.

Oh, the camp was nice, and all the American children were thrilled to be able to spend even a few weeks there, but for us refugees it seemed like an undeserved punishment. We longed for a home, a permanent residence where we could begin establishing our new life! We tried to communicate our feelings to Mrs. Carter, the head of the agency, in many different ways. At first we only pleaded with her orally; next, several of us wrote a formal request; after that was still of no avail, Hella and I hitchhiked and walked until the sheriff picked us up as runaways. One of the boys went as far as stealing a rifle somewhere, and threatened to shoot anyone who forced him to stay. But we were returned, the boy disarmed, and we were given no choice but to stay until the end of the summer.

On August 28 we were returned to Boston, and each of us was taken directly to our respective foster homes. I was placed with the Peters, a poor but warm-hearted Jewish family, residing in a three-bedroom apartment in Roxbury. They wanted me primarily as a companion for Reva, their sixteen-year-old only child. The Peters gave me their nicest room and catered to my every wish, that is, when I could express it. They spoke only English, my knowledge of which was what I had learned during my childhood — oh, ever so long ago! — and thus still rather limited. The previous five months had provided little practice, since refugees had come from various countries and spoke either our mother tongue or German among ourselves. But from now on I had to speak English, and learn it well and very fast, not only to communicate with the Peters and everyone else I came in contact with, but also since two weeks later I began attending Roxbury Memorial High School.

Based upon my scholastic background and a comprehensive examination, even though I had attended school for only three months during each of the past two school years, I was placed in the eleventh grade. My class schedule consisted of English literature, algebra, Latin, physics, and U. S. history. The middle three subjects gave me no trouble, especially since we had covered their contents in Hungary during the seventh and eighth grades, but

3

English was extremely difficult and history was simply impossible. (I had to look up twenty-three words of the first paragraph of the fifty-seven-page-long homework assigned on the second day of school!) With great regret I soon traded history for a second English class, which emphasized language structure, composition and public speaking. Wanting desperately to go to college, which necessitated the maintenance of a high grade-point average, I studied nearly around the clock. Only on Sunday afternoons did I take a break, to get together with my old buddies.

Making new friends was very difficult. Not only due to lack of time and the handicap of expressing myself fluently in English, but teen-agers used their own jargon, which was totally foreign to me. Further, my system of values and sphere of interest differed greatly from those of my peers. My foster sister Reva, not being able to identify with me, soon gave up making any attempt to get me involved with her friends and activities, and my classmates considered me more of a curiosity and source of information about a distant world than a potential friend.

One day in early October Reva came home bursting to tell me the news. One of the boys had been watching me for weeks, she said, and was determined to meet me. But! Franky had the reputation of being a "wolf", and sister Reva felt it was her duty to warn me of that fact. She advised me to refuse the introduction. I, on the other hand, reacted with delight. First, it flattered my female ego; next, I was anxious to make new friends. But mostly, after she explained the meaning of "wolf", I looked forward to the challenge.

Next day Reva returned from school later than usual. And, instead of storming up the stairs, she yelled up that I should step out on the porch. My heart went pitter-patter when I saw the handsome young gentleman standing beside her on the sidewalk. As his eyes fell upon me, they became fixated. He kept staring at me, motionless, without uttering a word. Feeling ill at ease, I broke the silence by inviting him in.

Franky walked up the staircase still in a daze. Upon entering, he

4

clumsily shook my hand and introduced himself. To make him feel more comfortable, I struck up a conversation about school and asked him to help me with my English home lesson. He was most eager to assist, and promptly offered to help each future day. Thus started my second platonic love affair.

Franky visited me every evening, for he worked after school as a soda jerk in a local drugstore. His income was of the essence, since his mother's meager salary from the factory was not enough to provide for even the bare necessities. His parents were divorced before Franky was born, and, since his father never contacted his ex-wife, he never even knew about his son. Franky's mother was middle-aged, not very attractive nor well educated, an introvert, but blessed with infinite patience, compassion, and a heart of gold. I felt a genuine love for her at first sight, and knew the feeling was mutual. His only other relative, Aunt Jerry, was also a poor factory worker, but single, more vivacious, modern, the worldly type. We, too, liked each other, but it was only Mother I considered like family.

Though Franky was blessed with a high I.Q., he had been nearly failing in school. For lack of a balanced home life and parental supervision, lonely and in want of attention, he had become the leader of the school's troublemakers. I, the bookworm, mature and motherly due to my past experiences, viewed Franky as an uncut gem, needing shaping, refining and polishing. Without his awareness, I set out to remold my new admirer.

Time made our relationship grow deeper and more profound. Though the world saw Franky only as my teen-age boyfriend, to each other we meant a great deal more. He bragged about his conquest of a "lady" who was beautiful, fascinatingly different, a year and a half older and, on top of it, "brainy". But deep inside he valued more my compassion, wisdom, depth of affection and sincerity. He looked up to me in every respect; he kept me on a pedestal and treated me as a knight would a princess. I needed exactly that. Alone in a strange country, penniless, totally controlled by and dependent on the agency, I desperately needed the complete acceptance, admiration and devotion of someone.

Franky and I soon became inseparable. Right after school, while he was at work, I did my algebra and Latin homework, learning the English equivalents of what I had already learned in Hungary. I studied my physics and literature with Franky in the evening, seeing to it that he, too, did his daily assignments. While Franky worked long hours during weekends, I studied or visited with my European friends. Our recreation consisted of an occasional movie, a school dance, or shopping for necessary clothes.

But we were happy just to be in each other's company. Franky dropped all his old companions, his grades shot up to A's and B's, and my English improved to the point that, by the end of the second quarter, I made the honor roll.

The future seemed to look rosier until early spring. I had had little contact with Mr. Peters, or with Reva, whose scope of interest and choice of friends were quite diverse from mine, but my relationship with Mrs. Peters was very close and warm. Though she was not well educated or learned in the social graces, she did possess a lot of common sense and worldly wisdom. She genuinely liked me and treated me as if I were her own teen-age daughter. While these should have been the ideal qualities for a happy relationship, the latter backfired. I had been alone, responsible for myself and even others for too long to revert to behaving as a young adolescent. Life had made me prematurely an adult. I was ready for the role of a mother, not that of a child.

One day in March, 1948, my foster mother and I had a silly argument. Melting slush had covered the ground on the eve when Franky was taking me to a school dance, and I foolishly refused to wear overshoes. Our argument had become so emotionally loaded that the next day we both called my social worker, independently, to arbitrate a peace treaty. Little did we realize that the head of the agency had long been waiting for just such an event.

Mrs. Carter, though an accredited psychologist, was an ivory-tower scholar, a poor judge of character, incapable of empathizing with, or even understanding, the emotional world of her orphaned remnants of the Holocaust. She catered to the seemingly weak and shy ones to the point of spoiling them with worldly goods, while allowing the more aggressive ones only the bare necessities. I had a monthly allotment of $15 for clothes, disbursed to me only upon the approval of my social worker, plus $3 weekly to cover cleaning or shoe repair bills, cosmetics and notions, transportation and recreation. (An inexpensive coat cost me then $45, while a lunch at the school cafeteria was $.50.) For those of us who were not adopted or sent to college or private school, the agency paid $60 monthly to the foster family.

I returned from school as usual on that crucial day and, not realizing that Mrs. Peters had called the agency also, I waited patiently for my social worker, Mrs. E., to arrive. She did, but to my surprise, not as an arbitrator. Without discussion she told me to pack right away, for she had been instructed to take me at once to a nearby orphanage. At first I thought she was joking, but she reiterated the order of her boss. Then I began to plead, and finally to cry. But all to no avail.

While the flowing tears saturated my clothes on their way to the suitcase, Mrs. E. stepped out to talk to my foster mother. Mere minutes had passed by when she burst into my room, threw her arms tightly around me, and with wet eyes and angry voice asserted that she would not let anyone take me away! Mrs. E. assured us that she too felt such action was not necessary, and promptly made a call to Mrs. Carter. All three of us alternately pleaded, cried and yelled, but the boss was unbendable. Without a chance to say good-bye to Mr. Peters, or even to Reva, I was off to the Bradshaw Street Orphanage.

My new home was a big old house, about a half-hour walk from my previous residence, shared at the time by a housemother and eight European children. Two of my old friends, Vera and David, were also staying there temporarily. Living in Bradshaw House

7

would have been almost pleasant, had it not been for the fact that "dear" Mrs. Carter forbade me to associate with Franky. My social worker brought me this news, as usual without an explanation, and simultaneously instructed our housemother that she was to bar Franky from entering the house.

Of course I pleaded and cried! But ours was not to reason why, ours was to do or . . . I did not know then what the alternatives were, only that the agency had the power to have us deported. — Back to Communist Hungary? Never! — A ward of a powerful government, penniless and friendless, in a strange country, only a sixteen-year-old-boy and his helpless mother to turn to, I had no choice but to obey.

While still attending the same school I saw Franky daily for a few brief minutes, but that was like putting salt on a fresh wound. We were by then everything to each other: buddies, tutors, advisors, siblings, and anticipated future mates. Our love was unselfish and pure, and though we both had healthy natural desires, my puritan upbringing said satisfaction of certain emotions must wait, so we never went beyond passionate kissing. To deprive us of each other's company, I felt was not just unfair, but outright cruel.

Even the beauty of budding trees and flowers, the glitter of butterflies and gay chirp of birds in the life-giving warmth of the fresh spring breeze did not relieve my deep depression. Finally, in early May Mrs. E. came to me with news. They had found a fabulous new foster home for me. I was to spend the coming weekend with the Shains.

AUTHOR.
BOSTON, 1948

FRANKY.
BOSTON, 1948

MY REFUGEE FRIENDS:
Hella, Vera, Edzia, Vera,
David, author, Laci
Boston, 1947.

AUTHOR. BOSTON, 1949.

CHAPTER 2: INTO SERVITUDE

The Shains were in their thirties, first generation Americans, and the Mrs. a descendent of well-to-do Russian Jews. Mr. was the assistant advertising manager of large supermarket chain. They had two children: Suzi, age five, and Marjorie, age ten. They lived in a three-bedroom, fairly new bilevel home, in a wealthy and beautiful area of Newton. Their home had a large garden and yard, and the house inside was furnished elegantly. My abode-to-be was a tiny corner room, a maid's room, downstairs. The Shains drove around to show me the highlights of the vicinity, and took me to meet some of their wealthy relatives and friends.

I did not take favorably to any phase of our first encounter. I could feel conceit, insincerity, and snobbery around me. Though they implied the opposite, I could feel their cold and calculated reason for wanting me: they needed a baby-sitting maid. Oh, I did plead not to be sent to the Shains; I even refused to pack, but of course to no avail. Next week I was relocated to Newton.

Although it was early May, my wish to finish the year in my old school was granted. I had to be in transit for nearly two hours each way, but at least I could manage to see Franky daily. Oh no, the bars had not been lifted; my undeserved sentence was not reduced.

As soon as the school year was over, Mrs. S., the children, and I moved into their summer home on Cape Cod. The house was in the woods, ten or so minutes walk from their beach. Only one other family lived close by, with children of Suzi's and Marjorie's age. They, too, brought along a teen-ager, referred to as ''mother's aid'', with whom, when time permitted, I could share my loneliness.

Free time for me was not abundant. The two brats woke me up at the crack of dawn, usually with their fighting. After breakfast: wash the dishes, clean the house, take the girls to the beach, run back for forgotten items, keep the kids entertained and out of fights, make and bring down sandwiches for lunch, cater to the children, help

9

prepare supper, wash dishes again, put the kids to bed, then finally collapse! If, after 9:00 p.m. I still had some energy, I could sit up and write or read, for nightly baby-sitting was part of my duties, and since I shared the children's room, reading in bed was tabu.

My big reward came on Sundays, when the neighbors' servant and I were driven to the nearby town, where we could walk around, sit in the ice cream parlor, or go to the movie; that is, if I had the money! For while the other girl got a weekly salary of $25, I had only the $3 the agency gave me . And most of that I saved, because the Kleins' baby had developed scurvy from malnutrition in the D.P. camp, and they had no one but me to ask for money and food supplements.

My only joy that summer was reading Franky's nearly daily letters. I kept them under my pillow and carried them with me to the beach, rereading each dozens of times. Near the end of August I received one that contained a very special message. Franky was planning to hitchhike down to the Cape, to visit me on my eighteenth birthday. I shouted with joy, singing and skipping along the mile-long road to the beach. But my happy tears soon turned into a heartbreaking sob. Mrs. S. promptly informed me that Franky was not allowed to even step into the house. Further, that neither was I permitted to leave the premises. Amidst pouring tears I stumbled back to the house, wondering whether the Shains' and Mrs. Carter's lack of compassion had indeed a limit.

Being too late to warn Franky not to come, I did my chores as usual the next day, but Saturday I refused to leave the house. My eyes swollen and red from crying, I was too embarrassed to be seen by the neighbors; I just sat near the window staring at the road. It was late afternoon, and everyone was down at the beach when Franky finally arrived. Hungry, dusty and sweaty, having been alternately riding and walking in the scorching sun since early morning, the poor dear could not even wash up or sit for a spell in the house. I walked with him and left him at a clearing in the woods, where I was to rejoin him after all the Shains were asleep. It was nearly midnight before I was able to sneak out, with my blanket and a sandwich in my hand. His clothes were wrinkled and damp from the dew, his body full of mosquito and ant bites, when rising from a deep sleep, hungry and thirsty, the first words he uttered were "Darling, I am so happy to be near you again!"

He reached into the arm bag he had carried, and handed me a neatly wrapped package. I knew it would be something I had long wanted, for Franky and I were atuned to feel each other's joys and sorrows, desires and dislikes. I would have cried from happiness if I had had any tears left, when in the bright moonlight I saw a little camera in its leather carrying case. Although I had never mentioned it, for it was sheer luxury on which our meager income was not to be wasted, I had long yearned for just such an object.

In fear that my absence would be discovered, I left Franky after a short while. I had managed to sneak back into "jail" inconspicuously, and to sob through the night without awakening anyone.

Since Mr. S. was with us on weekends, the next forenoon I was not needed at the beach. That gave me a chance to storm through my chores and fly to spend some time with Franky. We exchanged stories about insignificant incidents connected with our routine existence, interspersed frequently with the reiteration of our loneliness and love for each other. Near lunchtime we walked to the main road, kissed each other good-bye, and with head hanging low, Franky set out on his eighty-mile journey to Boston while I stumbled back to the house. And so did I spend my eighteenth birthday.

Labor Day weekend we packed and moved back to Newton. The following days were hectic; cleaning, shopping, washing and ironing, preparing for the new school year. I went to register, to be tested and counseled, and finally to enroll in English, U.S. history and government, Latin 2, chemistry and trigonometry.

The following weeks were even more busy. Since Newton High was a top-rated school, the competition was far more keen than at Roxbury Memorial. Getting excellent grades and learning my subjects well were essential in order to score high on the soon upcoming College Board Examination, to get into a highly rated institution. Thus, besides my studies and demanding household chores, I had little time to relax or socialize. Of the nine of us who had come to Boston together, the Polish and German Veras and Ester went to far distant schools; Edzia was adopted by a very wealthy family and thus pursued a different lifestyle; my best friend, Hella, went to a plush private school in Tanglewood in the Berkshire mountains; Beny and David had graduated and found employment; and my favorite, Larry, had entered Harvard University.

A while back Beny had introduced me to an American boy who was very persistent in wanting to date me. Jim was 26 years old, service manager for Frigidaire Company, quite good looking and very different from my European friends. I found him interesting, so I did go out with him three or four times during the autumn months.

Fate meanwhile had forced Franky to fade slowly out of my life. The Shains had been very adamant in following Mrs. Carter's order to keep us apart. Since he could not come to my house, and since we had to travel nearly two hours by streetcar and bus each way, we saw each other less and less frequently. Further, since he was barred from even phoning me, and my meager allowance hardly provided for calls from a pay phone, even talking to each other became most difficult.

Missing each other beyond expression, on a Saturday in October, when my foster parents had season tickets to the symphony and were sure to be out, Franky risked coming to my residence. We had barely spent an hour talking when, as if they had sensed it by telepathy, the Shains unexpectedly returned. Poor Franky jumped up and ran away instantly, as if he were a burglar having been caught red-handed, just as "dear" Mr. Shain picked up the telephone to call Mrs. Carter. With uncontrollable hate in my eyes, I speechlessly retired to my cubby-hole called a room. This did not prevent Mrs. S. from delivering a lengthy lecture and painting a horror picture of what could happen to me for breaking the agency's

12

rules. I cried through the night, feeling so weak and helpless that I began contemplating suicide.

The next week I called Franky, to meet me downtown on Saturday, to discuss our future course of action. We spoke for hours in a little coffee shop, hashing out all future possibilities. I still harbored a conditioned fear of authority, which rendered me unable to stand up to and challenge Mrs. Carter. To continue seeing each other secretly, at most once a month, we agreed would drive us nearly insane. To get married right then would have ruined both of our plans for the future. Franky, at age sixteen, would have had to seek full-time employment, and I, without any skill or training, some kind of part-time work. Neither of us, perhaps forever, would be able to go to college. Since I was a ward of the U.S. Government, therefore unable to disassociate myself from the guardian agency until age twenty-one or unless I got married, both of the above courses of action were detrimental. So, we reluctantly agreed to stop seeing each other for awhile.

A ray of sunshine penetrated my miserable existence around mid-November, when Larry invited me to a Harvard formal ball. I managed to borrow a lovely evening gown from one of my new girlfriends, appropriate accessories from another, and even dyed some old sandals to match the attire before I blurted out to Mrs. S. my exciting news. But oh, did she have a talent for ruining anything joyous in my drab existence! She instantly informed me that, since they had symphony tickets for Saturday nights, I was expected to baby-sit.

"But such an invitation may come only once in my lifetime! I'll pay for the baby-sitter, I'll even get my best girlfriend to stay! Or her mother!" I pleaded in desperation.

"We don't want strangers minding our children," said she abruptly. "The least you can do for your keep is to baby-sit!"

"But the agency pays for me," said I.

"Our family donates tenfold that sum! We are not accepting money for your keep. We took you in to give you a home, from the goodness of our hearts," was her stern reply.

No, I could not overcome such irrationality, such self-deception. The fact that each morning before school I had to make breakfast for the kids, after school mind them, then help prepare supper, wash the dishes, clean the kitchen and dining room, clean the downstairs each weekend, baby-sit every Saturday night and on many other evenings, etc., etc.; that I did as much as a paid maid, did not seem to even enter their minds. I felt like Cinderella, but my story did not have a happy ending. I stayed home on that memorable Saturday night.

To add to my misery, the following week I received a letter from Hungary. My guardian, Uncle Jenő, was informing me that, in order to meet the government's demands, he had to sell *all* my family's possessions, to make the necessary repairs on our house. A few months later, however, since the rightful owners — my parents or I — were not living in it, the house was confiscated by the state. I believed the loss of the five-unit house, but not that he had made repairs. But what was I to do? By then I felt so defeated and weak that even if he had been within reach, I would not have had the emotional strength to fight.

From late November on, I saw Jim weekly. Partly from lack of better male companionship, partly to spend my every free moment away from the house, but mostly because he was a 26-year-old adult, an established American male, who represented protection and security. But my guardians, in their "infinite wisdom" decided that Jim was to be treated as Franky.

Late in December I was notified that Mrs. Carter wished to confer with me. Upon my arrival she expressed her extreme displeasure that, against her distinct "desire", I was again "wasting time away from school work" by frequently dating. Then she asserted that if I did not qualify for a full scholarship, the agency would not finance my college education. I would have to go to work.

I was too young and naive then to realize that Mrs. Carter might have feared that I was promiscuous, that I might do something irrational which could affect my whole future, and, not wanting to discuss it in fear of putting ideas into my mind, used the denial of my education — which she knew meant so much to me — as a club to keep me away from boys. All I could think of at that time was Hella in a private school in Tanglewood, Larry at Harvard and living in a dormitory, several others attending various universities — all at the agency's expense — while I, working as a maid, would not be able to attend even a state supported college! This was the final straw!

When I reiterated the expired conversation to Jim, he at once offered to marry me and finance my education. His words dazed me. I did not love, nor did I feel I ever could love Jim. It was obvious to me that a one-sided love was not enough to overcome the tremendous differences in intellect, social background and personality between us.

On the other hand, my only goal in life was to fulfill my childhood dream and parents' desire, to become a degreed professional. I knew that the continuation of the status quo would lead me to a nervous breakdown or suicide. Further, since I was not the type who could "use" someone, that is, take Jim's money without giving him the only thing I had, *myself,* in my tormented mind I was not able to make a rational choice. I accepted Jim's offer without deliberation.

CHAPTER 3: TO SAVE MY SANITY

Jim felt much more confident about our future. He kept assuring me that his deep love and eternal devotion would make me so happy that my mere liking of him would eventually turn into love. But, although he did not pressure me to set the wedding date, he did insist on an early engagement. I resisted for awhile, but finally I agreed to set the date in February.

The formal engagement was to take place in his aunt's home, in the presence of all his relatives. For my friends I planned to give a party in my residence. But the Shains would not hear of it! They were concerned about the possible breakage of dishes and the "mess" in the house. Their only recourse, when I offered to use paper and plastic, to clean up and to reimburse them for any possible damage, was "What if something spills and ruins the rug?"

That did it! I went to the downstairs bathroom and began taking every pill in sight. Perhaps to attempt to justify their selfishness, or perhaps due to extrasensory perception, Mrs. S. burst into the bathroom, just as I was taking the first pill from the second bottle. I don't recall what the pills were, nor exactly how many I had already consumed, only that I was forced to drink some liquid, glass after glass. They made me walk from room to room until I passed out from the pills and exhaustion.

The next day I called my social worker and asserted that, do what they wished, I was leaving the Shains. My attempted suicide must have impressed members of the agency, for Mrs. E. offered to hold an engagement party for me in her own house, and Mrs. Carter personally moved me and my belongings to her private home.

The new arrangement eliminated many of my problems, but also introduced new ones. On the pro side, the house was still in Newton, so I did not have to change schools. My household duties were minimal, giving me much more free time. Besides Mrs. Carter, who was rarely home, there were three other European orphans living there, two of whom were quite nice.

The big disadvantage, however, was the third child. Dany was around eleven years old, from Poland, having spent the war years living in the woods with partisans. He was deeply disturbed and could not adjust to a normal society. He frequently ran away, necessitating all of us spending half the night searching the nearby woods. On several occasions he even stole Mrs. Carter's car, which made our search much more difficult. These escapades resulted in one of us having to supervise Dany constantly. This affected my performance in school severely, pushing me even closer to a nervous breakdown.

Meanwhile Franky found out about my engagement. Being young, lacking the wisdom and the maturity to fully understand my frame of mind, and feeling helpless to affect in any way the course of events, he decided to join the navy and request an out-of-town transfer. Oh, if he only knew that I had no love for Jim, that the engagement was only my mind's feeble attempt to save my sanity, that had he repeated his offer to marry me even after the engagement, I would have gladly accepted! But fate had other plans for us. He did ship out and dropped completely out of my life.

A ray of sunshine penetrated my miserable existence when in April the school's counselor informed me that I had passed the College Board Examination with flying colors, and further, that the local Women's Club had selected me to be the recipient of a scholarship. I would have been happy beyond words if Mrs. Carter had right then offered to send me to college. But she said only ''nice'' when I broke the news to her. This brought me to the irreversible conclusion that, at all cost, I had to get out of her clutches. Since the only way this could be done before my twenty-first birthday was for me to marry, I agreed to Jim's plea to set the wedding date for June 5, right after my graduation.

Had it not been the only way, I would never have married him. Jim and I had nearly nothing in common. His mother, of first generation Lithuanian descent with only a 6th grade education, his father a Russian refugee of World War I, with only a 4th grade education, were two people who had spent their entire lives running a seven-day local grocery store from 6:00 a.m. to 10:00 at night. They never traveled beyond the nearest town, had no hobbies, no friends, and no interest beyond making a mere living. They were not the type of people with whom I could ever have anything in common. Additionally, his mother was so neurotic that even her sister and brothers avoided her. Jim's father was kind and compassionate, but too weak to control his wife's constant griping, and too good to divorce or leave her.

Jim grew up on the streets. His parents were never around to supervise him, being too busy in the store even to be aware of what he was doing, much less what his thoughts, feelings and problems were. When World War II broke out, he enlisted in the navy and eventually became a First Class Pharmacist Mate. When the war ended he attempted to enter a college under the G.I. Bill, but his scores qualified him for only a business school, where he learned bookkeeping and accounting. Like his parents, he had no hobbies or special interests, nor did he have ambition to substantially improve himself. Jim had a dull personality and lacked social graces; he was weak, shallow, uncompassionate and irrational; he lacked confidence and was full of internal conflicts. His only assets were a meager but stable income, the $10,000 he claimed he had and was willing to spend for my higher education, plus the all-important fact that marrying him would make me independent of the government and the agency.

I had tried to influence Jim to read some of the basic classics, to go with me to concerts, ballets, exhibits, etc., but to no avail. Our typical recreational activities consisted of visiting his parents and relatives, and occasionally going to an inexpensive restaurant or movie. Since I had never been interested in sports, the scope of our conversational topics was extremely limited.

I weighed and balanced those facts daily in my mind, suggesting to Jim dozens of times that he cancel the wedding preparations, but each time he begged me to give marriage a chance, an opportunity for him to prove to me that his love would overshadow all those "minor differences". And so, against my better judgement, in my tormented emotional state, I jumped into a marriage that all my friends predicted would end in a disaster.

18

CHAPTER 4: THE "MIKVAH"

Preparing for the wedding was nothing but heartache for me. The agency assigned $200, as its final payment, for my trousseau. They allocated nearly half of that amount for sheets, towels, and other immediate household necessities, to be purchased without me by my social worker. The remaining half was for my going-away suit, shoes, accessories, underwear, etc., *plus* the wedding gown and veil. True, my future in-laws paid the entire cost of the wedding, but since out of the 150 guests only 8 of *my* friends were invited, I did not feel in their debt. But my mother-in-law-to-be felt differently. Her post-engagement criticisms and domineering ways kept increasing constantly.

The incident on the day before the wedding would have reversed my decision to marry, had I been even a little less lethargic. Ma, though only hypocritically and superficially religious, insisted that I go to the "mikvah". That is a religious tenet, practiced only by the very old-fashioned orthodox Jews, by which a bride goes to a special bathhouse to wash her body, symbolizing purity. To please Ma I unsuspectingly consented to go with her at the appointed time, the evening before the wedding. I finished manicuring my nails and having my hair beautifully set, just in time to meet our schedule. Not knowing anything about such orthodox dogmas, I did what I was told. The woman in charge instructed me to get undressed and to step into a small pool. That done, she told me to completely submerge. No way! I had just come from the beauty parlor! But Ma kept screaming that I must do as I was told. The stronger I objected, the more forcefully the woman kept pushing me in. I was under water up to my chin when finally in anger I shoved the old lady and ran for my clothes. Bodily blocking the exit, Ma ordered me to extend my hand for the nails to be cut. Not all ten, but part of a few were lost before I was able to shake the two women who were physically restraining me. One of my bridesmaids had to come in the wee hours of the next morning to reset my hair , patch up my nails, and put heavy makeup around my red , cried-out eyes, so I would not be too ashamed to attend my own wedding.

The constant premarital criticisms and insults of my mother-in-law were superseded only by those she dished out to me each time I saw her after the wedding. She never forgave me for being penniless, for not having paid for the wedding, and for intending to spend her son's money for my college education instead of getting a job. Her frequently voiced favorite expression was, ''You refugee should kiss the ground my son walks on, for having picked you out of the gutter!''

Our marriage started out even worse than I had anticipated. We set out to tour Canada in a rented car. We met our first obstacle at the border, when due to my naiveté and Jim's disorganized and irresponsible nature, we found out that, because I was not a citizen, I could not leave and reenter the U.S. without formal documents. Due to the kindness of the chief border guard, after several expensive phone calls to New York and Washington, D.C., and a day's delay, we managed to continue our trip.

My next disappointment came in Montreal, where instead of seeing historical sights, Jim insisted we attend the striptease shows. Furthering my displeasure, although I had my license, Jim would not allow me to drive the car. Yet, when we had a flat tire, I was the one who had to change it, because he didn't know how. Suffice it to say, I was glad to get home.

But to what home? Just before the wedding my husband had informed me that on his salary we could not afford to rent an apartment in his parents' vicinity, so I had to settle for a dark, tiny, furnished room with kitchen privileges.

Only the contents of two letters, which awaited my return from our honeymoon compensated for all my recent unhappiness. One was from the top-rated Brandeis University; the other from North Eastern University, one of the best engineering institutions. Both stated that I had been accepted. The former and more expensive even offered a scholarship. My joy was indescribable; my life's dream was to be fulfilled!

From the top of Mt. Everest to the valley below was the kind of drop I experienced when, near the end of July, I came down with a very high fever and had to go to the doctor. He took one look at me and asked in an angry voice: "Did your husband live up to his promise that he would protect you from pregnancy until I could provide you with the proper preventative?" In great embarrasment I had to admit that he had failed to do so on two occasions. "Well," the doctor said, "I will run a test, but I suggest you forget starting college this fall!"

When the test confirmed the doctor's suspicion, my mind was ready to snap. In anticipation of the many added expenses, Jim suggested that I earn some money by accepting part-time work in our landlady's cleaning store. Mainly to get out of our dark, depressing hole in the wall, I worked there each day for a month. Meanwhile I found an old house, where a cheap attic apartment was being constructed. After we had given notice to move and our room was rented, we were informed by the owner of the house that the construction had been delayed, and thus we had no place to live. Jim solved the problem the easy way; we moved in with my in-laws.

Ma made my life unendurable. No matter how sick I felt I had to rise at seven, eat every morsel of an enormous three-course break-fast, climb four flights of stairs and walk for miles to get exercise, do my share of the household chores, stuff myself again at lunch, repeat my constitutional in the afternoon, and listen to her unending criticism of everything I did or believed in. Since carrying "her grandchild" I had to eat supper for two again, after which I could collapse in another hole in the wall called our room, and listen to her constant ranting and raving at either Jim or her husband. Pa used to laugh it off feebly, while Jim would just stare, letting it go in one ear and out the other. Neither man had the guts to tell her off, or at least to make her stop. With everyone constantly on edge, Jim used to start an argument with me each night as soon as he could escape from Ma.

In three weeks I was at the end of my rope. One Saturday afternoon, amidst a big fight about my insistence that we move for the remaining weeks to a motel, Jim spoke to me in such a manner that I grabbed a bottle of lye, ran out of the house and into the bushy fence of the park across the street, fully intending to end my life. But the bottle cap was screwed on so tightly that by the time I found a rock and broke off the top, Jim had caught up with me and twisted the thing out of my hand. Thus ended my second attempt at suicide.

A week had passed when Ma made me the focus of her tirade during breakfast. I wasted no time looking for a poison. I just stormed out and up one flight, straight to the edge of the roof, to jump. Jim recalled the previous week and instantly ran after me. I already had a leg on the ledge when he reached up and pulled me off. Having tried and failed three times, my confidence was shattered. Even this means of escape no longer seemed possible.

Early in September we finally moved into our tiny, two-room attic apartment. We bought some inexpensive furniture on sale and fixed the place up to look quite pleasant. Before the year was over I had managed to save enough for even a cheap television. Since the agency had offered — as charity to a poor Jewish couple — to pay for the hospital cost if I gave up having a private doctor, Jim influenced me to become a hospital outpatient. Considering the saving as unexpected income, my dear husband decided to spend it to purchase a car, which, by the way, he never let me drive.

Shortly before the baby was due, my in-laws came to us with a business proposition. A nearby tobacco shop was for sale, and with Jim's help the three of them could purchase and manage it. The $10,000 Jim had promised for my college education turned out to be an annuity life insurance policy his parents were supposed to have turned over to him on his twenty-fifth birthday. Since they hadn't and it was still in their hands, they pressured Jim to invest it in the purchase of that store.

By then I felt so helpless and defeated that I would have raised no

22

objection to almost anything Jim wanted. But the store was to be opened seven days a week, from 6:00 a.m. to 11:00 p.m., requiring two people to man it nearly all the time, which meant that my husband would hardly ever be home. Further, it was difficult to predict how much the store would net, risking also a significant loss. To top it all, constant contact with his mother would have made Jim so nervous that even during those mere few hours at home he would constantly have picked fights with me. Foreseeing all of these, I vehemently opposed the joint venture.

In March, 1950, after a long and very agonizing labor I delivered a beautiful baby girl. On the way home from the hospital my husband abruptly broke the news: the tobacco shop was partly ours!

No ray of sunshine entered my life during the following months. Jim behaved exactly as I had anticipated. Nothing I did was right in his eyes. My cooking was not as good as his mother's; as hard as he worked I had no right to expect him to help me with any household chores; since from all the aggravation my weight had dropped to 95 pounds, I was too skinny; etc., etc. During that spring I often entertained the idea of a divorce, but by summer Jim and his mother had so destroyed my self-confidence that I no longer imagined myself capable of surviving alone, much less raising a child.

About then I began developing a phobia. Around ten o'clock if I was alone in the house when the street noise started to diminish, when the lights in the neighborhood gradually faded away, and when stillness and darkness finally enveloped the city, I began to sense the presence of a huge, muscular male — like a genie — floating behind me, ready to stab me in the back with his sword!

I used to lock all the doors and windows, shut off the TV to create total silence, turn every light on, and sit motionless on the couch, pressing firmly against its back. I was so mesmerized with terror that I did not dare get up to answer the phone, get a drink of water, or even go to the bathroom.

This paralyzing fear persisted until Jim walked through the door. I used to beg him again and again to exchange work schedules with his father, or to close the store earlier, but he only ridiculed my fear and ignored my plea.

CHAPTER 5: AN UNUSUAL DEDICATION

In August of 1950 the Korean war broke out. Since Jim was in the active reserve, it was predictable that he would be among the first to be called to active duty and be shipped overseas almost at once. He did not want to go, especially into combat. I, due to my past experiences, was also anxious to keep him home. As the word "war" brought to the surface all my deeply repressed memories, I thought of a scheme to achieve that end.

The day after Jim received his order to report to the nearby Chelsea Naval Hospital, I made an urgent appointment with a navy psychiatrist. I asserted that if my husband were sent into combat, I would kill the baby and commit suicide. I must have been convincing, for Dr. V. scheduled me for analysis and therapy, and at once requested my husband's official deferment from overseas duty. By our third session Jim's assignment to the Chelsea Hospital was confirmed, and I was deeply involved relating my life story. Once up to date, my doctor was ready to comment.

"Well, Georgia, this was quite a story! We certainly have some problems to resolve. To be totally honest with you, your wounds of the Holocaust are deep and very painful, and although with time they will *diminish,* they may *never* completely *heal.* Your marital problems are also severe, but at least helpable. However, that necessitates the cooperation of your husband and in-laws."

"Do not count on them, Dr. V. My mother-in-law has been in a rage, endlessly reiterating what a shame I have brought upon the family by going to a 'nut doctor', a stigma they will never be able to live down."

24

"And what about your husband? How does he react?"

"Nearly as antagonistically as his mother. I doubt that you could get him into therapy."

"I shall make an attempt, for he obviously needs help."

Dr. V. made several attempts to see Jim, but he managed to have an excuse each time. Finally my doctor succeeded, but only once, for the following week he was transferred. Under those negative circumstances, failing to see a reason to continue, I also stopped analysis.

The fact that Jim was stationed near Boston, that he was away from the store and his mother, that he was at home evenings and on weekends, plus the strength I had drawn from the sessions with Dr. V., helped me to begin to regain my sanity. Since I was no longer alone evenings, my phobia ceased to manifest itself and my arguments with Jim became less intense and frequent. My daughter Roberta became more enjoyable and easier to care for, and by the spring of 1951 I again viewed life as bearable.

In early April I received an unexpected telephone call. Franky wished to visit me, to introduce his bride. My heart began to throb. I was both happy and sad — happy to see him again and to know he had not forgotten me, and sad because his marriage destroyed even the minutest possibility of our ever belonging to each other.

Minutes after they arrived, the two of us knew the feelings and thoughts of the other. As soon as Shirley and Jim struck up a conversation, Franky and I simultaneously rose and went into the kitchen. Once alone, we uttered the words "You are not happy," concurrently. We spoke no further, just hugged one another tightly, sobbing quietly while we gently wiped away each other's tears. We parted after supper, perhaps never to meet again.

Having always longed for a brother or sister, thus not wanting Roberta to be an only child, during that spring I decided to conceive. The book, *Childbirth Without Fear,* was very popular at that time, so after having read it and several others on the subject, I decided to have my baby via the then revolutionary method, without anesthesia.

On my first visit to the dependents' medical unit in Chelsea Naval Hospital I was assigned to a doctor by the name of Roth. Glancing at the title page of the library book under my arm, my first question inside the office was, "Are you related to the author of this book?"

"Very closely," said the doctor with a chuckle, "I wrote it. Why?"

"I intend to have my baby via natural childbirth," was my reply.

"Good. Then practice the exercises described within. Oh yes, and make sure you go into labor when I am on duty," responded Dr. Roth with a grin.

Shortly before Christmas of that year a letter from Montreal arrived. I was thrilled to hear that the Klein family was finally able to leave the D.P. camp and immigrate to Canada. Imagining how lost and helpless they were, in spite of the dangers involved in driving 600 miles round trip on treacherous, icy mountain roads, I insisted on visiting them during the long holiday weekend. It was far from a luxury trip in an old Dodge coupe that had only front seats, with a 21-month-old baby and another due in five weeks, but the joy of the reunion made up for all the discomfort.

At dawn on February 4, 1952, I was awakened by cramps. By 8:00 a.m. the contractions had stopped, so I considered it a false alarm and went about my normal chores. Late that afternoon I had another pain, so after supper we leisurely drove to the hospital, to be assured that everything was progressing normally. To my great pleasure, who else but Dr. Roth was the chief obstetrician on duty.

After he examined me he remarked with a chuckle, "I can see you followed all my instructions. Even the one to time your labor so that I'd be here to deliver your child! It looks like very soon we will find out whether it's a boy or girl." At 2:00 a.m. I was in ecstacy, as I watched and helped my son enter the world.

At first Roberta seemed very happy about her new brother, but not for long. Although Don was a very good baby, he still demanded a great deal of my time and attention. Roberta was not willing to take second place. Two additional factors compounded

26

the problem.

Jim had received his discharge from the service and was looking for employment. By then his parents had sold the tobacco shop, never giving us any funds as our share of the investment. I had saved some from his navy salary, but not enough to live without an income for an extensive period of time. So, by July the tension caused daily arguments. Late in August Jim did accept employment in a bank, easy work and short hours, but the pay was minimal. To raise two children and support a car on such income required talent.

The second problem was more deeply rooted and serious. Don was a well-timed and wanted child, and I had no major emotional upsets during the pregnancy. Roberta's conception, on the other hand, had been a disaster. It prevented me from attending college, after all the sacrifices I had made to realize that lifelong ambition. It was too soon after the wedding, before Jim and I had a chance to settle down, to adjust to each other and the new life style. I was simply not ready for her physically, mentally, or emotionally. I was on the borderline of a nervous breakdown during, and for quite a while after, the pregnancy. Of course it affected her! She was very tense, demanding and difficult to handle from birth on.

As Don began to spend more and more time awake, taking me away from Roberta more often, and as the tension of Jim's unemployment increased, Roberta's resentments and their overt manifestations became more serious and intolerable. She started to cry and throw tantrums with increasing frequency. In June she added the refusal of meals. Around July she began crawling out of bed and getting into mischief several times during each night. The following month she started to mess in her pants every day. She had been toilet trained for over a year by then, and she was aware that her action was inappropriate, for as soon as she had done it she would cry out, "Mommy, don't come near me!" I changed her schedule, varied her food, spent my every free moment with her, but nothing reversed her intolerable behavior.

I kept hoping it was only a passing phase, but the next stage forced us to seek professional help. Roberta began throwing up every meal, every kind of nourishment, and as a consequence began rapidly losing weight. Our pediatrician subjected her to every examination and test even remotely germane to the displayed symptoms, but none gave even a clue. In final desperation he put her on sedatives, and since, even with large daily doses, her behavior did not change significantly, our pediatrician suggested psychotherapy. In October Roberta began seeing a psychiatrist at the Putnam Children's Center, three times a week.

Each time the doctor took Roberta into a huge room full of toys, where she was free to act out her emotions. Meanwhile Jim and I were assigned to a psychiatric counselor, who conferred with the child's doctor regularly. After a few joint sessions I was told to continue working with her, while Jim was reassigned to have weekly sessions with a psychiatrist. He did go a few times, then began finding excuses to cancel appointments or simply not show up.

Gradually Roberta's behavior changed, but not necessarily for the better. She stopped getting into mischief during the night, but started to be cruel to the baby. I had to watch her constantly, for she would kick Don, throw things at or batter him with hard objects, even step on his throat. Keeping both safe and separated in a tiny, one-bedroom apartment was an unachievable task.

We had applied for veterans' housing as soon as Jim was discharged from the navy, but when such a house became available, we found that on his meager salary, even its moderate cost was beyond our means. But our poverty qualified us for an apartment in a nearby, newly built, low-rent housing project. So, in February of 1953 we moved into a relatively nice two-bedroom apartment.

Since Jim was still avoiding the psychiatrist, neither Roberta's behavior nor our relationship improved. I was still very unhappy and deeply depressed, but had regained enough of my self-confidence to contemplate a separation. We had little in common before our marriage, and by now we had even less. Physical contact between the two of us was nearly nonexistent, communication pertained only to necessities, recreation consisted of a meal in an inexpensive restaurant or a drive-in movie at most once monthly, and getting together with friends even less frequently. What kept us married, besides the children and our low income, was our own inferiority complex, each of us fearing to face life's difficulties alone.

My health began to fail me during that spring. One night I was awakened by a pain that felt as if someone were cutting my stomach open. Keeling over, I could not move nor speak. Since nearly an hour later the pain still persisted, I woke Jim to call our physician. Instead, he wrapped me in a blanket and carried my rigid body to a nearby hospital. I know not what they did, for by then I was unconscious from the pain.

The next day I had a series of tests. When the results were in, the doctor informed me that the upper wall of my stomach was ulcerated. Having reviewed my other complaints and medical history, he put me on a special diet and eating schedule, prescribed a heavy dose of sedatives, and scheduled me for a seemingly unending series of additional examinations and tests. Except for the ulcer, a cyst and an allergy, I was found to be in good physical health.

Shortly after the consumption of the last sedative, I had another similarly severe attack. The internist concluded that the gastric convulsions were brought on by nervous tension, and were likely to reoccur whenever I was under severe pressure. He dismissed me with prescriptions, plus the advice to avoid tension-provoking situations if I wished to live long enough to raise my children.

"Don't aggravate yourself," my friends used to say, while failing to instruct me as to how it was to be accomplished. Since neither our financial nor our marital situation showed any improvement, one day in October, after an all-night argument, I simply packed all Jim's personal belongings, put the suitcases outside the door, and when he came home, refused to let him in. He kept phoning and knocking on the door hourly during that night and the next day, promising to change and begging me to take him back. Persistently pursuing that behavior, he wore me out so that after a week I let him move back.

Meanwhile, after the long summer vacation, Roberta returned to her psychiatrist. This time the doctor insisted that the father attend weekly also. After our reunion Jim began to cooperate, even with that request. It looked like a divorce might be avoided. But, unfortunately, not for long.

As typical in therapy, the subject's emotions and behavior fluctuate, so just as Roberta had been going from one extreme to the other, from being angelic to a holy terror, my husband began displaying alternating behavior patterns. By the early spring of 1954 he had regressed to being more impossible to live with than ever before. Worst of all, he had stopped seeing the psychiatrist regularly, and had started to drink and lie to me frequently.

In September I requested therapy in place of counseling. I needed to think out loud, to put things in their proper perspective, to see how much I was to blame.

By no means was I easy to live with. I was an overzealous perfectionist, demanding from myself and others flawless performance in all endeavors. I was a race-horse who never relaxed, trying to capture those experiences encountered by normally maturing pre- and young-adults, denied me by the events of the Holocaust. Its additional effect, a weakly developed nervous system — due to the lack of proper nutrients and excessive strain during the formative years — caused me often to over-react. I was a physiological and emotional invalid, needing a lot more than I was able to give.

I felt inadequate as a wife, as a mother, even as a person. I had long ago lost contact with my old buddies, and had found no one who really understood me, with whom I could identify. I had tried desperately to think, to act, and react as my American friends, but my upbringing, value system, and past experiences were so vastly different that the gap could not be spanned. No parents or relatives to turn to for uncritical acceptance; no empathetic friend with shoulders to cry on; a loveless and incompatible marrige not likely to improve; a new country with foreign customs and a way of life difficult to adjust to; I felt like a trapped fugitive — a misfit, hopelessly lonely, helpless and weak.

As I related my life story to the psychiatrist, describing my feelings during and after the war, my problems and emotions after arriving in this country, I became aware of something that had not occurred to me for many years. All through my childhood, and even through the Nazi era, I believed strongly in God. It always gave me hope and strength. But after the war I began to lose faith. By the time of my engagement I was like Jim, an atheist.

Since then I had been heading steadily, although with some fluctuation, toward a nervous breakdown. My marital problems were far less devastating than my problems during and after the war, yet I felt more depressed, less able to face life, and less desirous even to live than ever before. I became consciously aware of my need to turn to God. But it was easier said than done.

One day in mid-November, 1954, Jim's psychiatrist called. He said he had been waiting a full hour, but his patient had not shown up. When my husband got home, red-nosed and smelling like a beer barrel, I asked how his session with the doctor went. With a perfectly straight face and honest tone of voice he asserted that everything went as usual, as well as could be anticipated. When I reiterated what the doctor had said on the phone, Jim became furious, yelling and referring to the doctor with profanities, while calling him an outright liar. I quietly asked him if he was drunk, which enraged him even more, till he accused me of being a lunatic, belonging in an insane asylum.

That did it! Next day I contacted a lawyer and applied for a legal separation. On December 23 the decree was delivered and Jim moved back to the heart of his problems, his parents.

The children's reaction was the opposite of everyone's prediction. Roberta, the problem child, whom I had frequently punished and whom Daddy had always defended, became very compassionate and well-behaved. We spent a lot of time together each day after she returned from kindergarten, and she became a real companion to me. Don, the angelic, well-adjusted toddler, on the other hand, turned into a cry-baby. My reaction was also different from what I had anticipated. Strangely, instead of feeling lonely, I enjoyed my newfound freedom.

During the months of January and February Jim called and visited me a few times, on each occasion confessing his weaknesses and faults, apologizing for his past wrongdoings, promising a total change and begging to be allowed to return. Trusting his vows, I let him move back in March.

But as after the first separation, my sweet and loving husband, soon after he achieved what he wanted, began regressing. By summer we existed just like the year before. I had attempted to pray a few times, mainly in despair, but, since miracles did not follow, my belief was superficial.

My doctor at the Center had left and was replaced by a psychiatric counselor, a very intelligent, compassionate elderly lady. During our third session, after I had briefed her about Roberta's original problems, the child's behavior through the past three years and her current overt display of emotions, she asked a significant question.

"Have you ever tried the old-fashioned remedy of a thorough spanking on the rear end?" I admitted sheepishly that I had felt like doing it many times, but since my husband and "dear" Ma considered physical punishment of a child criminal, I used other nonphysical punitive devices.

"Yet she still persists being frequently outright cruel to her little brother?" My answer, of course, had to be "yes."

"For the next few weeks, try a new approach. Each time you catch your daughter doing something dangerous or purposely cruel to the baby, pull down her pants and spank her till her rear end is pink. Do it without a word, without emotion, in a totally matter-of-fact way. Then go about your business as if nothing had happened. But do it right after the event, and consistently. Make her feel the pain she has caused; not for an instant, but an extended period of time.''

During the next two weeks I followed my case-worker's advice on many occasions; the third week the procedure was necessitated only a few times; the following week only once. Like a miracle, Roberta seemed to be cured.

During the last session of August, 1955, my new advisor was subjected to my outburst about my latest fight with Jim, followed by my lengthy and emphatic complaint about feeling constantly exhausted. Knowing of the correspondence course I had been taking in dress designing, she interrupted me, asserting, ''You need to get a job!''

At first I thought she was joking, but she continued in a firm voice, ''I know the owner of an expensive boutique who is looking for a sample maker. You could make arrangements with her to pick up and deliver, doing the sewing at home. This would at least get you out of the house occasionally, give you a small but independent income, and most important, build up your self-confidence. I will now make an appointment and you be sure to keep it!''

Without giving me a chance to respond, she picked up the phone, recommended me very highly, and arranged for me to pick up work the next day. At first I gasped for air, then I listened totally bewildered, and finally I concluded that either it was all my imagination or she was crazy. I left that day in a daze. But I did keep my appointment the next day, dragging both children along, and arranged for pickup and delivery bi-monthly, commencing after the school year began.

Roberta was entering first grade and Don a nearby nursery, which gave me time to make the samples and finish my designing course. Encouraged by my success, I promoted myself to dressmaker, taking in alterations from friends and neighbors in the housing project.

Roberta made an excellent adjustment to school, with her disposition rapidly changing for the better. By early October, upon her doctor's advice, she ceased going to the Center. My therapy was terminated also, but Jim's doctor firmly advised analysis, or at least continuation of therapy. My husband would not even entertain the thought. I did not make it an issue, for by then I had other plans.

Before the month was over, I had filed for a divorce. As soon as Jim received the official papers, he proceeded with his previous routine of begging, pleading and promising to change. Because of his concurrent improved behavior, my deep concern for the children's probably negative reaction, and my still rather low self-confidence, I decided to leave the application on file, but not press for a court date.

This time I was acting more logically, less emotionally than before. Feeling convinced that the divorce was inevitable, I tried to time it advantageously for me. Concerned about my future financial situation, one day in January I sat down to compute our total assets. Our furniture was cheap and old, almost worthless. Our car's worth was insignificant. I then looked for the savings account booklet, since Jim had always handled the transactions. Having had no reason to doubt his financial honesty, I had never examined the bank book, his wallet, or his private papers. I was in for a shock.

The bank book showed no entry for the several hundred dollars my husband was supposed to receive upon his discharge from the navy. But it did show frequent small withdrawls within the past months. Among his papers I found a form, dated over a year earlier, showing a loan on the car. Although when faced with it he confessed to drinking and petty gambling, the pattern of the withdrawals made me doubt his confession and suspect involvement with another woman.

During the following spring and summer both of us underwent significant changes. Jim became increasingly antagonistic and defiant, while my emotions and reactions, both positive and negative, kept decreasing in intensity.

By September I had completed the dress-designing course. With Don in kindergarten and Roberta in the second grade, I was less tied down and began making new friends through my business. My self-confidence had also improved by my small but independent income, and the compliments of friends and customers. I purchased a very old car — all mine — and was ready to end my hopeless marriage.

In March of 1957, Judge Mahoney decreed the divorce. Jim did not contest it, but did appear in court. As I exited the courthouse he stepped up to me, looked at me with great fury and bitterness, and, with a hand on his heart, he said: "I swear on my children's happiness that you will pay for this. I am dedicating my life to making you miserable."

CHAPTER 6: MY SECOND LOVE REVISITED

Adjusting to my new life was much easier than I had expected. After the 1956 revolution nearly 100,000 Hungarians escaped from communism, and more than 10,000 found refuge in the U.S.A. Among them was Erika Viltschek, the sister of my childhood love, Bandi. She came to Boston and stayed with us for awhile, giving me great comfort during the trying times of my divorce. Getting her settled put me in touch with my old agency, and later, when dozens of lonely Hungarians began to arrive, I became a volunteer interpreter for various agencies, hospitals, factories, and even the police. Through this activity I met some influential people and made some valuable and lifelong friendships. Among them was a girl named Gitta, who soon became my closest friend.

I also met Dave, a gentleman who owned a factory, and was in need of a sample maker. He hired me on a part-time basis, and as we worked closely together, we soon became friends. One day he called me into his office and said he had decided that the job was not for me.

I nearly broke out in tears, but he quickly continued, "You need a business of your own, to spend more time at home with your children and earn more money." My brows rose and jaw dropped in amazement as he went on. "Hush. I have it all figured out. Continue doing dressmaking, but triple all your prices. Cater to the wealthiest women in Boston and render a special service: pick up, fit and deliver in their homes. Here is how it will work. I will recommend you to several very rich ladies. You will go to their homes, do the initial work well and fast, and when you return their clothes, explain that instead of charging extra for your travel, you require your customers to have at least six items to be altered each time they call you. Assuming that women often need only one or two articles to be fixed and always in a hurry, suggest that they invite their friends and neighbors with their dressmaking needs to make up the six items. Picking up new customers that way rapidly, you will soon have more work than you can handle."

I followed Dave's advice, and it turned out just as he predicted. I handled the customers while the children were in school, fixing the clothes during the afternoons and evenings. Business picked up so rapidly that by summer I had to hire a helper.

Through the multitude of new acquaintances, my social life also expanded. I had friends and dates and could pursue any type of recreation my heart desired. The word "happy" would have appropriately described my emotional state had it not been that Jim was fulfilling his vow successfully.

The children spent each Sunday afternoon with their father. The tactic he used at first, while the divorce could still be absolved, was literally crying, reiterating how miserable and lonely he was without them, and encouraging them to influence me to let him move back with us. The children used to come home hateful and upset, telling me how cruel I was for "kicking Daddy out."

Since the method failed to serve its intended purpose, Jim, with the very able help of his mother, managed to convince the children that I did not really love or want them. Roberta, then about seven and a half, returned on Sundays with stories like, "Mommy, is it true that you hate me so much that when I was a baby you tried to drown me?"

As time went on Jim tried every means his twisted mind could think of to alienate the children. One that impressed them most was his convincing them that they were little angels, incapable of doing anything bad. Consequently, my punishing them was due to my own bitterness and hatred. Whenever I caught either child doing something dishonest or dangerous — such as lying, hurting each other, or playing with the stove or sewing machine — they would instantly exclaim, "Don't you dare hit me! I'll tell Daddy and he'll have you deported to Hungary!"

What could I do to stop that man? Did he not realize that though he was hurting me, he was doing much more and irreparable harm to the children, the ones he claimed to love? What was I to say to a seven- and a five-year-old? Again I turned to God, in despair, but still without belief. I seemed to draw strength and serenity each time I prayed, but only temporarily.

Summer turned to fall and fall to winter; pre-Christmas snow covered the ground and the streets were filled with busy holiday shoppers, when one day on the street someone behind touched me on the shoulder. I nearly fainted as I turned around and saw none other than my old love, Franky. We embraced and kissed, blocking the sidewalk, amidst a flood of happy tears. I purposely did not blurt out that I was divorced, letting him be the first to bring me up to date.

"After our last meeting, on my honeymoon in 1951, Shirley and I moved to Chicago and later to Forest Park, where I worked as a hospital corpsman at the navy torpedo factory. In December of 1953 I was assigned to the U.S.S. Midway, an aircraft carrier, for a year, followed by a six-month duty on the U.S. New Jersey, a battle ship. Finally I was transferred to Baltimore, where I work currently at the recruiting station, still in the same capacity. Meanwhile our three children were born; David in 1952, Nick in 1954, and Susan a year later. For the last two years I've been moonlighting with various jobs in the evenings, partly to make ends meet, and partly to get away from the house.''

''I take it that you are not happy,'' I said with mixed emotions.

''How could I be, Georgia? It is you whom I love, have and shall always love. There is no other woman, including my wife, I could ever be truly happy with. Besides, like you and Jim, we have conflicting philosophies and personalities. But what's the use to talk about it. We both have cast the die.''

His story over, it was time for mine. I briefly related the highlights of the past five years, concluding with the statement that I had recently been divorced. Franky's reaction was extreme. ''At last you will be mine! This time I will not let you go,'' said he excitedly.

Oh, how I longed to hear those words! But I knew they represented only wishful thinking.

''I'll get a divorce. My navy pay will more than support Shirley and the children, and my part-time earnings, plus your income, will be sufficient for us. Well, at least . . .''

''No, my dear,'' said I, ''there are more important things to consider. To mention a few, is your love as deep for me as it is for your three children? And what about Shirley? Would she give you a divorce? Is she strong enough to raise three children alone? Go home, Franky, and think everything over. If you do get a divorce, it will have to be based on your own unhappiness, independent of my problems and marital status. I could not be happy with you knowing that I broke up your home.''

We parted in tears and I spent one sleepless night after another. I knew I could sway him to make or break his marriage. When I could barely hold up under the weight of my own post-marital problems, suddenly the responsibility for the effect of my words upon the future of eight people rested on my shoulders. My heart yearned for Franky, but my conscience said, ''No! He belongs to his own family.''

Exchanging letters did not satisfy Franky, for I was determined not to advise him. So, a month later he arranged to come to Boston for nearly a week. We talked and talked and talked, as my psychiatrists and case-workers used to do with me, but without my tipping the scale, it stayed right in the center. Franky had to go through the torture of making the decision, and he had to do it alone.

His letters kept coming for over a year, sometimes as often as twice a week. One said he could not stand the fights with his mate any longer, the next that his wife was on the verge of a mental breakdown, the third that he would leave as soon as Shirley was stable again, then a pause in our correspondence. Then the whole cycle started over again. One week it looked as if my love was ready to come to me, the next week it seemed he needed only a little more time, then the letdown that I would never see him again, followed by the sudden hope of the next cycle.

All this was more than I could take. "Oh Lord, if you exist, why do you punish me so? I did not ask you to tear my wounds open! It would have been better never to see Franky again. What have I done to deserve all this agony?"

During 1958 I worked nearly around the clock, partly necessitated by my growing business, partly to keep my mind off my personal problems. Jim had not been satisifed with just alienating the children. He was determined to get custody. A few times he tried being late or not even paying the due alimony, but when he was ordered by the court to pay the past due amount, he gave up that attempt. His next brainchild was taking me to court, trying to prove that I was an unfit mother. He had built an asinine case, charging me with drunkenness and relying on the testimony of a witness who could claim no more than having seen two bottles of liquor in my cabinet. The case, of course, was thrown out of court in minutes, with fees and embarrassment to him, but great stress to me.

After that costly failure he tried something even more hairraising. Roberta came home on a Sunday, saying, "Mommy, Daddy knows all your boyfriends! When he thinks you are out on a date or have male company, he parks his car on the other side of the street and watches for when our lights go out. Then, when he sees your date get into his car, Dad writes down the number of his license plate and the next day finds out who owns the car and where he lives. Isn't my father clever?''

I would have considered it only a child's imagination, but soon the story was substantiated. I had met a very nice young psychologist, who was only five feet tall and weighed about a hundred pounds. He took me home from our third date and set another for the following week. But he called me the next evening to break the date. He said that when he had left my house a big man came up to him, said he was my husband, and threatened to beat him up if he ever attempted to see me again. I stuttered some words in response, but he hung up, saying he did not wish to cause nor get into any trouble.

Before the end of that year I had met a very fine young Hungarian gentleman, Andy, who was my match in all respects. Since, by then I was losing hope that Franky would get a divorce, and since I did not want to influence his decision by letting him know how much I needed the love and strength of a husband, I had decided to give my new friend a chance. He came to our home several times, took me and the children out, and within the span of a couple of months, became a possible candidate for a future mate. Then one day the unforeseen happened.

Andy called me in the middle of the night, accusing me of not having been honest with him. He said my husband had just left his house, asserting that he and I were separated but not divorced, crying like a child while begging him to break up with me, in hopes that if I would get lonesome I might take him back. Because Andy was a very compassionate person, he felt that we should give Jim a chance and not see each other for a while. This drove me into another deep depression.

Not until March of 1959 was I willing to go out on a date again. F.J.M. was different from the companions I had chosen in the past. He was not a mild-mannered intellectual, but a muscular tool and die maker, of hot-tempered Irish descent. He was opinionated and determined, afraid of nothing and no one. Just at that time I needed someone like him. Our friendship started slowly, as we saw each other at most once a week.

Franky and I were still corresponding, but a year of his fluctuating decisions became an intense emotional strain, which, in addition to my other problems, I could hardly bear. I could not simply cut him off, partly because I felt he needed me as in the past I had needed my psychiatric social workers, as a "spiritual wastebasket" and occasional advisor; partly because I felt that I was, to some extent, the cause of his current trauma; but mostly because of my deep love for him. It became increasingly obvious to me that he was not ready for a divorce. He needed a complete disassociation from me to give his marriage a final chance to work. Without it he could not resolve his stalemate. Ignoring my heart, my conscience said I had to tip his scale.

So, my letters in 1959 spoke mainly of my conquests. Suppressing all my internal sufferings, I wrote mostly about my business success and new exciting boyfriends. Playing on his deep-rooted self image as head of the household, a good provider and protector of his dependents, my plan was to imply that I did not need him as either, and wanted him gradually less and less. My plan — unfortunately — worked. He finally committed himself in his last letter in March, stating that his family was not emotionally strong enough to be left on their own. He did, however, insist on seeing me once in April to, as he put it, "explain the reasons and details."

That was torture for me. Not only did I have to refrain from mentioning Jim's cruel behavior, but I had to put on a convincing act to stay in character with the image I had created. Without his knowledge, F.J. had a role in the play. He was present at my final encounter with Franky, and before my true love left, I had convinced him that F.J. was my husband-to-be. Once again, Franky and I parted forever.

Feeling a neurotic need to get away from everything, I arranged a summer trip to Europe. While Roberta and Don attended a private summer camp for a month and a half, I toured the western part of my old war-torn continent. Rejuvenated by the change of pace and environment, I felt strong enough to handle my foreseeable problems again. But fate had a few more unbearable surprises in store for me. Shortly after my return papers were served to me, announcing that my ex-husband wished to see me in court again. "What is it this time?" my soul cried out in desperation. The comments of my children after the Sunday visitation gave me a clue.

F.J. had spent a lot of time with me shortly before the trip. As a safety measure against possible burglary, I had asked him to move into our apartment during my long absence. But not wishing to worry the children, they were not told that Mother was to be overseas, out of their reach, during the time they were at camp. Instead, that Mother planned to be out a lot and take occasional overnight trips, during which time F.J. would be staying in our home. So, when the children told their father that F.J. would be living in Mother's apartment, he planned to request custody, charging me with being unfit, based on immoral behavior.

Finding this out was the last straw for me. I had to go back to a psychiatrist. He said Jim sounded psychotic, not even fit to visit the children, but no doctor could diagnose and testify unless he voluntarily sought treatment. After several daily sessions the doctor advised that both the children and I should cease to be exposed to him, and suggested that we move far away.

My next trip was to my lawyer, inquiring about the legal implications of such a move. Mr. Perlman informed me that a long-distance move might result in divided custody. "The mother usually gets the children during the school year, and the father during the summer vacation; in your case, probably not at all. But even the former would be better than the weekly torment for the children, and endless upset for you!"

The only place I had always hoped to live was around Los Angeles, California. But the thought of having to support myself and the children, and raise them in a strange environment without a partner or even friends, kept deterring me from moving. That evening I spoke of my dilemma to F.J., who at once offered a solution.

If I became his wife before the impending custody hearing, my ex-husband would not have a case. Nor could he continue annoying me. During the Christmas vacation Jim could have the children, while we moved to Los Angeles (L.A.) and got established. Since he would support me, I could stay home to attend to my children, and if I still wished, I could gradually start a new dressmaking business.

This sounded ideal, except for the fact that I did not love the man. But what were my choices? The status quo, which was about to result in insanity; moving to a strange city with only my two small children, having no place to live nor a job, not even someone to turn to in an emergency; or jump into a second loveless wedlock, with a man who again was not my type.

The last choice seemed the least evil. The price was high, but in my tormented emotional state, the foreseeable benefits appeared to warrant it. And so, in October of 1959 I dove into my second disastrous marriage.

PART II: A NEW BEGINNING

CHAPTER 7: GO WEST YOUNG LADY

The custody hearing went just as F.J. predicted; it was thrown out of court with great embarrassment to Jim. But the hell that was yet to come began as soon as we left Boston in December.

While driving across country, I kept coming upon empty vodka bottles in hotel wastebaskets and in various crevices of the car. When faced with it, F.J. claimed no knowledge of their origin. I suddenly became aware of my new husband's two major faults, until then unrevealed. He was a heavy drinker and an inveterate liar.

In Los Angeles we soon found a suitable furnished apartment, to be exchanged for a larger one as soon as my furniture and children arrived. But F.J. seemed to have difficulty finding a job. A few days after our arrival, while looking through the paper's "Help Wanted" section, an attractive ad struck my eyes: "Dance analyst wanted. Sales experience necessary, skills we will teach. Veloz and Yolanda School of Dancing." I responded to the ad.

The studio was plush and the owners seemed intelligent and refined. The job entailed teaching new customers five dance lessons, meanwhile determining their weaknesses, then enrolling them in various additional courses. I was to receive a moderate salary plus a substantial commission on the sale of the courses. My working hours were 7:30-11:00 p.m., learning variety and style at my convenience during the day. Since dancing was my favorite recreation, I was happy to accept the job.

In January of 1960 I had to return to Boston, to pack and ship out my furniture, attend the custody hearing my lawyer had set up, and drive back in my car with the children. When it was time to purchase the flight tickets, F.J. blurted out that he was penniless. I had to return to Boston alone.

44

The children remained with their father while I sold, packed and shipped all our belongings, ready to start on our cross-country journey right after the hearing. My lawyer opened the case by stating that I had moved to California. Judge Mahoney, who had presided over most of our litigations, including our divorce, interrupted him at once, asserting that since he had no jurisdiction outside the state, he would not let the children leave Massachusetts. Their sole custody would go to the remaining parent, until the mother returned. Without allowing a response the judge got up, walked out of the room and I fainted.

By the time my lawyer revived me, everyone, including my children, was gone. I dropped my car off at the nearest dealer, authorizing him to sell it. My lawyer's partner drove me straight to the airport while we talked. He claimed he had never heard of such a decision and advised me to appeal.

I know not how but I managed to get back to the apartment in L.A. I was half insane, penniless, burning up with a 104° fever from influenza. F.J. was at home, still without a job, drunk as a derelict.

Fearing to give my mind time to think about my personal problems, and in dire need of money, I went to work the next day and asked to be scheduled to learn or work from 10:00 a.m. to late at night. Once the reason was told, I could count on my employers' cooperation.

Next I managed to locate Gitta, my dear friend with whom I had lost contact when she had moved to Beverly Hills, nearly a year before. F.J. and I moved to a larger apartment as soon as my furniture arrived, and were sharing it and the rent with John, a Hungarian friend of Gitta. I was anxious to have him move in with us, for I had begun to fear F.J. and his violent, almost psychotic behavior when drunk.

I had gotten suspicious about him during our trip, so while back in Boston for the hearing, I had asked an old friend to investigate his background. The letter reporting the findings gave reason for both my suspicion and fear. "F. J. M. was found guilty of carnal abuse in .... He served a three-year sentence in the ... penitentiary for armed robbery in .... He is currently a fugitive of the law for non-support of his ex-wife and four children ...." — How much more punishment was I destined to take?

As soon as I was settled and assured of an income sufficient for self-support, I faced F.J. with the proposition that we get a divorce. Drunk as usual, and giving me no chance to continue, he ran into the kitchen and grabbed a butcher knife. Seeing the weapon in his hand, I ran into John's room. My husband pursued me, seemingly determined to kill. John jumped in front of him, bodily cornering him, giving me a chance to escape from the house. I spent the night with Gitta, then returned the next day for my clothes and to make arrangements to move out.

I was astounded as F.J. greeted me as if nothing had happened. More in fear of attempting to walk out with clothes in my arms than to stay, I acted like a loving wife and remained.

The next night at work we had a couple to process, so it was way after midnight by the time the owners drove me home. My mind still on the sale and the substantial commission, I failed to notice the empty quart of vodka on the coffee table, or that my husband was not in bed.

When I entered the bathroom he jumped out from behind the door, began to yell and curse, accusing me irrationally of all sorts of things, and then proceeded to beat me mercilessly. I tried to claw my way out of his clutches, but he had grabbed my neck, squeezed it powerfully, suffocating me. Feeling death near I gave a mighty kick, which forced him to momentarily release me. I kept screaming hysterically as I flew out the door and through the front gate.

Someone must have called the police, for by the time I reached the next building the officers were there to help. I had related the events by the time we returned to the apartment. The two policemen speedily handcuffed the violently resisting F.J., and requested that I prefer a charge of "attempted manslaughter". That, I could not do.

But I did agree to an "assault and battery" charge, and my deranged mate was taken to jail.

During the night I packed as much as I could, and by morning had moved in with Gitta. By the time I got to work everyone knew that my husband was in jail. He had tried to reach me, to come and bail him out. Pitying him, I rushed to the courthouse, where a judge released him in my custody, with the provisions that he was not to drive for thirty days, was to seek psychiatric help, and attend sessions of Alcoholics Anonymous.

I drove him to both places, left him at the meeting, then returned to work. The last lesson over, my favorite student, Gary, walked with me to my car. But my parking space was empty, the car nowhere in sight. Sympathetically Gary offered to drive me home.

He patiently listened to my problems during the ride, and urged me to let him drive me home each night until the situation with F.J. settled. The next day I sought and got permission from the owners to be seen with a student outside the studio, since the job forbade socializing with customers. Thus, the 5'2", 110-pound little Hawaiian Gary became my nightly escort and bodyguard.

On the day when I met the movers in my old residence, the missing television and my coin and stamp collection were the only signs that F.J. had been there during the past three days. Poor Gitta's tiny furnished apartment looked like a junk shop with all my furniture and belongings piled ceiling high. I often wondered how much it must have bothered such a pedantic perfectionist, but she used to say, "That is the least I can do for a friend."

For the following several weeks I had no peace. F.J. kept calling me in the studio, in Gitta's house, waiting for me on the street before and after work, alternately pleading or making a scene, wanting me to return to the apartment. Each time he did all the talking, for I refused to get involved in any way with him again. Finding me unresponsive, he tried to get me back through fear. Night after night he hid in the bushes under our window, making noises like a burglar would. He would jump from behind doorways, shine a flashlight into my face, then run away; he would make hourly obscene phone calls, not letting me nor Gitta sleep. I notified the court and got released of my obligation, but without knowing his address, the police could not arrest him. We called the police on several occasions, but each time he managed to avoid being caught. Finally, in early March everything stopped. F.J. had vanished.

During all this time Gary kept driving me home. He never came in, nor did he invite me out. We learned a great deal about each other during the rides, and the more I found out about him the more I admired and liked him. He was of Korean descent, but born and raised in Honolulu. His father had been a teacher, historian, and newspaper publisher before he passed away, leaving three small children behind.

When Gary became of age, his family pinched pennies and sent him to Massachusetts Institute of Technology (MIT). After receipt of his bachelor's degree he moved to L.A., and while working as a scientist for Space Technology Laboratories, he acquired his master's degree at the University of California (UCLA). Gary was a year or so younger than I, shy yet charming, brilliant yet modest, instantly liked by everyone, yet without real friends. He admired, respected and trusted me, and the feeling was mutual.

With F.J. out of the picture, and Gitta's place too crowded, it was time for us to move. We found a suitable apartment in Hollywood, sufficiently close to work for both of us.

I needed a car badly, and my fairly new Oldsmobile in Boston was still not sold. I also wanted desperately to see my children, but lacked funds for the flight. Gary came up with a gallant proposition. He claimed he needed a brief vacation and change of scenery, so he offered to lend me money and fly to Boston with me, then drive back cross-country in my car. I happily accepted his offer, and near the end of May we took off on our whirlwind trip. A reduced-fare night flight, a trip to the lawyer to proceed with the appeal, a few hours with the children, then, alternating drivers and stopping only to eat, we returned to L.A. within our available five days.

Looking forward to the luxury of driving to work in my own car, the next morning I cockily walked to my subterranean garage. I rubbed my eyes twice, but my car was nowhere in sight. I searched the neighborhood, called the police, but my car had vanished without a trace.

Three days later I had a bizarre experience. During the night I dreamt that I was a child of nine, on a Friday night in the temple, praying in Hebrew. I woke, but went right back to sleep. When the alarm rang the next morning, I began rattling off the "Sheh Mah" (Hebrew prayer) without conscious design, just as I used to in my childhood. I had an eerie feeling as I looked around the room, as if seeing each object for the first time. Taking it as some kind of premonition, I relaxed and let my thoughts flow. I recall having mumbled something like: "Dear God, I have had just about enough! Now it is up to You to straighten my life out! I have no one to turn to 'cause You took my parents away; now You must take their place. I've been suffering more than anyone deserves. I can not endure any more. Stop punishing and start helping me again!"

When I ceased mumbling I was aware of everything I had said or thought, yet it seemed as if having listened to or having read someone else's mind. The strangest thing was, however, that I felt a sense of serenity and contentment, physical and mental strength, and best of all, complete faith that I had passed the turning point and my life was about to change for the better. I felt I had found God again, and that He would guide and watch over me, as He had during the Holocaust.

Just then the telephone rang. "We found your car at the bottom of a deep embankment, all banged up but still running fine. You can take it from our station's lot any time you wish," said the police chief.

Not sure whether to believe what I had heard, I ran excitedly to the nearby station. Sure enough, there was my car, just as the voice on the phone had described it!

CHAPTER 8: VEXATIONS AND VICTORIES

From that memorable day on my life had indeed changed. Gitta and I got along as twin sisters, and enjoyed the car and our new apartment. Gary and I became inseparable. I was successful in my job, earning substantial commissions. I soon saved enough to repay Gary, and hire a lawyer to file for an annulment. I even got news about F.J. that put my mind completely at ease.

One day a man appeared at our door. He showed me his FBI identification, then a photo of F.J.M. He asked if I could give some information about the man. Having told everything I knew, it was my turn to ask, and the agent was kind enough to bring me up to date.

F.J. was wanted by the Los Angeles police for contempt of court, driving without a license, nonpayment of rent, and writing checks on a closed account; by the California police for stealing televisions, a license plate, and forging checks; by the Boston police for not making alimony and child support payments; and by the FBI for interstate theft. He had just been caught in New York with a stolen car. I asked the agent how long a sentence could be anticipated, to which he responded that in view of his previous record, a minimum of ten years.

With F.J. out of the way, the only pain I still had to endure was not having my children with me. We frequently had long conversations on the phone, but those were worse than salt on an open wound. In September my lawyer informed me that my appeal was rejected; Judge Mahoney would not change his decision. This time, however, my reaction was different. Instead of going into an apathetic depression, I felt it was an omen that I was destined to have a different role in life.

My first objective was to earn and save a substantial amount of money, to be able to reduce my work load when I did regain the children, and to finance my future college education. During the winter I changed employment; a similar position, but with higher base pay and better opportunity for large commissions. By the summer of 1961 I had saved enough to visit my children, and to rehire the lawyer to appeal for custody again.

Shortly after my return, one of my co-workers asked me a favor. He had been hearing a lot about computers and wanted me to help him investigate the requirements and opportunities in the field. It took us little time to find out that the rapidly growing new field offered an enormous variety of employment, with unusually high salaries. Having taken several aptitude tests upon which both of us scored high, I too decided to enter the computer field. So, in September we both enrolled in an intensive programming course.

The course was very demanding. We attended daily classes from early morn till 1:00 p.m., worked from then until midnight, and studied between clients and all day on Sundays. The effort was worth it, for we became competent programmers in a mere three months.

Two weeks after the completion of the course my friend found employment. I was not so lucky. Interested in scientific application, being a woman and without a degree, my opportunities were limited.

As if being rejected time after time without even an interview had not been upsetting enough, I got a letter from my lawyer in Boston, stating: "The judge not only rejected our appeal, but asserted that if you could prove that the father is incompetent, the children would be placed in an orphanage. During our talk in his chambers he explained that if he decreed partial custody and you did not turn the children over to the father at the specified time, the father would have no legal recourse. You could lose the right to custody, even be charged with contempt of court, but prosecuted only when you re-entered the state of the decree, or the father established residence in California. Assuming that in your case, where both parents desperately want custody, the aforementioned situation is likely to arise, the judge intends to prevent it by not allowing the children to leave Massachusetts.''

I felt crushed, but not defeated. I had faith by then that the Lord was guiding my life, that everything that was happening was part of a greater design, all eventually in my best interest. Thus, to keep my mind off my sorrow, I continued filling out applications, going on interviews, and teaching as many students as time permitted. Finally, in January of 1962, Todd Shipyards hired me.

At first I felt very much out of place. The yard had over 2,000 male employees. Our section had about fifty male engineers and executives, my group five male researchers, all balanced by a grand total of *three* female secretaries. During the first week my co-workers were determined to have me do the most undesirable and menial jobs, or to get rid of me. However, when they found out that, although I had no knowledge of ship engineering, I knew significantly more about our computer than they did, each respected and accepted me as his equal. I enjoyed my job immensely, but soon felt the need and urge to go to college. So, the next month I began attending two evening courses at Los Angeles City College (LACC).

In April a minor miracle finally happened. While speaking on the phone long distance with Roberta, she kept saying how much she and her brother missed me. Without logical reason, I said, ''I don't believe you! You never write that in your letters!''

''We can't, Mommy. Dad won't let us! He said he would punish us something awful if we'd ever write that to you,'' replied my daughter. Her comment gave me an idea, so to force the issue I called her a liar. Among sobs and tears she kept insisting that it was the truth. I posed the same assertions to Don, who verified his sister's statement.

Upon my insistence, my ex-husband reluctantly came to the phone. I repeated to him what my children had claimed, which he, of course, denied, accusing them of not telling the truth. That triggered a war between the three! That was all I needed.

I informed Jim that not only was the entire conversation taped, but a friend of mine was on the extension phone listening to every word. I then threatened him that if he dared to oppose my having the children during the summer vacation, I would use every means to take away not only custody, but also his visitation rights. Jim realized that he had unintentionally given me a weapon, so without further discussion he agreed to the summer visit. I immediately called my Boston lawyer and authorized him to attend to the necessary legal details.

Even though Jim's attorney notified the court that the father was raising no objections, heartless Judge Mahoney made the visit almost impossible. He allowed the minors to leave the state for no more than three weeks, all expenses to be paid by me, and ordered a $5,000 "security deposit" with said court, the amount to be forfeited if the minors were not returned within the specified time. Again Gary came to my rescue. He loaned me all I needed, and my children were soon on their way.

It would have been my most joyous summer had it not been dampened by two events. Gitta got married, leaving me with a two-bedroom apartment which, though ideal during the children's visit, was too costly without a roommate for the rest of the year. Second, at work my group's federal fund was depleted, thus our research terminated. My co-workers, naval engineers, were simply transferred to another department, but for me, in spite of the efforts of my superiors, there was no suitable position in the yard. So, just days before the children arrived, I had to face the enormous expenses without a job and income.

To utilize the summer, when chances for new employment were almost null, I enrolled in three math courses at LACC. Fulfilling my lifelong ambition to get a degree, anticipating the return of my children, with faith that God was guiding my destiny, I faced autumn with optimism and confidence.

In September I found an excellent position, working through a consulting firm for Douglas Aircraft Company's Space Division, as a consultant and programmer systems analyst. The pay was unusually high and the working conditions were excellent. Our team of eleven was charged with the selection of a multi-million dollar computer complex, which was to be connected with and be in control of all major testing equipment of newly designed space models. Hardware chosen, we proceeded to write the software. My primary assignment was to develop the Test Language Compiler, which translated English words to machine language, enabling any research engineer without programming knowledge to communicate with and/or put the computers in charge of controlling test procedures.

Everything went well for a while. I found a superb roommate, continued my college studies, even pursued learning to fly.

I had just received my temporary pilot license when Douglas had a multi-million dollar government contract cancelled, necessitating the layoff of over 10,000 employees. Thus terminated my wonderful position during the spring of 1963. Being so near to summer and the chance to find employment meager, I enrolled in three college courses and spent two delightful months with my children.

Right after Labor Day I was offered an excellent position at General Precision Inc. The mother company manufactured computers, and our division wrote the library routines and special programs requested by the customers. Our department head gave us the assignments, otherwise we worked independently. This enabled me to attend a physics course given only in the daytime, while at night I took three of my favorite subjects: math, psychology and philosophy.

Having an outstanding instructor for the latter, several of my classmates and I decided to form a club. We christened it Eta Phi Chi, Evening Philosophy Club. Various professors became our monthly speakers, their presentations followed by group discussions lasting often beyond midnight. The club soon became popular, so I, as its founder, received a "Service to the College Award." But more meaningful was the recognition bestowed upon me the next June, citing me as a "Departmental Outstanding Student" for the year.

From then on new accomplishments and further recognitions followed in rapid succession. Both my lifestyle and personality began to undergo a change.

Next September I was pressured to accept a post on the LACC Evening Division Executive Board, to function as the program chairman. After receiving my associate of arts degree at the end of the fall semester, while still maintaining my job and taking transferable courses, I was drafted to organize and launch the LACC Alumni Association. Before the summer ended I had terminated my job and had moved to West L.A., near UCLA, where I started my last undergraduate year as a full-time student.

Meanwhile my friend Gary had become famous for his research, computing the exact ellipticity of the earth around the equator. He spent literally all his time either at work or writing his dissertation. Both of us being so very preoccupied, our relationship suffered to the extent that after five years we remained only casual friends.

Due to my reputation as an organizer and one with first-hand experience about Naziism and communism, in March of 1966 I got an invitation to be a key speaker in Chicago, at the founding convention of the Jewish Society of Americanists (JSA). The group consisted of prominent patriotic Jews from all parts of our country. Having participated in drafting the new organization's constitution and by-laws, statement of purpose and a list of intended activities, I happily accepted the office of JSA West Coast Director.

During that spring I passed the UCLA's Graduate Record Examination, qualifying me to enter the master and doctoral programs. But I decided to change my major and plan for the future. To advance in my computer career, a degree in mathematics, the sciences or in engineering was necessary. Thus far I had majored in math and minored in psychology. But my profession, though highly paid, had two grave disadvantages: one, duration of employment was unpredictable, and two, long hours and frequent stressful situations were unavoidable. By then I was beginning to feel my age and the effects of the many hardships I had endured, so I searched for a new profession that gave me more security, more time to relax, and was more emotionally satisfying. After suffering through a course with another greatly incompetent math professor, I knew exactly what goal to set. I decided to concentrate on educational psychology, with the intention of teaching and doing research in the field.

Since I had regained my faith in God, I had also regained my mental and emotional balance and self-confidence. Although with relentless determination I had been attaining my goals, the roads leading to them were full of weird obstacles; not just the typical hardships most people encounter occasionally, but a multitude of incidents which very rarely happen. One such occurred in June, one week before completion of my undergraduate studies.

The administration office sent me a letter, stating that I could not yet graduate, because I was lacking a *half* unit in high school math. Thinking that the letter was a mistake, before the third of five finals scheduled for the same day, I ran to see a counselor. She pulled my records and confirmed the contents of the letter.

"But Miss K., I have completed 48 units in math, my major on the college level! I had recently scored in the 97th percentile in that topic on the Graduate Record Exam," said I in total bewilderment.

"Sorry," replied the lady as she motioned me to leave the room, "take an adult education course in a high school, and graduate next semester."

Too angry to even comment, I charged into the chief administrator's office. Ignoring politeness, I slammed the letter on his desk, repeated my counselor's comments, adding that I was qualified to teach, not attend a high school. I stopped him discourteously when he said: "My hands are tied, the rules . . ." Asserting that I was not willing to fulfill such an asinine demand, that I intended to go, if

56

needed, to the dean, chancellor, or even the news media, his tone immediately changed. Minutes later my name was added by hand to the posted graduation list.

CHAPTER 9: THAT WAS MY DESTINY

I spent a delightful summer with my children again that year, while taking the last two courses required for my teaching credential. Rejuvenated, by the fall I was ready to take a full load, leading to my master's degree, plus begin student teaching algebra in University High School. Completely drained of funds, I applied to be an intern, starting the following spring. That meant full-time teaching for five-sixth of the normal salary, the balance going to the supervising teacher. Such a position was scarce and in great demand, so applicants had to qualify via a heterogeneous series of examinations. I was already optionally hired to teach in a mid-city minority school when scheduled for the last phase, filling out papers and taking a physical.

In January of 1967, nine days before my much anticipated employment began, the few of us lucky ones stood in various lines from 8:00 a.m. until 4:00 p.m., arriving finally at our last stop, where a nurse charted our height and weight. Exhausted but happy that all had gone well, I stepped on the scale. But lo and behold! I registered only 98 pounds.

The nurse ran frantically for the doctor. He looked twice, then shook his head and said, "Sorry, we can not allow you to teach. You are *seven* pounds underweight."

"But doctor, this has been my normal weight for over twenty years! It has nothing to do with my ability to teach," said I totally bewildered.

"Sorry, my child, rules, you know, are rules!" The shock brought angry tears to my eyes. Sympathetically the doctor advised me to eat fattening foods for a week, then to return.

During the next five days I called and asked all my past and present gentlemen friends to take me out to highly rated restaurants for lunch and for dinner. Stuffing myself made me gain nearly four pounds, but on the sixth day I became ill with an unforgettable diarrhea. A day before my appointment I weighed again exactly 98 pounds. In desperation I decided to cheat. Stuffing my underwear with the last bits of my savings, $60 worth of silver dollars and halves, I went to the cafeteria before seeing the doctor. After consuming three of each, orange juice, water, tea, and bowls of clear soup, I was ready to step on the scale.

"Made it!" exclaimed the doctor," And now . . ."

"Hold it!" I interrupted," I simply *must* run," said I with great relief, as I flew toward the ladies' room.

My new job had its share of problems, but I overcame all by my love of children, mathematics and teaching. I knew I had found the career which I would happily pursue for the rest of my life.

While still attending UCLA in the evenings, I came across a bulletin of great interest. The National Science Foundation was offering large grants to forty carefully selected applicants for Claremont Graduate College's Summer Institute in Psychology. I quickly filled out an application, attached several letters of recommendation, mailed it and prayed to be one of those chosen. My prayer was answered in May, when the confirmation letter stated that my tuition and all living expenses for nearly the entire summer would be covered by the grant.

By the fall of 1967 I was a full-fledged, credentialed math/psychology instructor, and before the following year was over, I had completed my master's thesis. The chairman of the committee was so impressed with the research that not only did he approve my first draft, but suggested that I submit a condensed version for publication in one of the leading research journals.

It was clear to me by then that I was destined to succeed — perhaps not in my love life, but in my careers. The thought began to haunt me that perhaps the Lord had protected me during the Holocaust because he had chosen me to accomplish something special, which could not be done had I been just a content mother and housewife. Atypical circumstances parted me from both of the only two males I ever loved — Bandi and Franky, who both married meanwhile someone else in rebound — and forced me into two unsuccessful marriages. On the other hand, I had succeeded beyond expectations in all my highly diversified undertakings: as a dressmaker, dance analyst, programmer, organizational leader, student, teacher, and even as a researcher. A broad pattern emerged, but not yet the clear sight of my eventual destiny.

One success or recognition kept following the other. During the spring of that year Senator Richardson, whom I had never even met, while in the process of drafting revisions to the California Educational Code, requested me to serve on his advisory committee. A month or so later, when several veterans' organizations were arranging a "Loyalty to God and Country" parade, I was invited to sit on a float, representing Jewish participation. During the summer several prominent Jews and past officers of the JSA appointed me the national director and chief editor of the Jewish Right (JR), an organization larger and more prestigious than the old JSA. 1968 ended with my receiving the master of arts degree.

Oh, the joy of being able to relax evenings and on weekends! To do occasionally nothing else but watch television! To visit with friends without feeling guilty for not studying instead! I felt like a mountain climber who had just reached the top of Everest.

Next year Roberta and I spent a glorious summer traveling around the West Coast and Hawaii. She traded places with Don, who moved to L.A. in late August, to start attending college here. In September I traded my teaching job in the big and impersonal L.A. school system for a position in a small and beautiful suburban community.

The following June I flew to Boston, to calm Roberta during the last two weeks prior to her wedding. Then quickly back, to prepare my home for the arrival of the newlyweds. Within a month they, too, found an apartment in the vicinity, and so by the fall of 1970 I was again living alone, but richer for having both of my children nearby.

While contemplating the future one night, I plotted the emotional curve of my past. It formed an interesting pattern. The sharp incline through my childhood, followed by the steep decline during and after the war; the gradual up-trend after my escape from the horrors of communism, culminating with the happiness I had attained with Franky, succeeded by the slow-down trend until my divorce; a bit of zigzagging in the pit, then a positive, still rising incline to the present. An eery feeling passed through me, realizing that of the three people I loved most, although in reverse order — first Don, my second born, then Roberta, my first born — had returned into my daily life. But there was *one more to go*.

While still contemplating, I realized something else. I had attained all my planned goals. Setting new ones was necessary. But first I had to decide what I really wanted to achieve. — Riches? No. My job offered me security and a comfortable existence. Another husband? No, I was not ready yet. More education? Not really. I had taken several courses toward my doctorate, enough to put me on top of our salary scale. Besides, I felt saturated, like a glass of water ready to overflow.

All through the years I had been absorbing, like a sponge, both from instructors and from my highly heterogeneous acquaintances. Teaching gave me a great deal of satisfaction, for it allowed me to pass on knowledge, like letting a narrow stream of air escape from a ready-to-burst balloon. Writing I enjoyed too, for the same reason, but in that area I still lacked confidence. Recalling that my highest grades were always on term and research papers, the encouraging advice of several of my past instructors to become an author, and finally Dr. Keislar's assertion that my thesis warranted publication, my next goal suddenly emerged.

During the following months I spent all my spare time on the research report. I wrote and rewrote, revised and re-revised. I even prepared half a dozen self-addressed envelopes, expecting at least that many rejections. In May I finally mustered enough courage to address one to the California Journal of Educational Research (CJER). — To such a highly rated journal? Where only professors' articles appear? Inexperienced, with only a fair command of the English language? How dare I shoot for the stars! But why not? At worse it would be rejected. I would submit it to a lesser rated journal, again and again. — Those thoughts rushed through my mind. Pleased with my determination and courage, I stamped and mailed the envelope.

Like raindrops dancing in the summer sunshine, happy tears dripped from my eyes when three weeks later I read the letter of unconditional acceptance. A sudden burst of energy flooded my body. As I recalled one of my advisor's comments, "To reinforce your conclusions and broaden their inferences the experiment should be identically repeated with an oppositely skewed atypical set of subjects," I realized that by coincidence my current students represented precisely that type of statistical population. Thus, my next goal became the retesting of my hypotheses.

By the time my article appeared in the March, 1972, issue of the CJER, my second experiment was well on its way. During that summer I analyzed my preliminary data and — lo and behold — the trend was the same. To strengthen the research I decided to use one more set of subjects, so I waited to write up the study until after the following school year.

Before that year was over something else worthy of mention had occurred. A publishing company sent me a personal data form and asked for my permission to print the information if their editorial board found it of interest. Due to my organizational position, I had by then made so many speeches, appearances, publicity releases, etc., that during that busy weekend, without reading the enclosures

I just filed them away, and returned the completed questionaire.

The next summer, instead of working on my research, since both Roberta and I felt the need for a vacation, we decided to visit my homeland. It was to be a highly emotional journey, which I had long desired but feared to undertake.

It was painful to see what had become of my old friends in communist Hungary. Bitter, afraid of their own shadows — people didn't live, they just existed. Every able-bodied woman worked, not only because it was compulsory, but to enable them to buy even the bare necessities for their families.

We visited Magda, my deceased uncle's 69-year-old wife, who was still living in my grandmother's prewar apartment with her 83-year-old ex-employer, once manager of the City Bank. I had to look twice upon entering, for each room had three tree-trunks wedged between the floor and ceiling. The explanation was much simpler than I thought. The trees were supporting the ceiling beams, preventing the cave-in of the roof!

The answer to my question of why she and János had lived together for nearly thirty years without wedlock was also, at least to them, very obvious. If they had married, Magda would have lost her 200 forint ($10) weekly pension, and on his subsidy alone the two would have literally starved. Besides, Magda said, if they had married, due to the housing shortage — nearly 30 years after World War II had ended — they would have had to share their one-bedroom apartment with a stranger.

When I looked at the rags they wore, I offered to send packages of some good, used clothes. At first they begged me not to do so, but when I insisted, they explained that they simply could not spare the money to pay the required import tax on them.

Among my childhood friends we visited a few who lived almost comfortably, but most were what we in the U.S. call poverty-stricken. The wealthiest, who lived like middle-class Americans, were my old love Bandi and his wife, she a high-positioned, active member of the communist party.

After our return I published an article about life in Hungary: pre-, during, and post-World War II. Almost by return mail I was flooded by requests for reprints. As the word got around, I began to get dozens of invitations to speak about my first-hand experiences. Each speech was a success. Audiences often kept me until the wee hours of the morning, wanting to hear more and more. Acquaintances began to encourage me to write a book. Although I felt still somewhat incompetent, the thought kept recurring.

Before 1973 was over, I had completed my second research and needed a new goal. As I mailed it to the CJER, I decided that its acceptance would be an omen that I should write my life story. But before it even reached the editors, via special delivery Providence gave me the sign.

A package marked "book" arrived. "I had ordered no book, it must be a mistake," said I. Since the name and address were correct, the mailman insisted on leaving it. Upon removal of the wrapping I was even more puzzled. The book's title was *Who's Who in California*. No letter, no signature, why would it be sent to me? Curiosity made me look through the list of V.I.P.'s, in search of someone I perhaps knew. I nearly fainted when my eyes fell upon a photograph and description of me.

I had not yet recovered fully from the shock when the letter of acceptance of my study arrived. I knew then that I had to write this book. *That was my destiny!*

CHAPTER 10: HIS SELF-IMPOSED EXILE

Writing this book was a major and painful undertaking. I relived each incident when I looked at my old pictures and diary. And relived them again when putting it on paper. Then came the problem of what to do about those incidents that were hazy in my mind, and time periods to which my diary made no reference. Twice I needed to travel to Hungary, to revisit pre- and postwar sites, locate and reminisce with old acquaintances, and research scores of out-of-print books and almost inaccessible documents. But everything I needed in connection with this book just fell into my lap, like manna from heaven.

A day after my arrival the second time I returned to Hungary, a friend took me to the retail outlet of the famous Herend porcelain factory. As I leaned on the counter to point at a figurine, my eyes fell upon two silver medallions, so out of place amidst the multitude of porcelain items. I recognized what they depicted, but not believing my eyes I asked the manager to take them from the locked showcase. Yes, one really was the carved portrait of Ann Frank, the Dutch Jewess whose diary had become so well-known, and the other a replica of the Dohány Temple, the site of my escapes from the ghetto during the war. I asked what those objects were doing in his store. He said they had come from the Tourists' Shop in Budapest, but why they were sent and why to his outlet, he did not know.

This incident was followed by innumerably more unexplainable and highly unlikely occurrences. In Budapest, a stranger I stopped to ask directions turned out be a retired professor, currently compiling information on Hungarian ghetto survivors; an information-packed book about the war years I had for days been searching for, I found lying on top of the trash at my residence; the director of the city's Jewish Museum turned out to be the editor of three books, documenting all the anti-Jewish laws issued during the Holocaust, and also former co-worker of my father at the Jewish Central Council during 1944.

Interpreting all of those to be positive signs, I felt encouraged to write my life story. But as I reread my manuscript, I felt it went on and on, just going nowhere. It needed a focus and a powerful finish. I could have created a fictitious ending, but that would have spoiled the authenticity of my autobiography. This time not just an omen, but almost a miracle was needed.

For many years I had felt that my life was guided, my successes and failures predetermined. Perhaps my heavenly Father did want me to write my life story, to alert present and future generations to the pains modern men can inflict upon each other, and of the sufferings of those people who still live under the yoke of atheistic totalitarian systems. If so, He gave me the urge to write this book. And if so, He would also provide the finish.

And He did! Soon and unexpectedly, a strange looking envelope arrived; no name or return address, but the chirography I could at once recognize. My hands were shaking and my heart throbbing as I read the eight-page letter that started: "My Dearest Kitten: Oh, how long since I have uttered these words! After you read this letter you may prefer not to answer. I would not blame you; I would understand. I have lived an eventful life, attained success and moderate riches, fulfilled all my desires but one. I am writing to you now because for thirty years not one week has passed without you on my mind, and I feel unable to continue to live in this self-imposed exile."

The rest of the letter informed me that after Franky had retired from the navy, he had been employed by Los Alamos Scientific Laboratory, a position he traded in 1969 to work at the Puget Sound Naval Shipyard as a health physicist. He was currently supervising the radiological controls involved in the refueling and overhauling of nuclear surface ships and submarines. Sue had attended Olympic College and was now working for Pan American Airlines; David was married and a lieutenant in the navy; Nick was at Brigham Young University and the father of three children. The letter concluded that he had tangible assets, including his home and ten rental properties, all of which he was willing to give to Shirley in a divorce settlement if I still loved and wished to marry him.

What a question? Of course I did! Upon receipt of my answer Franky accepted a brief assignment in San Diego, where we met again after eighteen long years. We did not speak for a long time; there was no need for words. We knew each other's unspoken thoughts and feelings, as we had thirty years before.

In June Franky returned to Washington. While I traveled to Hungary to do the final research for this book he terminated his job, gave up his assets, dissolved his marriage, and moved to Los Angeles. By November of 1978 the two of us had turned time back thirty years, and realized our dreams of getting married. *This, too, was part of my destiny.*

Author's family.
Testimony to the failure of Hitler's goal,
the destruction of the world's Jewry.

BIBLIOGRAPHY

Benoschofsky, Ilona, and Karsai, Elek. Vádirat a Nácizmus Ellen. Budapest: Magyar Izraeliták Országos Képviselete, Vol. 1: 1958; Vol. 2: 1960; Vol. 3: 1967.

Bernadac, Christian. Devil's Doctors. Geneva: Ferni Publishing House, 1978.

Braham, Randolph L. The Destruction of Hungarian Jewry. New York: World Federation of Hungarian Jews, 1963, Vols. 1 and 2.

Dimont, Max I. The Indestructible Jews. New York: The New American Library, Inc., 1971.

Hitler, Adolf. Mein Kampf. New York: Reynal and Hitchcock, 1939.

Horthy, Nicholas. Memories. New York: Robert Seller and Sons, 1963.

Karsai, Elek. Fegyvertelen Álltak Az Aknamezőkön. Budapest: Magyar Izraeliták Országos Képviselete, 1962. Vols. 1 and 2.

Lévai, Jenő. A Pesti Gettó Történette. Budapest: Magyar Téka, 1946.

Lévai, Jenő. Zsidósors Magyarországon. Budapest: Magyar Téka, 1948.

Levin, Nora. The Holocaust. New York: Thomas Y. Crowell Co., 1968.

Manvell, Roger and Fraenkel, Heinrich. The Incomparable Crime. New York: G. P. Putnam and Sons, 1967.

Montgomery, John Flournoy. Hungary, The Unwilling Satellite. New York: Devin-Adair Co., 1947.

Morse, Arthur D. While Six Million Died. New York: Random House, 1967.

Neuhausler, Dr. Johann. What was it like in the Concentration Camp at Dachau? Munich: A. G. Manz, 1960.

Pór, Dezső and Zsadányi, Oszkár. Te Vagy A Tanu. Budapest: Szikra Irodalmi És Lapkiadóvállalat, 1947.

Sachar, Abram L., Ph.D. A History of the Jews. New York: Alfred A. Knopf, 1965.

Shirer, William L. The Rise and Fall of the Third Reich. New York: Simon and Schuster, 1960.

Smith, Marcus J. The Harrowing of Hell. University of New Mexico Press, 1972.

Száraz, György. Egy Előitélet Nyomában. Budapest:Magvető, 1976.

Teleki, Éva. Nyilas Uradalom Magyarországon. Budapest: Kossuth, 1974.